Magic, White and Black

The Science of Finite and Infinite Life

CONTAINING

Practical Hints for Students of Occultism

By Franz Hartmann, M.D.

This Edition Includes all Original Tables and Illustrations

PANTIANOS
CLASSICS

Published by Pantianos Classics

ISBN-13: 978-1545379943

The Fourth Edition was published in 1888

Franz Hartmann

Contents

Description of the Frontispiece .... *vi*

Preface to the Fourth Edition .... *viii*

Preface .... *xi*

Introduction: Spiritual Law in the Natural World .... *xiii*

Chapter I - The Ideal 30

Chapter II - The Real and the Unreal 43

Chapter III – Form 55

Chapter IV - Life 73

Chapter V - Harmony 82

Chapter VI - Illusions 97

Chapter VII - Consciousness 112

Chapter VIII – Unconsciousness 125

Chapter IX - Transformations 140

Chapter X - Creation 156

Chapter XI - Light 172

Chapter XII - Theosophy 184

Appendix 204

"For in our searching are fulfilled all our desires, and we obtain the victory over all worlds."

— ***Khand. Upanishad***

Description of the Frontispiece

AT the foot of the picture is a sleeping Sphinx, whose upper part (representing the higher principles) is human; while the lower parts (symbolising the lower principles) are of an animal nature. She is dreaming of the solution of the great problem of the construction of the Universe and of the nature and destiny of Man, and her dream takes the shape of the figure above her, representing the Macrocosm and the Microcosm and their mutual interaction.

Above, around, and within all, without beginning and without an end, penetrating and pervading all, from the endless and unimaginable periphery to the invisible and incomprehensible centre is Parabrahm, the unmanifested Absolute, the supreme source of every power that ever manifested or may in the future manifest itself as a "thing," and by whose activity the world was thrown into existence, being projected by the power of His own will and imagination.

The Omega (and the Alpha in the centre) represent the "Son," the Absolute having become manifest as the Universal Logos or The Christ, also called Buddhi, or the sixth principle, the cause of the beginning and the end of every created thing. It is One with the "father," being manifested as a Trinity in a Unity, the cause of what we call Space, Motion, and Substance. Its highest manifestation is Self-consciousness, by which it may come to the comprehension of Man. The spiritual man whose matrix is his own physical body, draws his nutriment from this universal spiritual principle as the physical foetus is nourished by means of the womb of the mother, his soul being formed from the astral influences or the soul of the world.

Out of the Universal Logos proceeds the "invisible Light" of the Spirit, the Truth, the Law, and the Life, embracing and penetrating the Cosmos and becoming manifest in the illuminated soul of Man, while the visible light of Nature is only its most material aspect or mode of manifestation, in the same sense as the visible sun is the reflex of its divine prototype, the invisible centre of power or the great spiritual Sun.

The circle with the twelve signs of the Zodiac, enclosing the space in which the planets belonging to our solar system are represented, symbolises the Cosmos, filled with the planetary influences pervading the Astral Light, and which are caused by the interaction of the astral emanations of the cosmic bodies and their inhabitants.

The activity in the Cosmos is represented by the interlaced triangle. The two outer ones represent the great powers of creation, preservation, and destruction, or Brahma, Vishnu, and Siva, acting upon the elements of Fire, Water, and Earth -- that is to say, upon the original principles out of which ethereal, fluid and solid material substances and forms are produced.

The two inner interlaced triangles refer more especially to the development of Man. B, C, and D represent Knowledge, the Knower, and the Known, which trinity constitutes Self-knowledge. E, F, and G represent the Physical Man, the Ethereal or Inner Man, and the Spiritual Man. The centre represents the divine Atma, being identical with the Universal Logos. It is, like the latter, a Trinity in a Unity.*(Of the three interlaced A's only one is distinctly drawn in the figure.)* It is the spiritual seed implanted in the soul of man, through whose growth immortal life is attained. Its light is the Rose of the Cross that is formed by Wisdom and Power. But below all is the realm of Illusion, of the most gross and heavy materialised thoughts, sinking into Darkness and Death, where they decompose and putrefy, and are resolved again into the elements out of which the Universe came into existence.

Preface to the Fourth Edition

This book was originally written for the purpose of disenchanting certain credulous inquirers, who fancied that the exercise of spiritual powers could be taught by teaching them certain incantations and formulas. It was to prove that spiritual powers must be developed before they can be exercised, and to explain the conditions necessary for their development.

Since the appearance of the previous edition, a little additional knowledge, gained by the experiences of my own inner life, has enabled me to make certain corrections; to sift out much of what was irrelevant, and to remodel a great deal of what was incorrectly expressed. Moreover in this edition an attempt has been made to answer the numerous questions which have been addressed to me by the readers of "Magic."

The most serious objection which has been made against this book has been on account of its title; but the causes which induced me to select such a title were suggested by the purpose for which the book was intended; nor would I at present be able to find one more appropriate for it, for "Magic" means that divine art or exercise of spiritual power by which the awakened spirit in man controls the invisible living elements in the soul-substance of the universe; but, above all, those in his own soul, which are the ones nearest to him.

If we desire to master any forces whatever, it is, above all, necessary to know what they are and how they originate, and as we have no better means to study the qualities of any internal forces, than by observing those which are active within ourselves, the perception of the processes going on within our own psychic organism, will be the means to accomplish our object. The art Magic is the exercise of spiritual power, to be obtained by practising self-control, and this power cannot be acquired in any other way; nor is it possible to teach any one how to exercise a power which he does not possess, because he has not developed it; we can only indicate the way in which the psychic powers latent in every human constitution may be developed. The constitutions of all men are fundamentally the same, and in each human being are contained magical powers germinally or in a latent condition; but they cannot be said to exist before they become active and manifest themselves, first interiorly, and afterwards in an outward direction.

It was not my object, in composing this book, to write merely a code of ethics, and thereby to increase the already existing pile of moral precepts, but to assist the student of Occultism in studying the elements of which his own soul is composed, and to learn to know his own psychical organism. I want to give an impulse to the study of a science, which may be called the "anatomy and physiology of the soul" which investigates the elements of which the organism of the soul is composed, and the source from which man's desires and emotions spring.

Physical science has advanced with great strides in the realm of superficial phenomena and external illusions, but the science of the real interior and invisible man is still very little known. The mechanical and chemical forces of nature have been made subservient to physical science. She has laid the yoke upon the neck of the giant Steam and chained Electricity to her triumphal chariot; she made mechanical motion, heat, and light, and magnetism the obedient slaves of men; she made discoveries which make man to a certain extent independent of the conditions imposed upon him by space and time; she succeeded in realising certain ideas and to put them into practical execution, ideas which a century ago were believed to belong merely to the realm of the fancies of the visionary and the dreamer.

Why should we stop here? Why should it not be possible for us to advance still further, and to enchain those semi-conscious and conscious forces which pervade our own soul, and also the soul of the world? Why should it be impossible to condense into forms by the omnipotent power of Will the living but formless Elementals; to concentrate and give shape to living and universal principles, which, although they are at present invisible for us, nevertheless exist? Such things have been accomplished by the Eastern sages thousands of years ago, and may be accomplished by ourselves, provided we attain the same state of perfection which characterises these Adepts.

To arrive at this end the merely superficially intellectual reading of books on Occultism is entirely insufficient. The divine mysteries of nature are above and beyond the power of conception of the limited intellect. They must be grasped by the power of the spirit. If we cannot by our own soul perception perceive a spiritual truth with the eye of the spirit, intellectual reasoning and book learning will not enable us to perceive it clearly. Books, dealing with such subjects, should not be masters to us; they should merely be our assistants. They are merely useful to describe the details of things which we already know in the depths of our soul; they are merely servants to hold up before our eyes magnifying mirrors, wherein we see the truths whose presence we feel in ourselves.

Jackob Boehme, the great theosoph, says in regard to the study of Occultism: "If you desire to investigate the divine mysteries of nature, investigate first your own mind, and ask yourself about the purity of your purpose. Do you desire to put the good teachings which you may receive into practice for the benefit of humanity? Are you ready to renounce all selfish desires, which cloud your mind and hinder you to see the clear light of eternal truth? Are you willing to become an instrument for the manifestation of Divine Wisdom? Do you know what it means to become united with your own higher Self, to get rid of your illusive Self, to become one with the living universal power of Good and to die to your own shadowy insignificant terrestrial personality? Or do you merely desire to obtain great knowledge, so that your curiosity may be gratified, and that you may be proud of your science, and believe yourself to be superior to the rest of mankind? Consider, that the depths of Divinity can only be searched by the divine spirit itself, which is active within you. Real knowledge must come from our own interior, not merely from externals, and they who seek for the essence of things merely in externals may find the artificial colour of a thing, but not the true thing itself."

Again this self-taught philosopher says: "The intellect should be developed, but above all the heart. We should attempt to understand intellectually the laws of everything; but our own still fallible intellect should not be made the starting-point in our investigations. Man should not be governed by his reasoning from appearances; but he should govern his mind, so that the light of divine wisdom may illuminate his intellect. If our judgment becomes free of all selfish taint, and the vibrations of our soul are made to vibrate in harmony with the eternal spirit, our perishable intellect will be penetrated by the imperishable light of divine wisdom; and we will be able to perceive and to solve the deepest problems of nature. If our desire and reason cling to the sphere of self, we shall see merely the illusions which we ourselves have created; but if we become free by being obedient to the universal law, we will become one with the law and see the truth in its purity."

And to this we will add, as a warning to all inquirers, that a scientific investigation of the occult mysteries of nature, without that firm foundation furnished by the development of true spirituality, is exceedingly dangerous and leads to deplorable consequences. The perception of things which belong to the spirit is a faculty of the spiritually developed man and not within the reach of the semi-material mind. He who continually pores over things which he cannot comprehend lives in the realm of his dreams; he becomes an unpractical person, incapable to fulfil his duties in life, and often insanity and suicide is the result. The school of the occultist is only for those who have graduated in the school of terrestrial life.

Let, therefore, those who wish to acquire spiritual or divine power, follow this advice: let them rise spiritually into the highest regions of thought and remain therein as its permanent residents. Let them cultivate their physical bodies and their mental constitutions in such a manner that the matter of which they are composed will become less gross and more penetrable to the divine light of the spirit. Then will the veils that separate them from the invisible world become thinner; then will they become aware of the fact that the circle which limits their terrestrial and phenomenal existence is merely a small segment of that grand circle wherein their existence as self-conscious beings on the spiritual plane is enclosed, and as they increase in transcendental knowledge they will grow in spiritual power, until, by the understanding of the divine laws of the universe, they will become the co-operators of God, and God will perform his miracles in and through them.

The following pages are an attempt to show the way how Man may become an instrument of the Divine Power whose product is Nature; they constitute a book which may properly bear the title of "Magic," for if the readers succeed in practically following its teachings, they will be able to witness the greatest of all magical feats, the spiritual regeneration of Man.

Preface

OUR age is the age of opinions. The majority of our educated people live, so to say, in their heads, and the claims of the heart are neglected. Vanity is king, and wisdom is only permitted to speak when it does not come into conflict with selfish considerations. The guardians of a narrow limited science delude themselves with a belief of being capable to bring the infinite truth within the grasp of their finite understanding, and whatever they fail to comprehend is asserted not to exist. Our speculative philosophers refuse to recognise the eternal power of universal love whose light is reflected in the human soul; they wish to examine eternal truths by the flickering candle-light of their logic, reasoning from the basis of sensual observations; they forget that Humanity is a Unity, and that one individual cannot encompass the All; and the ignorant asks scientific reasons why man should be faithful and true, and why he should not consider his own personal interests above those of the rest of mankind.

It is universally admitted that man's final destiny cannot depend on the theories which he may have formed in his mind regarding Cosmology, Pneumatology, plans of salvation, &c., and as long as he possesses no real knowledge, one set of beliefs or opinions may perhaps be as good as another; but it cannot be denied, that the sooner man frees himself of the erroneous opinions of others and opening his own eyes recognises the real truth, the less will he. be impeded by the obstacles which are in the way of his higher evolution, and the sooner will he reach the summit of his final perfection.

The most important question seems, therefore, to be: "Is it possible that a man should actually know anything transcending his sensual perception, unless it is told to him by some supposed authority? Can the power of intuition be developed to such an extent as to become actual knowledge without any possibility of error, or shall we always be doomed to depend on hearsay and opinions? Can any individual man possess powers transcending those which are admitted to exist by modern science, and how can such transcendental powers be acquired?"

The following pages were written for the purpose of attempting to answer such questions, by calling the attention of those who desire to know the truth to a consideration of the true nature of Man and of his position in the Universe. Those who already know these things of course will not need the instructions which these pages contain, but to those who desire to know they may be of some use, and to the latter we recommend the advice given by Gautama Buddha to his disciples: "Believe nothing which is unreasonable, and reject nothing as unreasonable without proper examination."

This book was not written for the purpose of convincing sceptics of the fact that phenomena of an occult character have taken place in the past and are occurring at present; though an attempt has been made to prove the possibility of mystic occurrences, by offering some explanation in regard to the laws by which they may be produced. No space has been devoted to lengthy illustrative examples of phenomena. Those who require them will find such evidence in the books whose titles have been given at the foot of the pages.

Introduction: Spiritual Law in the Natural World

"There is no religion higher than truth."

The Highest Science

WHATEVER misinterpretation ancient or modern ignorance may have given to the word Magic, its only true significance is The Highest Science, or Wisdom, based upon knowledge and practical experience.

If you doubt whether there is any such thing as Magic, and if you desire any practical illustration about it, open your eyes and look around you. See the world, the animals, and the trees, and ask yourself whether they could have come into existence by any other power than by the magic power of nature. Magical power is not a supernatural power, if by the term "supernatural" you mean a power which is outside, beyond, or locally above nature. To suppose the existence of such a power is an absurdity and a superstition, opposed to all our experience; for we see that all organisms, vegetable and animal ones, grow by the action of internal forces acting outwardly, and not by having something added to their substance from the outside. A seed does not become a tree, nor a child a man, by having substance added to its organism by some outside workman, or like a house which is built by putting stones on the top of each other; but living things grow by the action of an internal power, acting from a centre within the form. To this centre flow the influences coming from the universal storehouse of matter and motion, and from there they radiate again towards the periphery, and perform that labour which builds up the living organism.

But what else can such a power be, except a spiritual power, because it penetrates to the very centre of material things. It acts according to law, and builds up organisms according to a certain order, and is therefore superior to blind mechanical force. It cannot be a mere mechanical force; for we know that a mechanical force ceases as soon as the impulse which originated it ceases to act, while the stream of life is inexhaustible, and only the forms in which it becomes manifest die. It cannot be a chemical force, for chemical action ceases when the chemical combination of the substances which were to combine has taken place. It must therefore be a living power, and as life cannot be a product of a dead form, it can be nothing else but the power of the One Life, acting within the life centres of the forms.

Nature is a magician, every plant, animal, and every man is a magician, who uses his powers unconsciously and instinctively to build up his own organism; or, in other words, every living being is an organism in which the magic power of the spirit in nature acts; and if a man should attain the knowledge how to control this power of life, and to employ it consciously, instead of merely submitting unconsciously to its influence, then he would be a magician, and could control the processes of life in his own organism, and perhaps in that of other beings. Now the question is: Can any man obtain such a power as to control the processes of life? The answer to this question depends on what you mean by the term "man." If you mean by "man" an intellectual animal, such as we meet every day in the streets, then the answer is: No ! for the majority of the men and women of our present generation, including our greatest scientific lumens, know absolutely nothing about their own inner nature or about the universal power of the One Life, and many of them have not even made up their minds whether or not they will believe in the existence of their own soul. They can neither see it nor feel it objectively, and therefore they do not know what to make of it.

But if you mean by "man" that intelligent principle, which is active within the organism of man, and which constitutes him a human being, and by whose action he becomes a being very distinct from and superior to animals in human or animal form, then the answer is: Yes! for the divine power which acts within the organism of man is the same and identical power which acts within the centre of nature. It is an internal power of man, and belongs to man's true self, and if man once knows all the powers which belong to his essential constitution, and knows how to use them, then he may enter from the passive into the active state, and employ these powers himself.

Absurd as it may seem, it is nevertheless a logical consequence drawn from the fundamental truths about the constitution of man. that if a man could control the universal power of life acting within himself, he might prolong the life of his organism as long as it pleased him; if he could control it, and knew all the laws of his nature, he might render it dense or vaporous, concentrate it to a small point, or expand it, so as to occupy a great deal of space. Verily, truth is stranger than fiction, and we might see it, if we could only rise above the narrow conceptions and prejudices which we have inherited and acquired by education and sensual observation.

The most strange things happen continually in nature, and hardly attract our attention. They do not seem strange to us, although we do not understand them; merely because we are accustomed to see them every day. Who would be so "foolish" as to believe that a tree could grow out of a seed -- as there is evidently no tree in the seed -- if his experience had not told him that trees grow out of seeds in spite of all arguments to the contrary? Who would believe that a flower would grow out of a plant, if he had not seen it, for observation and reason show that there is no flower in the stalk? Nevertheless, flowers grow, and cannot be disputed away.

Everywhere in nature the action of a universal spiritual law is manifest, but we cannot see the law itself. Everywhere we see the manifestations of wisdom; but those who seek for the origin of wisdom within their own brains will seek for it in vain.

The Art of Magic

The Art of Magic is the art of employing invisible or so-called spiritual agencies to obtain certain visible results. Such agencies are not necessarily invisible entities, flitting about in vacant space, ready to come at the command of anyone who has learned certain incantations and ceremonies; but they consist principally in the unseen but nevertheless powerful influences of the Emotions and the Will, of desires and passions, thought and imagination, love and hate, fear and hope, faith and doubt, &c., &c. They are the powers of what is called the Soul; they are employed everywhere and by everybody every day, consciously or unconsciously, willingly or unwillingly, and while those that cannot control or resist such influences, but are controlled by them, are passive instruments, "Mediums" through which such unseen powers act, and often their unwilling slaves; those who are able to guide and control such influences by gaining control over themselves, are, in proportion to their controlling capacity, active, and powerful, and true Magicians, and may employ their powers for good or for evil. We see, therefore, that with the exception of irresponsible persons, every one who has any will power is, in so far as he exercises that will power, an active Magician; a white magician if he employs them for good, a black magician if he uses them for the purposes of evil.

There are people in the East and some in the West, through whom extraordinary feats, such as are usually classified as "Magic," are performed; but it does not logically follow that such people are therefore conscious Magicians; it only shows that the power which acts through their organism, is a magic power, and the supposed "Magician" may be merely the instrument through which invisible intelligent powers perform such feats, and he may not even know who or what such a power is.

We all cannot honestly say "we have life"; for life does not belong to us, and we cannot control or monopolise it. All we can say without arrogance and presumption is that we are instruments through which the universal One Life manifests itself in the form of a human being. We are all Mediums, through which the universal One Life acts. Only when we know our own selves and can control the life-principle within ourselves, can we become our own Masters. He who thinks that he has any power whatever of his own, thinks foolish: for all the powers he has are lent him by nature, or -- more correctly speaking -- by that eternal spiritual power, which acts in and from the centre of nature, and which men have called "God," because they have found it to be the source of all good; the one Reality within the universe and within every being.

No one will deny that Man, besides having physical powers, is also temporally endowed with mental and even spiritual energies. We love, respect, or obey a person, not on account of his superior bodily strength, but on account of his intellectual and moral worth, or while we are under the spell of some real or imaginary authority, that we may believe him to possess. A king or a bishop has, as a person, not necessarily any more physical power than his lackey or butler, and must make himself known before he will be obeyed; a captain may be bodily the weakest man in his company and still his soldiers obey him. We love beauty, harmony, and sublimity, not on account of their usefulness for material purposes, but because they satisfy a corresponding inner sense, which does not belong to the physical plane; civilisation gains ground, more by moral and intellectual influences than by the power of the bayonet, and it is a true saying, that in our age the pen is mightier than the sword.

What would be a world without the magic power of love of beauty and harmony? How would a world look if made after a pattern furnished by modern science? A world in which the universal power of truth were not recognised could be nothing else but a world of maniacs and filled with hallucinations. In such a world art and poetry could not exist, justice would become a convenience, honesty be equivalent with imbecility, to be truthful would be to be foolish, and the idol of "Self" the only god worthy of any consideration.

Magic may be said to be that science which deals with the mental and moral powers of man, and shows what control he may exercise over himself and others. In order to study the powers of man it is necessary to investigate what Man is, and what relation he bears to the universe, and such an investigation, if properly conducted, will show that the elements which compose the essential man are identical with those we find in the universe; that is to say, that the universe is the Macrocosm, and man -- its true copy -- the Microcosm.

Microcosm and Macrocosm

Microcosmic man and the Macrocosm of nature are one. How could it be possible that the Macrocosm should contain anything not contained within the Microcosm or that man should have something within his organism, which cannot be found within the grand organism of nature? Is not man the child of nature, and can there be anything within his constitution which does not come from his eternal father and mother? If man's organisation contained something unnatural, he would be a monster, and nature would spew him out. Everything contained in nature can be found within the organism of man, and exists therein either in a germinal or developed state; either latent or active, and may be perceived by him who possesses the power of self-knowledge.

We are born into a world in which we find ourselves surrounded by physical objects. There seems to be still another -- a subjective -- world within us, capable of receiving and retaining impressions from the outside world. Each one is a world of its own, with a relation to space different from that of the other. Each has its days of sunshine and its nights of darkness, which are not regulated by the days and nights of the other, each has its clouds and its storms, and shapes and forms of its own.

As we grow up we listen to the teachings of science to try to find out the true nature of these worlds and the laws that govern them, but physical science deals only with forms, and forms are continually changing. She gives only a partial solution of the problems of the objective world, and leaves us in regard to the subjective world almost entirely in the dark. Modern science classifies phenomena and describes events, but to describe how an event takes place is not sufficient to explain why it takes place. To discover causes, which are in themselves the effects of unknown primal causes, is only to evade one difficulty by substituting another. Science describes some of the attributes of things, but the first causes which brought these attributes into existence are unknown to her, and will remain so, until her powers of perception will penetrate into the unseen.

Besides scientific observation there seems to be still another way to obtain knowledge of the mysterious side of nature. The religious teachers of the world claim to have sounded the depths which the scientists cannot reach. Their doctrines are supposed by many to have been received through certain divine or angelic revelations, proceeding from a supreme, infinite omnipresent, and yet personal, and therefore limited external Being, the existence of which has never been proved. Although the existence of such a being is -- to say the least -- exceedingly doubtful, yet men in all countries have bowed down in terror before its supposed dictates; ready to tear each other's throats at a sign of its supposed command, and willing to lay down their money, their lives, and even their honour at the feet of those who are looked upon as the confidants or deputies of a god. Men and women are willing to make themselves miserable and unhappy in life for the purpose of obtaining some reward after they live no more. Some waste their life in the anticipation of joys in a life of which they do not know whether or not it exists; some die for fear of losing that which they do not possess. Thousands are engaged in teaching others that which they themselves do not know, and in spite of a very great number of religious systems there is comparatively little religion at present upon the Earth.

Religion

The term Religion is derived from the Latin world religere, which may be properly translated "to bind back," or to "relate." Religion, in the true sense of the term, implies that science which examines the link which exists between man and the cause from which he originated, or in other words, which deals with the relation which exists between man and God, for the true meaning of the term "God" is Supreme First Cause, and Nature is the effect of its manifestation. True religion is therefore a science far higher than a science based upon mere sensual perception, but it cannot be in conflict with what is true in science. Only what is false in science must necessarily be in conflict with what is true in religion, and what is false in religion is in conflict with what is true in science. True religion and true science are ultimately one and the same thing, and therefore equally true; a religion that clings to illusions, and an illusory science, are equally false, and the greater the obstinacy with which they cling to their illusions the more pernicious is their effect.

A distinction should be made between "religion" and "religionism"; between "science" and "scientism"; between "mystic science" and "mysticism."

The highest aspect of Religion is practically the union of man with the Supreme First Cause, from which his essence emanated in the beginning.

Its second aspect teaches theoretically the relations existing between that Great First Cause and Man; in other words, the relations existing between the Macrocosm and Microcosm.

In its lowest aspect religionism consists of the adulation of dead forms, of the worshipping of fetiches, of fruitless attempts to wheedle oneself into the favour of some imaginary deity, to persuade "God" to change his mind, and to try to obtain some favours which are not in accordance with justice.

Science in her highest aspect is the real knowledge of the fundamental laws of Nature, and is therefore a spiritual science, based upon the knowledge of the spirit within one's own self.

In its lower aspect it is a knowledge of external phenomena, and the secondary or superficial causes which produce the latter, and which our modern scientism mistakes for the final cause.

In its lowest aspect scientism is a system of observation and classification of external appearances, of the causes of which we know nothing.

Religionism and Scientism are continually subject to changes. They have been created by illusions, and die when the illusions are over. True Science and true Religion are one, and if realised by Practice, they form, with the truth which they contain, the three-lateral pyramid, whose foundations are upon the earth, and whose point reaches into the kingdom of heaven.

Mystic science in its true meaning is spiritual knowledge; that is to say, the soul knowledge of spiritual and "super-sensual" things, perceived by the spiritual powers of the soul. These powers are germinally contained in every human organisation, but only few have developed them sufficiently to be of any practical use.

Mysticism belongs to the vapoury speculations of the brain. It is a hankering after illusions, a desire to pry into divine mysteries which the material mind cannot comprehend, a craving to satisfy curiosity in regard to what an animal ought not to know. It is the realm of fancies, of dreams, the paradise of ghost-seers, and of spiritistic tomfooleries of all kinds.

But which is the true religion and the true science? There is no doubt that a definite relationship exists between Man and the cause that called humanity into existence, and a true religion or a true science must be the one which teaches the true terms of that relation. If we take a superficial view of the various religious systems of the world, we find them all apparently contradicting each other. We find a great mass of apparent superstitions and absurdities heaped upon a grain of something that may be true. We admire the ethics and moral doctrines of our favourite religious system, and we take its theological rubbish in our bargain, forgetting that the ethics of nearly all religions are essentially the same, and that the rubbish which surrounds them is not real religion. It is evidently an absurdity to believe that any system could be true, unless it contained the truth. But it is equally evident that a thing cannot be true and false at the same time.

The truth can only be one. The truth never changes; but we ourselves change, and as we change so changes our aspect of the truth. The various religious systems of the world cannot be unnatural products. They are all the natural outgrowth of man's spiritual evolution upon this globe, and they differ only in so far as the conditions under which they came into existence differed at the time when they began to exist; while his science has been artificially built by facts collected from external observation. Each intellectual human being, except one blinded by prejudice, recognises the fact that each of the great religious systems of the world contains certain truths, which we intuitively know to be true; and as there can be only one fundamental truth, so all these religions are branches of the same tree, even if the forms in which the truth manifests itself are not alike. The sunshine is everywhere the same, only its intensity differs in different localities. In one place it induces the growth of palms, in another of mushrooms; but there is only one Sun in our system. The processes going on on the physical plane have their analogies in the spiritual realm, for there is only one Nature, one Law.

If one person quarrels with another about religious opinions, he cannot have the true religion, nor can he have any true knowledge; because true religion is the realisation of truth. The only true religion is the religion of universal Love; this love is the recognition of one's own divine universal self. Love is an element of divine Wisdom, and there can be no wisdom without love. Each species of birds in the woods sings a different tune; but the principle which causes them to sing is the same in each. They do not quarrel with each other, because one can sing better than the rest. Moreover, religious disputations, with their resulting animosities, are the most useless things in the world; for no one can combat the darkness by fighting it with a stick: the only way to remove darkness is to kindle a light, the only way to dispel spiritual ignorance is to let the light of knowledge that comes from the centre of love shine into every heart.

All religions are based upon internal truth, all have an outside ornamentation which varies in character in the different systems, but all have the same foundation of truth, and if we compare the various systems with one another, looking below the surface of exterior forms, we find that this truth is in all religious systems one and the same. In all this, truth has been hidden beneath a more or less allegorical language, impersonal and invisible powers have been personified and represented in images carved in stones or wood, and the formless and real has been pictured in illusive forms. These forms in letters, and pictures, and images are the means by which truths may be brought to the attention of the unripe Mind. They are to the grown-up children of all nations what picture-books are to small children who are not yet able to read, and it would be as unreasonable to deprive grown-up children of their images before they are able to read in their own hearts, as it would be to take away the picture-books from little children and to ask them to read printed books, which they cannot yet understand.

Very uninteresting and insignificant would be the stories contained in the Bible, and in other religious books, if the personal events described therein were referring merely to certain occurrences having happened in the lives of certain individuals who lived some thousands of years ago, and whose biography can seriously interest no one to-day. What do we care now about the family affairs of a man called Adam or Abraham? Why should we want to be interested in knowing bow many legitimate or illegitimate children the Jewish Patriarchs had, and what became of them? What is it to us whether or not a man by the name of Jonah was thrown into the water and swallowed by a whale? What happens to-day in the various countries of Europe is more interesting and important for us to know than what happened at the court of Zerubabel or Nabuchodonoser. But fortunately for the Bible and -- if we only knew how to read it -- fortunately for us, the stories contained therein are by no means merely histories of persons who lived in ancient times, but they are allegories and myths having always a very deep meaning, of which our expounders of the Bible, as well as its critics, usually know very little.

The men and the women of the old and new "testament" are much more than mere persons supposed to have existed at that time. They are personifications of eternally active spiritual forces, of which physical science does not even know that they exist; and their histories give an account of their action, their interrelations within the Macrocosm and its counterpart the Microcosm; they teach the history of the evolution of mankind in its spiritual aspect.

If our natural philosophers would study the Bible and the ancient religious books of the East, in their esoteric and spiritual aspects, they might learn a great many things which they desire to know. They might learn to find out what are the true powers of the still sleeping "Inner Man," which are required to produce occult phenomena at will; they might find instruction how to transmute lead or iron into pure gold, and to transform animals into gods.

Truth Based on Natural Law

But it is a truth, based upon natural laws, that man can see nothing except that which exists in his mind. If a man closes his eyes, he sees nothing, and if his mind is filled with illusions, he will have no room for the truth, and the deepest of symbols will be pictures without meaning to him.

If our children -- the big ones as well as the little ones -- are only looking at the pictures without learning the text, they are apt to grow to believe the pictorial representations to be the very things they are intended to represent; they become accustomed to forget that forms are only illusions, and that formless realities cannot be seen. It is so much easier to believe than to think. Children should not linger over their picture-books so long as to neglect their higher education. Humanity has outgrown the infancy of its present cycle, and asks for more intellectual food; the age of superstition is passing away, and the demand is not for opinions but for knowledge, and knowledge cannot be obtained without an effort. If we examine the various religious systems we may find a great deal of truth, but we cannot recognise it without knowledge, and real knowledge can only be obtained by practical experience. The expressed opinion of one person can only give rise to conviction in another, if corroborated by the same or a similar experience of the latter. A person can only truly believe that which he knows himself, and he can only actually know himself that which he has experienced himself.

There is a great difference between believing and understanding the truth. We may believe the truth with our heart and reject it with our brain. In other words: We may feel the truth intuitively, and not see it intellectually. If our present generation would cultivate the faculty of knowing the truth by heart, and afterwards examine that which they know by means of their intellect, we would soon have a far better and happier state of society everywhere. But the great curse of our age is that the intellectual faculties reject the truth in the heart. The science of the brain suppresses the knowledge of the soul, and tries to grasp that which only the heart can touch.

Men, instead of living in the sanctuary of the temples which they inhabit, are continually absent from there, and reside in the garret under the roof, looking out through the windows of the garret after scientific theories and other illusions of life. Day and night they stand there and watch, careful that none of the passing illusions may escape their observation, and while their attention is absorbed by these idle shows, the thieves enter the house and the sanctuary without being seen, and steal away the treasures. Then at the time when the house is destroyed, and death appears, the soul returns to the heart and finds it empty and desolate, and all the illusions that occupied the brain during life fly away, and man is left poor indeed, because he has not perceived the truth in his heart.

The real object of a religious system should therefore be to teach a way by which a person may develop the power to perceive the truth himself, independent of anybody's opinion. To ask a man to believe in the opinion expressed by another, and to remain satisfied with such a belief, is to ask him to remain ignorant, and to trust to another person more than to his own experience. A person without knowledge can have no real conviction, no true faith. His adoption of one particular theory or system depends on the circumstances under which he is born, or brought up, or surrounded. He is most liable to adopt that system which his parents or neighbours have inherited or adopted, and if he changes from one to another, he, generally speaking, does so from mere sentimentalism, or on account of some selfish consideration, expecting to obtain some benefit to himself by that change.

From a spiritual standpoint he will gain nothing under such circumstances; because to approach the truth, he must love the truth for its own sake, and not on account of the personal advantage that it may bring; from an intellectual standpoint he will gain little or nothing by exchanging one superstition for another. The only way by which Man can hope to arrive at the truth is to love the truth on account of its being the truth, and to free his mind from all prejudices and predilections, so that its light may penetrate into the mind.

"What is the religionism of to-day, but a religion of fear? Men do not wish to avoid vice, but they wish to avoid the punishment for having indulged in vice. Their experience teaches them that the laws of nature are unchangeable, but nevertheless they continue to act against the universal law. They claim to believe in a God who is unchangeable, and yet they implore his assistance if they desire to break his own law. When will they rise up to the true conception that the only possible God is that universal power which acts in the law, which is itself the law of the spirit in nature, and cannot be changed? To break the law is identical with breaking the God within ourselves, and the only way to obtain forgiveness after he is broken is to restore the supremacy of the law, and to create a new God within ourselves."

It may be well to study the opinions of others, and to store them up in the book of our memory, but we should not believe them to constitute self-knowledge. Even the teachings of the world's greatest Adepts, unimpeachable as they may be, can only instruct us, but give us no real knowledge. -They can show the way, but we must take ourselves the steps on the ladder. Were we to recognise their dictum as the final aim, to be accepted without any further internal investigation, we should again fall back into a system of belief for the sake of authority. Knowledge gives strength, doubt paralyses the will. A man who does not believe that he is able to walk will not be able to walk as long as he does not believe; a man who knows by experience that he can command himself will be able to do so. He who can command himself can command that which is below him, because the low is controlled by the high, and there is nothing higher than Man having obtained a perfect knowledge of Self.

Knowledge of Self

The knowledge of Self is identical with Self-knowledge, i.e., with one's own Soul knowledge independent of any dogmas or doctrines, no matter from what external authority they may proceed. If we study the teachings of any supposed authority external to our own selves, we at best know what the opinion of such an authority is in regard to the truth, but we do not necessarily arrive thereby at a self-knowledge of the truth. If we, for instance, learn what Christ taught about God, we are only informed of what he knew or believed to know; but we cannot know God for all that, unless we awaken to a realisation of God's presence within our own heart. The knowledge of even the wisest of all men, if communicated to us, will be to us nothing more than an opinion, as long as it is not experienced within our own selves. As long as we cannot penetrate within the soul of Man, we can know little more about him but his corporeal form; but how could we penetrate within the soul of another as long as we do not know our own? therefore the beginning of all real knowledge is the knowledge of Self; the knowledge of the Soul and not the vagaries of the brain.

Does external science confer any true knowledge of Man? The range of her power of observation is limited by the perceptive power of the physical senses, assisted by physical instruments; she has no means to investigate that which transcends physical sense, she cannot enter the temple of the unseen, she only knows the external form in which the reality dwells. She only knows what man appears to be, but not what he is, she knows nothing whatever of the essential and real man, and sometimes denies his existence. In vain shall we look to her for the solution of the problem, which thousands of years ago the Egyptian Sphinx propounded. Do the popular religious systems confer any true knowledge of Man? The conception which the average theologian has of the mysterious being called Man is as narrow as that of the professor of modern science. He looks upon man as a personal being, isolated from other personal beings around whose infinite little personality centres the interests of the infinitely great. He forgets that the founders of the principal religious systems taught that the original and essential man was a universal power, that the real man is a whole and cannot be divided, and that the personal form of man is only the temporary temple in which the spirit dwells. *(Bible: Corinth, iii. 16.)*

The misconceptions arising from ignorance of the true nature of Man are the cause that the popular religious opinions held by the average theologians in Christian and Pagan countries are based upon selfishness, contrary to the spirit of that which true religion teaches. "Christians" and "Heathens" clamour for some benefit to be conferred by some imaginary person upon that insignificant soap bubble, called the "personal self," either here or in the hereafter. Each one of such shortsighted nothings wants to be saved personally himself above all, the salvation of the rest is a matter of second consideration. They expect to obtain some benefit which they do not deserve, to wheedle themselves into the favour of some personal deity, argue their case before God, cheat the "devil" of his just dues, and smuggle their imperfections into the kingdom of heaven.

The only reasonable object which any external religious system can possibly have, is to elevate man from a lower state to a higher one, in which he can form a better conception of his true dignity as a member of the human family. If there is any possibility of imparting to a man a knowledge of his true self, the churches are the places where such a knowledge should be imparted; but to accomplish this the claims of the truth should predominate over those of the form, the interests of religion and the interests of the "church" would have to cease to be interchangeable terms, and the church should again be founded upon the rock of self-knowledge, instead of the craving to obtain some selfish personal benefit in this world or in the problematical hereafter.

Selfish Considerations

He who is led by selfish considerations cannot enter a heaven where personal considerations do not exist. He who does not care for heaven but is contented where he is, is already in heaven, while the discontented will in vain clamour for it. To be without personal desires is to be free and happy. "Heaven" can mean nothing else but a state in which freedom and happiness exist. The man who performs beneficial acts induced by a hope of reward is not happy unless the reward is obtained, and if his reward is obtained his happiness ends. There can be no permanent rest and happiness as long as there is some work to be done and not accomplished, and the fulfilment of duties brings its own reward,

A man who performs a good act with the hope of reward is not free. He is a servant of Self, and works for the benefit of Self and not for his God. It is, therefore, not the power of God which will reward him, he can only expect that reward from his own temporary surroundings.

The man who performs evil acts, induced by a selfish motive, is not free. He who desires evil and is restrained by fear is not his own master. He who recognises the supreme power of the universe in his own heart has become free. He whose will is swayed by his Personal self is the slave of his person, but he who has conquered that so-called "self" enters the higher life and becomes a power.

The science of Life consists in subduing the low and elevating the high. Its first lesson is how to free oneself from the love of self, the first angel of evil, or, according to Edwin Arnold:

"The sin of self, who in the universe
As in a mirror sees her fond face shown,
And crying 'I,' would have the world say 'I,'
And all things perish so if she endure."

-- Edw. Arnold: "Light of Asia."

Elementals

This lower Self is an unreal thing, composed of a great many illusive egos, of which each one has his peculiar claims, and whose demands grow in proportion as we attempt to satisfy them. They are the semi-intellectual forces of the soul that would rend the soul to pieces if they were allowed to grow, and which must be subdued by the power of the real Master, the superior "I" -- the God.

These "I's" are the Elementals, of which has been said so much in occult literature. They are not imaginary things, but living forces, and they may be perceived by him who has acquired the power to look within his own soul. Each of these forces corresponds to some animal desire, and if it is permitted to grow is symbolised by the form of the being which corresponds to its nature. At first they are thin and shadowy, but as the desire which corresponds to them is indulged in, they become more and more dense within the soul, and being nourished by the will, they gain great strength as our desires grow into a passion. The lesser Elementals are swallowed by the bigger ones, the little desires are absorbed by the stronger ones, until perhaps at last one Master Passion, one powerful Elemental remains. They form the dreaded Dwellers of the Threshold, who guard the garden of the paradise of the soul. They are described as having the form of snakes and tigers, hogs, insatiable wolves, &c., but as they are often the result of a mixture of human and animal elements, they do not merely exhibit purely animal forms; but frequently they look like animals with human heads or like men with animal members; they appear under endless varieties of shapes, because there is an endless variety of correlations and mixtures of lust, avarice, greed, sensual love, ambition, cowardice, fear, terror, hate, pride, vanity, self-conceit, stupidity, voluptuousness, selfishness, jealousy, envy, arrogance, hypocrisy, cunning, sophistry, imbecility, superstition, &c., &c.

These Elementals live in the soul-realm of man as long as he lives, and grow strong and fat, for they live on his life-principle, and are fed by the substance of his thoughts. They may even become objective to him, if during a paroxysm of fear or in consequence of some disease they are enabled to step out of their sphere. They cannot be killed by pious ceremonies, nor be driven away by the exhortations of a clergyman; they are only destroyed by the power of the spiritual Will of the divine man, which annihilates them as the light annihilates darkness, or as a stroke of lightning seems to rend the clouds.

Only those who have awakened to divine spiritual consciousness can have that spiritual will, of which the non-regenerated knows nothing. But those who are not yet so far advanced may cause those elementals to die slowly, by withdrawing from them the food which they require, that is to say, by not desiring or enjoying their presence; by not giving to their existence the consent of the will. They will then begin to wane, to get sick, die and putrefy like a member of the body which has become mortified. A line of demarkation will be formed in the soul-body of man, there may be "inflammation" and suffering. A process, similar to that which occurs if a gangrenous part of the physical body is thrown off, takes place; and at last the putrid carcass of the Elemental drops off and dissolves.

These descriptions are neither fancies nor allegories. Theophrastus Paracelsus, Jackob Boehme, and many other writers on Occultism write about them, and a due appreciation of their doctrines will go far to explain many occurrences mentioned in the history of witchcraft, and in the legends of the lives of the saints.

But there are not merely animal germs within the realm of the soul of man. In each human constitution there are also the germs which go to make up a Shakespeare, a Washington, Goethe, Voltaire, a Buddha, or Jesus of Nazareth. There are also the germs which may grow to make a Nero, Messalina, or Torquemada; and each germ has the latent power to develop, take a form and ultimately find its expression and reflection in the outward body, as much as the density of the material atoms, which are slow to transform, will permit; for each character corresponds to a form, and each form to a character.

Man's microcosm is a garden in which all kinds of living plants grow Some are poisonous, some are wholesome. It rests with man to decide which germs he wants to develop into a living tree, and that tree will be himself.

Becoming Spiritual

To accomplish the task of becoming spiritual it is not necessary to be a misanthrope and retire into a jungle there to feed on the products of one's own morbid imagination; the struggle caused by the petty annoyances of everyday life is the best school to exercise the will power for those that have not yet gained the mastery over Self. "To renounce the vanities of the world" does not mean to look with contempt upon the progress of the world, to remain ignorant of mathematics and logic, to take no interest in the welfare of humanity, to avoid the duties of life or neglect one's family. Such a proceeding would accomplish the very reverse of what is intended; it would increase the love of self, it would cause the soul to shrink to a small focus instead of expanding it over the world.

We must attain a state before we can outgrow it. A misanthrope cannot attain the love of God, if he does not first rise up to the love for mankind. "To renounce one's self" means to conquer the sense of personality and to free one's self of the love of things which that personality desires. It means to "live in the world, but not cling to the world," to substitute universal love for personal love, and to consider the interests of the whole of superior importance than personal claims. The renunciation of that self which is only a mask, is necessarily followed by spiritual growth. As we forget our personal self, we attach less importance to personalities, personal things, and personal feelings. We begin to look upon ourselves not as being permanent, unchanging and unchangeable entities, standing isolated among other isolated entities, and being separated from them by impenetrable shells, but as manifestations of an infinite power, which embraces the universe, and whose powers are concentrated and brought to a focus in the bodies which we temporarily inhabit, into which bodies continually flow and from which are incessantly radiating the rays of an infinite sphere of light, whose circumference is endless and whose centre is everywhere.

Upon the recognition and realisation of this truth rests the only true Law, the Religion of the Universal Love of God in all Beings, As long as man takes only his own little self into consideration in his thoughts and acts, the sphere of his mind becomes necessarily narrow. All our popular religious sects are based upon selfish considerations. Each of our religious sectarians specu- lates to obtain some spiritual, if not material, benefit for himself. Each one wants to be saved by somebody; first he, and then perhaps the others ; but, above all, he himself. The true religion of universal Love knows of no "self."

Even the high and laudable desire to go to heaven or enter the state of Nirvana is, after all, but a selfish desire, and as long as man has any selfish desires what- ever, his mind perceives only his own self. Only when he ceases to have a limited illusive "self" will his real god become unlimited and be omnipresent, like the spirit of Wisdom. He who desires unlimited knowledge must rise above limitation.

Looked at from that height, the personality appears exceedingly small and insignificant, and of little im- portance. Man appears as the centralisation of an idea, persons and peoples like living grains of sand on the shore of an infinite ocean. Fortune, fame, love, luxury, &c, assume the importance of soap-bubbles, and t]ie soul has no hesitation in relinquishing them as the idle playthings of children. Neither can such a renuncia- tion be called a sacrifice, for grown-up boys and girls do not "sacrifice" their popguns and dolls, they simply do not want them any longer. In proportion as their minds expand, do they reach out for something more useful, and as a man's soul expands, his surroundings, and even the planet on which he lives, appear to him small as a landscape seen from a great distance, or from a high mountain, while at the same time his conception of the infinite grows larger and assumes a gigantic form. This expansion of our existence "robs us of a country and a home" *(Bulwer-Lytton : "Zanoni,")* by making us citizens of the grand universe; it separates us from the fancied affections for the impermanent forms of our mortal parents and friends, to unite us with their true in- dividualities for ever as our immortal brothers and sis- ters ; it lifts us up from the narrow confines of the illusory to the unlimited realm of the Ideal, and releas- ing man from the prison-house of insignificant clay, it leads him to the sublime freedom and splendour of Eternal and Universal Life.

Focus of Energies

Every form of life, the human form not excepted, is nothing more than a focus in which the energies of the universal principle of life are concentrated, and the more they are concentrated and cling to that centre, the less are they able to manifest their activity, to grow and expand. Self-satisfied man, who employs his ca- pacities only for his own selfish purpose, contracts them into himself, and as he contracts he becomes more and more narrow-minded and insignificant, and as he loses sight of the whole, the whole loses sight of him. If, on the other hand, a person lives only in dreams, sending his forces into the region of the unknown, scattering them through space, without having obtained intellectual strength, his thoughts will wander like shadows through the realm of the infinite and become lost. Neither the self-conceited realist nor the visionary dreamer requires expansion along with a corresponding accumulation of energy.

Some persons are possessed of great intellectual power, but of little spirituality; some have spiritual power, but a weak intellect; those in whom the intel- lectual energies are well supported by a strong spirit are the elect. To become practical, we must first learn to understand the thing we want to practice, by obser- vation and receiving instruction. Understanding is a result of assimilation and growth, not a result of memory. The truth must nourish the soul. It is an awakening to a state of consciousness of the nature of the thing that comes to be a part of our own being. A person coming to a strange country in the evening will, when after a night's rest he awakes in the morning, hardly realise where he is. He has, perhaps, been dreaming of his home and those that are left there, and only after he opens his eyes and awakens to a full sense of con- sciousness of his new and strange surroundings, will the old impressions fade away, and he will begin to realise where he is. In the same manner old errors must dis- appear before new truths can be realised. Man only begins to exist as conscious a spiritual being when he begins to experience spiritual life.

To become spiritual, physical health, intellectual growth, and spiritual activity should go hand in hand. Intuition should be supported by an unselfish intellect, a pure mind by a healthy form. How to accomplish this can neither be taught by a science which deals only with illusory effects, nor by a religious belief based upon illusions; but it is taught by Theosophy, the Wisdom Religion of the ages, whose foundation is truth, and whose practical application is the highest object of human existence.

This Wisdom Religion has been, and is to-day, the inheritance of the saints, prophets, and seers, and of the illuminated ones of all nations, no matter to what external system of religion they may have given their adherence. It was taught by the ancient Brahmins, Egyptians, and Jews in temples and caves, Gautama Buddha and Jesus of Nazareth preached it, it formed the basis of the Eleusinian and Bacchic mysteries of the Greeks, and the true religion of the eternal Christ is resting upon it. It is the religion of Humanity, that has nothing to do with opinions and forms. Now, as in times of old, its truths are misunderstood and misrep- resented by men who profess to be teachers of men. The Pharisees and Sadducees of the New Testament were the prototypes of modern churchmen and scientists existing to-day. Now, as then, the truth is daily crucified between superstition and selfishness and laid in the tomb of ignorance. Now, as then, the spirit has fled from the form, being driven away by those that worship the letter and ignore the spirit. Wisdom will for ever remain a secret science to the idolators adoring the form, even if it were proclaimed from the housetops and preached at a market-place. The dealer in pounds and pennies, absorbed by his material interests, may be sur- rounded by the greatest beauties of nature and not com- prehend them, the speculative reasoner will ask for a sign and not see the signs by which he is continually surrounded. The tomb from which the Saviour will arise is the heart of mankind; if the God in Humanity awakens to self-consciousness of his Divinity then will he appear as a sun, shedding its light upon a better and happier generation.*(See "Bhagavad Gita," cap xi.)*

"Black Magic"

The existence of the magic power of good will probably be denied by few; but if the existence of benevolent or White Magic, is admitted, that of malevolent, or Black Magic, is not any more improbable.

It is not man who exercises good or evil magic powers, but it is the spirit in him who works good or evil through the organism of man. God in his aspect as the great cause is good or evil according to the conditions under which he acts; for if God did not include evil as well as good, he would not be universal. God performs good or evil deeds according to the mode in which he must act; in the same way as the sun is good in spring- time when he melts the snow and assists the grass and flowers to crawl out of the dark earth, and evil, if he parches the skin of the wanderer in tropical Africa and kills persons by sun-stroke.

God causes the healthy growth of a limb and the unhealthy growth of a cancer by the power of his unintelligent material nature which acts according to law and not according to whims. Divine wisdom does not become manifest in that which is not divine or spiritual. Consciousness cannot become revealed in an unconscious body. Only when the spirit in Man has awakened to consciousness and knowledge, will man be able to control his own spiritual power and employ it for good or for evil.

A person having created (or called into consciousness) in himself a spiritual power may employ it for good or for evil. Every day we may read of persons who have used high intellectual powers for vile purposes. We see persons making use of the vanity, greediness, selfishness, or ambition of others to render them subservient to their own purpose. We see them commit murder and instigate wars for the benefit of their own purposes or to attain some object of their ambition. But such events belong more or less to the struggle for existence. They do not necessarily belong to the sphere of black magic because they are usually not caused by a love for absolute evil, but by a desire of a personal benefit of some kind.

The real black magicians are those that are doing evil for the sake of doing evil, who injure others without expecting or receiving any benefit for them-selves. To that class belong the habitual backbiter and slanderer, traducer and seducer, those who enjoy to create enmity in the bosom of families, oppose progress and encourage ignorance, and they have been rightly called the Sons of Darkness, while those who do good for the sole purpose of doing good have been called the Children of Light.

The struggle between Light and Darkness is as old as the world; there can no light become manifest without Darkness and no evil without good. Good and evil are the light and shadow of the one eternal principle of life, and each is necessary if the other is to become manifest. Absolute good must exist, but we cannot know good without knowing the presence of evil. Absolute evil cannot exist, because it is held together by the power of good. A soul in which there were no good whatever would rage against itself, the forces constituting such an entity would combat each other and rend it to pieces. Man's Redeemer is his power for good. This power attracts him to that which is good, and at the end, when the supreme source of all power, from which life emanated in the beginning, withdraws that activity into itself, the powers of darkness will suffer, but the crea- tures of Light will be one with their own source.

This is the law of evolution, that the lower should develop' into something higher; but this can be accom- plished only by the power of the highest of all germin- ally contained within the form, and acted upon by itself from without. The soul requires nutriment as much as the physical form, and the nutriment of the soul descends from above like the rain ; while the earth below furnishes the conditions for its assimilation. This is the law of the spirit in the natural world, that all nature .should receive it and by a spiritual unfolding rise up to the spirit, while matter is to furnish the steps upon which to ascend. This unfolding and uprising takes place in proportion as the spirit of God becomes self-conscious in man, endowing him with a sense of its divine nature, which will ultimately lead him to a recognition of God.

Chapter I - The Ideal

"God is a Spirit, and they that worship him must worship him in spirit and in truth."
-- John iv. 24

The Highest Desire

The highest desire any reasonable man can cherish and the highest right he may possibly claim, is to become perfect. To know everything, to love all and be known and beloved by all, to possess and command everything that exists, such is a condition of being that, to a certain extent, may be felt intuitively, but whose possibility cannot be grasped by the intellect of mortal man.

A foretaste of such a blissful condition may be experienced by a person who -- even for a short period of time -- is perfectly happy. He who is not oppressed by sorrow, not excited by selfish desires, and who is conscious of his own strength and liberty, may feel as if he were the master of worlds and the king of creation; and, in fact, during such moments he is their ruler, as far as he himself is concerned, although his subjects may not seem to be aware of his existence.

But when he awakes from his dream and looks through the windows of his senses into the exterior world, and begins to reason about his surroundings, his vision fades away; he beholds himself a child of the Earth, a mortal form, bound with many chains to a speck of dust in the Universe, on a ball of matter called a planet that floats in the infinity of space. The ideal world, that perhaps a moment before appeared to him as a glorious reality, may now seem to him the baseless fabric of a dream, in which there is nothing real, and physical existence, with all its imperfections, is now to him the only unquestionable reality, and its most dear illusions the only things worthy of his attention. He sees himself surrounded by material forms, and he seeks to discover among these forms that which corresponds to his highest ideal.

The highest desire of a mortal is to attain fully that which exists in himself as his highest ideal. A person without an ideal is unthinkable. To be conscious is to realise the existence of some ideal, to relinquish the ideal world would be death. A person without any desire for some ideal would be useless in the economy of nature, a person having all his desires satisfied needs to live no longer, for life can be of no further use to him. Each one is bound to his own ideal; he whose ideal is mortal must die when his ideal dies, he whose ideal is immortal must become immortal himself to attain it.

Each man's highest ideal should be his own higher spiritual self. Man's semi-animal self, which we see expressed in his physical form, is not the whole of man. Man may be regarded as an invisible power or ray extending from the (spiritual)

Sun to the Earth. Only the lower end of that ray is visible, where it has evolved an organised material body; by means of which the invisible ray draws strength from the earth below. If all the life and thought-force evolved by the contact with matter are spent within the material plane, the higher spiritual self will gain nothing by it. Such a person resembles a plant developing nothing but its root. When death breaks the communication between the higher and lower, the lower self will perish, and the ray will remain what it was, before it evolved a mortal inhabitant of the material world.

Interior and External Worlds

Man lives in two worlds, in his interior and in the exterior world. Each of these worlds exists under conditions peculiar to itself, and that world in which he lives is for the time being the most real to him. When he enters into his interior world during deep sleep or in moments of perfect abstraction, the forms perceived in the exterior world fade away; but when he awakes in the exterior world the impressions received in his interior state are forgotten, or leave only their uncertain shadows on the sky. To live simultaneously in both worlds is only possible to him who succeeds in harmoniously blending his internal and external worlds into one.

The so-called Real seldom corresponds with the Ideal, and often it happens that man, after many unsuccessful attempts to realise his ideals in the exterior world, returns to his interior world with disappointment, and resolves to give up his search; but if he succeeds in the realisation of his ideal, then arises for him a moment of happiness, during which time, as we know it, exists for him no more, the exterior world is then blended with his interior world, his consciousness is absorbed in the enjoyment of both, and yet he remains a man.

Artists and poets may be familiar with such states. An inventor who sees his invention accepted, a soldier coming victorious out of the struggle for victory, a lover united with the object of his desire, forgets his own personality and is lost in the contemplation of his ideal. The extatic saint, seeing the Redeemer before him, floats in an ocean' of rapture, and his consciousness is centred in the ideal that he himself has created out of his own mind, but which is as real to him as if it were a living form of flesh. Shakespeare's Juliet finds her mortal ideal realised in Romeo's youthful form. United with him, she forgets the rush of time, night disappears, and she is not conscious of it; the lark heralds the dawn and she mistakes its song for the singing of the nightingale. Happiness measures no time and knows no danger. But Juliet's ideal is mortal and dies; having lost her ideal Juliet must die; but the immortal ideals of both become again one as they enter the immortal realm through the door of physical death.

But as the sun rose too early for Juliet, so all evanescent ideals that have been realised in the external world vanish soon. An ideal that has been realised ceases to be an ideal; the ethereal forms of the interior world, if grasped by the rude hand of mortals and embodied in matter, must die. To grasp an immortal ideal, man's mortal nature must die before he can grasp it.

Low ideals may be killed, but their death calls similar ones into existence. From the blood of a vampire that has been slain a swarm of vampires arises. A selfish desire fulfilled makes room for similar desires, a gratified passion is chased away by other similar passions, a sensual craving that has been stilled gives rise to new cravings. Earthly happiness is short-lived and often dies in disgust; the love of the immortal alone is immortal. Material acquisitions perish, because forms are evanescent and die. Intellectual accomplishments vanish, for the products of the imagination, opinions, and theories, are subject to change. Desires and passions change and memories fade away.

He who clings to old memories, clings to that which is dead. A child becomes a man, a man an old man, an old man a child; the playthings of childhood give way to intellectual playthings, but when the latter have served their purpose, they appear as useless as did the former, only spiritual realities are everlasting and true.

In the ever-revolving kaleidoscope of nature the aspect of illusions continually changes its form. What is laughed at as a superstition by one century is often accepted as the basis of science for the next, and what appears as wisdom to-day may be looked upon as an absurdity in the great to-morrow. Nothing is permanent but the truth.

The Germ of Truth

But where can man find the truth? If he seeks deep enough in himself he will find it revealed, each man may know his own heart. He may let a ray of the light of intelligence into the depths of his soul and search its bottom, he will find it to be as infinitely deep as the sky above his head. He may find corals and pearls, or watch the monsters of the deep. If his thought is steady and unwavering, he may enter the innermost sanctuary of his own temple and see the goddess unveiled. Not every one can penetrate into such depths, because the thought is easily led astray; but the strong and persisting searcher will penetrate veil after veil, until at the innermost centre he discovers the germ of truth, which, awakened to self-consciousness, will grow in him into a sun that illuminates the whole of his interior world.

Such an interior meditation and elevation of thought in the innermost centre of the soul, is the only true prayer. The adulation of an external form, whether living or dead, whether existing objectively or merely subjectively in the imagination, is useless, and serves only to deceive. It is very easy to attend to forms of external worship, but the true worship of the living God within requires a great effort of will and a power of thought, and is in fact the exercise of a spiritual power received from God. God in us prays to himself. Our business consists in continual guarding of the door of the sacred lodge, so that no illegitimate thoughts may enter the mind to disturb the holy assembly whose deliberations are presided over by the spirit of wisdom.

How shall we know the truth? It can be known only if it becomes revealed within the soul. Truth, having awakened to consciousness, knows that it is; it is the god-principle in man, which is infallible and cannot be misled by illusions. If the surface of the soul is not lashed by the storms of passion, if no selfish desires exist to disturb its tranquillity, if its waters are not darkened by reflections of the past, we will see the image of eternal truth mirrored in the deep.

To know the truth in its fulness is to become alive and immortal, to lose the power of recognising the truth is to perish in death. The voice of truth in a person that has not yet awakened to spiritual life, is the "still small voice" that may be heard in the heart, listened to by the soul, as a half-conscious dreamer listens to the ringing of bells in the distance, *(See H. P. Blavatsky: "The voice of the silence.")* but in those that have become conscious of life, having received the baptism of the first initiation administered by the spirit of God, the voice heard by the new-born ego has no uncertain sound, but becomes the powerful Word of the Master. The awakened truth is self-conscious and self-sufficient, it knows that it exists. It stands higher than all theories and creeds and higher than science, it does not need to be corroborated by "recognised authorities," it cares not for the opinion of others, and its decisions suffer no appeal. It knows neither doubt nor fear, but reposes in the tranquillity of its own supreme majesty. It can neither be altered nor changed, it always was and ever remains the same, whether mortal man perceives it or not. It may be compared to the light of the earthly sun, that cannot be excluded from the world, but from which man may exclude himself.

We may blind ourselves to the perception of the truth, but the truth itself is not thereby changed. It illuminates the minds of those who have awakened to immortal life. A small room requires a little flame, a large room a great light for its illumination, but in either room the light shines equally clear in each; in the same manner the light of truth shines into the hearts of the illumined with equal clearness, but with a power differing according to their individual capacity.

It would be perfectly useless to attempt to describe this interior illumination. Only that which exists relatively to ourselves has a real existence for us, that of which we know nothing does not exist for us. No real knowledge of the existence of light can be furnished to the blind, no experience of transcendental knowledge can be given to those whose capacity to know does not transcend the realm of external appearances.

Truth, the Highest Ideal

There is nothing higher than truth, and the acquisition of truth is therefore man's highest ideal. The highest ideal in the Universe must be a universal ideal. The constitution of all men is built according to one universal law, and the highest ideal must be the same to all and attainable to all, and in its attainment all individuals become reunited. As long as the soul of man does not recognise the highest ideal in the Universe, the highest one which he is able to recognise will be the highest to him; but as long as there still exists a higher one than the one he perceives, the higher will unconsciously attract him, unless he forcibly and persistingly repulses its attraction.

Only the attainment of the highest ideal in the Universe can give eternal and permanent happiness, for having attained the highest there is nothing left that could possibly be desired. As long as there is still a higher ideal for man, he will have aspirations to reach it, but having reached the highest all attraction ceases, he becomes one with it and can desire nothing more.

There must be a state of perfection which all may reach and beyond which none can advance, until the Universe as, a whole advances beyond it. All men have the same right to reach the highest, but not all have the same power developed, some may reach it soon, others may lag on the road, and perhaps the majority may fall and have to begin again at the foot of the ladder. Each ripe acorn that falls from an oak has the inherent capacity to develop into an oak; but not each finds the same conditions for development. Some may grow, a few may develop into trees, but the majority will enter into decomposition to furnish material out of which new forms may be developed.

The highest truth in its fulness is not known to man in the mortal form. Those that have attained to a state of perfect consciousness of infinite truth are not imprisoned in a limited form, they belong to a formless tribe; they could not be one with an universal principle if they were tied by the chains of personality; a soul expanded, so that the prison-house of flesh can hold it no more, will require that prison-house no longer. Flesh and blood is only required to shelter the spirit in the infancy of his development, as long as he has not attained full power. The "clothes of skin"*(Bible: Genesis iii. 21)* were needed to protect him against the destructive elementary influences of the sphere of evil as long as he could not rise above evil. Having attained the knowledge of evil and the power to subdue it, and having by the realisation of the truth "eaten from the tree of life and attained substantiality,"*(Bible: Genesis iii. 22.)* he can protect himself by his own power, and requires his clothes of flesh no longer.

Direct Perception

Imperfectly developed man, unless he has become degraded, feels intuitively that which is true, but does not know the truth by direct perception. The externalist who reasons only from the plane of sensual perceptions is farthest from a recognition of the truth, because he mistakes the illusions produced by his senses for the reality, and repulses the revelations of his own spirit. The philosopher, unable to see the truth, attempts to grasp it with his logic, and may approach it to a certain extent; but he, in whom the truth has attained its own self-consciousness, knows the truth because he is himself one with it.

Such a state is incomprehensible to the majority of men, to scientists and philosophers as well as to the ignorant; nevertheless, men have existed, and exist to-day, who have attained it. They are the true Theosophists, but not everyone is a Theosophist who goes by the name of "Theosophist," nor is everyone a Christ who is called a Christian. But a true Theosophist and a true Christian are one and the same, because both are human forms in which the universal spiritual soul, the Christ or the light of Divine Wisdom, has become manifest.

The terms "Christian" or "Theosophist," like so many other terms of a similar kind, have almost entirely lost their true meaning. A "Christian" now-a-days means a person whose name is inscribed in the register of some so-called Christian Church, and performs the ceremonies prescribed by that social organisation; while a "Theosophist" is said to be a visionary or dreamer.

But a real Christian is something entirely different from a merely external one. The first Christians were a secret organisation, a school of Occultists, who adopted certain symbols and signs, in which to represent spiritual truths, and thus to communicate them to each other.

A real Theosophist is not a dreamer, but a most practical person. By purity of life he acquires the power to perceive higher truths than average man is able to see, and he understands the things which he sees, because he possesses a spiritual knowledge gained by many a life of self-denial in repeated reincarnations.

As fundamental truth, the life of all things is only one; men in all countries, having attained self-consciousness in it, have the same perception. This explains why the revelations of the sages are identical with each other. The truths revealed by a Jackob Boehme, Eckhart, or Paracelsus in Germany, are essentially the same as those revealed by the Thibetan Mahatmas, they only differ in extent and in mode of expression.

A true Christian saint in England or France would tell the same tale as a real Brahmin in India or a truly wise red Indian in America; because all three, being in the same state of clear perception, would exactly see the same thing. The truth is there, visible to all who possess it, but each will describe what he sees according to his mode of thinking and in his own fashion.

If -- as the ignorant believe -- all the visions of saints and lamas, sanyaasi, and dervishes, were only the result of hallucinations and fancies, not two of them, having never heard of each other, would have the same vision. A tree will be a tree to all who are able to see it, and if their sight is clear no arguments will change it into an oyster; a truth will be seen as a truth by all who are able to see it, and no sophistry will change it into a lie. To know the whole truth is to know everything that exists; to love the truth above all is to become united with everything; to be able to express the truth in its fulness is to possess universal power; to be one with immortal truth is to be for ever immortal.

Tranquillity of Soul

The capacity of perceiving the truth depends on the tranquillity of the soul. The soul not being true cannot realise truth, it can at best dream of it as of something existing in another world. The sound of the voice of the truth cannot penetrate through the noise caused by the turmoil in the heart; its light cannot break through the clouds of false theories and the smoke of opinions which inhabit the brain.

To understand that voice and to behold that light distinctly and without any foreign admixture, heart and head should be at rest. To perceive the truth, purity of heart and self-control should go hand in hand, and it is therefore taught that men must become as unsophisticated as children and strong as lions before they can enter the sphere of truth. Head and heart, if united, are One, but if they act against each other they form the absurd Two that produces illusions.

The emotional maniac is only guided by his heart, the intellectual fool only listens to the dictates of his head, he lives in his head and knows not the heart. But neither the revelry of the emotions nor intellectual fanaticism discloses the truth; only in the "stillness that follows the storm,"(*Light on the Path,*" by Mabel Collins.) when the harmony of both is restored, can the truth be discovered.

A man who only follows the dictates of his emotions, resembles one who in ascending a mountain peak becomes dizzy, and losing his power to control himself, falls over a precipice; a man who is only guided by his sensual perceptions influencing his intellect is easily lost in the whirlpool of multifarious illusions. He is like a person on an island in the ocean examining a drop of water taken from the ocean, and being blind to the existence of the ocean from which that drop has been taken. But if heart and head are attuned to the divine harmonies of the invisible realm of nature, then will the truth reveal itself to man, and in him will the highest ideal see its own image reflected.

We sometimes hear some people boast that they are controlled by their intellect, others are guided by their emotions; a free man is not controlled by either of the two; he is his own master guiding his heart and his mind. By the power of the god in him he controls the intellectual workings of his brain no less than the emotions of his heart. Heart and brain are not ourselves. They are instruments which have been lent to us by our Creator. They should not govern us; but we should govern them, and use them according to the dictates of his wisdom.

Material man, entombed in his chrysalis of clay, can only feel, but not see, the spiritual rays that radiate from the sun of infinite truth; but if he bids his emotions be still! and commands his reasoning power be not deluded! he may stretch his feelers into the realm of the spirit. In dealing with the unseen, his heart should be used as a touchstone to examine the conclusions arrived at by the brain, and the brain should be employed like scales to weigh the decisions of the heart; but when the light of divine wisdom comes to his aid, there will be no more difference of opinion between the head and the heart, the perceptions of the one will be in harmony with the aspirations of the latter, because both will be joined in the light.

Man is usually guided principally by his intellect, woman by her emotions; man represents intelligence, woman the will. To reason from external appearances has become a necessity to men in consequence of their material organisation, which like a shell surrounds their soul; but if the innermost spiritual man, sleeping in every heart, awakens to life, he emits a light that penetrates through the veil of matter and illuminates the mind. If this germ of divinity, hidden in the centre, awakens, it emits a spiritual light, which reaches from man to the stars and to the utmost limits of space, and by the help of that divine light the mind may perceive and penetrate into the deepest mysteries of the Universe. Those who are able to know the truth by direct perception do not need to be informed of it by others, the whole of the visible and invisible realm lies open before them, like a book in whose pages they may read the whole history of the world. They know all the manifestations of life, because they are one with the source of life from which all forms were born, they need not study letters, because the Word itself is living in them. They are the instruments through whom eternal wisdom reveals itself to those who are entombed in matter. These are the true Saviours, Adepts, Illuminates, Rosicrucians, Mahatmas, and Theosophoi; not those pretenders who merely fancy to be what they not really are.

The Vanity of the "Learned"

How pitiful must appear to the enlightened the war of opinions raging among those whom humanity believes to be the keepers of knowledge and wisdom; how insignificantly small appear those lights before the sun of divine truth. What appears as a light to the ignorant, appears to the illuminated seer as darkness and smoke, and the wisdom of the world becomes foolishness*(1 Cor. iii. 19)* before the eye of the truth.

The oyster in its shell may believe itself at the pinnacle of perfection, and that there is no higher existence than that which it enjoys in the ocean-bed; the self-conceited, proud of his learning, is swelled with vanity, knowing little how little he knows.

Many of the representatives of modern science forget that the greatest inventions have been made, not by the professed guardians of science, but by men with a clear perception, and upon whom they looked with contempt. They ought to remember, that many useful inventions were made and introduced, not with the assistance, but in spite of the opposition of the learned.

It may be disagreeable to call up unpleasant memories, but we cannot close our eyes to the fact that the inventors of railroads, steamships, and telegraphs have been ridiculed by professors of science, that men of science have laughed at the belief in the rotundity of the earth, and that some of the appointed keepers of the truth have often been conspicuous on account of their misunderstanding of the laws of nature, and of their opposition to truth, whenever it conflicted with their preconceived opinions.

Many useful discoveries have been made through the power of intuition; some have been made by logical reasoners without intuition, and their results are still a curse to mankind. For centuries the learned professions have been thriving on human suffering, and many of their followers, mistaking the low for the high, have prostituted their knowledge.

The fear of an illusory devil external to man has served to swell the money-bags of Brahmins and priests, while the real internal devils, residing in the passionate nature of man, were allowed to grow. For centuries many of the self-appointed servants of the Supreme have only served the golden calf, residing in their animal nature, feeding their followers with false hopes of immortality, and speculating on the selfish propensities of men.

Those to whom humanity looks for protection against bodily ills, and who therefore -- more than anybody else -- should understand the real constitution of man, still experiment with the physical form to seek the cause of disease, being ignorant of the fact that the form is an expression of life, the product of the soul, and that external effects cannot be effectually changed without changing the internal causes. Many of them refusing to believe in Soul, seek the cause of diseases in its external expression, where it does not exist.

Diseases are the necessary results of disobedience to the laws of nature, they are the consequences of "sins" that cannot be forgiven, but must be atoned for by acting again in accordance with natural laws. In vain will the ignorant ask the guardians of health for their assistance to cheat nature out of its dues. Physicians may restore health by restoring the supremacy of the law, but as long as they know only an infinitesimal part of the law they can only cure an infinitesimal part of the diseases afflicting mankind; they sometimes suppress the manifestation of one disease by calling another and more serious one into existence. In vain will such investigators seek for the cause for epidemic diseases in places where such diseases may be propagated, but where they are not created. The soul of the world in which such causes reside cannot be seen with microscopes, it can only be recognised by a man capable of perceiving the truth.

The Constitution of Man

A true conception of the nature of man will lead to the comprehension of the fact that man, being as a microcosm the true image, reflection and representative of the macrocosm of nature; Nature has the same organisation as Man, although not the same external form. Having the same organs and functions, and being ruled by the same laws, the organism of Nature is liable to experience diseases similar to those experienced by the organism of man. Nature has her dropsical swellings, her nervous tremblings, her paralytic affections by which civilised countries turn into deserts, her inflammatory affections, her rheumatic contractions, spells of heat and cold, eruptions and earthquakes. If our physicians knew the nature of man, they would also know the organisation of Nature as a whole, and understand more about the origin of epidemic diseases, of which they now know merely the external effects.

What does modern medical science know of the constitution of man, whose life and safety is made to depend on that knowledge? It knows the form of the body, the arrangement of muscles, and bones, and organs, and it calls these constituent parts by names which it invented. Having no supersensual perceptions it does not know the soul of man, but believes that his body is the essential man.

If its eyes were open it would see that this visible body is only the material kernal of the "immaterial," but nevertheless substantial real man, whose soul-essence radiates far into space, and whose spirit is without limits, and that the spirit is not merely within the body, but rather the body within the sphere of the spirit. They would know that in the life-principle resides sensation, perception, consciousness, and all the causes that produce the growth of the form. Labouring under their fatal mistake they attempt to cure that which is not sick, while the real patient is unknown to them.

Under such circumstances it is not surprising that the most enlightened physicians of our time have expressed the opinion that our present system of medicine is rather a curse than a blessing to mankind, and that our drugs and medicines on the whole do vastly more harm than good, because they are continually misapplied. This is an assertion which has often been made by their own most prominent leaders.

The ideal physician of the future is he who knows the true constitution of man, and who is not led by illusive external appearances, but able to examine into the hidden causes of all external effects. To him the acquisitions of external science are not the guides but only the assistants, his guide will be his own knowledge and not a theory, and his knowledge will endow him with power.*(Such a physician was Theophrastus Paracelsus, the great reformer of medicine in the sixteenth century.)*

If our medical students were to apply a part of the time which they employ for amusements for the development of a love for the truth, they would become able to know certain processes within the organism of man, which are at present to them a mere matter of speculation, and which are not discoverable by any physical means.

But even the modern physician acts wiser than he knows. He may say that he does not believe in faith, and yet it is only faith that upholds him and by which he exists, because if men had no confidence in him they would not employ him, and if his patients did not believe that he could benefit them they would not follow his directions. A physician without spiritual knowledge, having no confidence in himself, and in whom no one else has any faith, is perfectly useless as a physician, no matter how much he may have learned in schools.

There is nothing whatever that can be accomplished without the power of Faith, and there is no faith possible without spiritual knowledge. We can only accomplish that of which we are confident that we can accomplish it, and we can only be truly confident if we know by experience that we have the power to do it.

The Mind

What does popular science know about Mind? According to the usual definition, Mind is "the intellectual power in man," and as "man" means a visible body, this definition makes of mind something confined within that visible form. But if this conception were true, there could be no transmission of will to a distance and no transmission of thought.

No sound can be heard in a space from which the air has been exhausted, and no thought can travel from one individual to another without a corresponding "ether" existing between them; but the possibility of thought-transference is now an universally admitted fact; its truth has been perceived long ago by children who make practical use of it in some of their games, and it has now been admitted as a fact even by the most sceptical and superficial observers. *(Report of the Society for Psychical Research." London, 1884.)* Moreover, any one who doubts its possibility has it in his power to convince himself by either impressing his thoughts silently upon others, or by letting others impress their thoughts upon him.

How infinitely more grand and how much more reasonable is the conception of ancient philosophical science, according to whose doctrines everything that exists is an expression of the thoughts of the Universal Mind, pervading all space! This conception makes Mind a power in the realm of infinity, acting through living and intelligent instruments, and of Man, an intellectual power, an expression of the Universal Mind, able to receive, reflect, and modify the thoughts of the latter, like a diamond that becomes self-luminous through the influence of the Sun.

There is no reason why we should delude ourselves with a belief that an intelligent mind can exist only in a form which is visible and tangible to the external senses of man. There may be, for all we know, untold millions of intelligent or semi-intelligent beings in the universe, whose forms are constituted differently from ours, living on another plane of existence than ours, and who are therefore invisible to our physical senses, but may be perceived by the superior power of perception of the inner man. Nor is their existence a matter of mere speculation, for they have been perceived by those who have the power of interior perception.

All we know of external objects is the images which they produce in the sphere of our mind. Astral or spiritual beings produce no reflection upon the retina, but their presence may be known when they enter the mental sphere of the observer and they may be perceived with the eye of the soul.

The ideal scientist of the future having attained the power of inner perception, will recognise this truth.

If we believe that the object of life is simply to render our material Self satisfied and to keep it in comfort, and that material comfort confers the highest state of possible happiness, we mistake the low for the high and an illusion for the truth. Our material mode of life is a consequence of the material constitution of our bodies. We are "worms of earth" because we cling with all our desires and aspirations to earth.

If we can enter upon a path of evolution, by which we become less material and more ethereal, a very different order of civilisation would be established. Things which now appear indispensable and necessary would cease to be useful; if we could transfer our consciousness with the velocity of thought from one part of the globe to another, the present mode of communication and transportation would be no longer required. The deeper we sink into matter, the more material means for comfort will be needed; but the essential inner man is not material -- in the usual acceptation of this term -- and independent of the restrictions of matter.

What are the real necessities of life? The answer to this question depends entirely on what we imagine to be necessary. Railways, steamers, electric lights, &c., are now a necessity to us, and yet millions of people have lived long and happy knowing nothing about them. To one man a dozen of palaces may appear to be an indispensable necessity, to another a carriage, another a pipe, or a bottle of whisky.

But all such necessities are only such as man himself has created. They make the state in which he now is agreeable to him, and tempt him to remain in that state and to desire for nothing higher. They may even hinder his development instead of advancing it. If we would rise into a higher state, in which we would no longer require such things, they would cease to be a necessity, and even become undesirable and useless; but it is the craving and the wasting of thought for the augmentation of the pleasures of the lower life which prevent man to enter the higher one.

The Great Arcanum

To raise the evanescent man to a state of perfection enjoyed by the permanent ideal man is the great Arcanum, that cannot be learned in books. It is the great secret, that may be understood by a child, but will for ever be incomprehensible to him who, living entirely in the realm of his dreams, has no power to grasp it. The attainment of a higher consciousness is the Magnum opus, the great work, of which the Alchemists said that thousands of years may be required to perform it, but that it may also be accomplished in a moment, even by a woman while engaged in spinning. They looked upon the human mind as being a great alembic,* in which the contending forces of the emotions may be purified by the heat of holy aspirations and by a supreme love of truth. They gave instructions how the soul of mortal man may be sublimated and purified from earthly attractions, and its immortal parts be made living and free.

The purified elements were made to ascend to the supreme source of law, and descended again in showers of snowy whiteness, visible to all, because they rendered every act of life holy and pure. They taught how the base metals -- meaning the animal energies in man -- could be transformed into the pure gold of true spirituality, and how, by attaining spiritual knowledge and spiritual life, souls could have their youth and innocence restored and be rendered immortal. Their truths shared the fate of other truths; they were misunderstood and rejected by the ignorant, who continually clamour for truth and reject it when it is offered, and ridiculed by fools. Theology and Masonry have -- each in its own manner -- continued the teachings of the Alchemists, and fortunate is the Mason or the priest who spiritually understands that which he teaches. But of such true disciples there are only few. The systems in which the old truths have been embodied are still in existence, but the cold hands of Sophistry and Materialism have been laid upon the outward forms, and from the interior the spirit has fled. Doctors and clergymen see only the outward form, and not the hidden mystery that called these forms into existence. The key to the inner sanctuary has been lost by those that were entrusted with its keeping, and the true password has not been rediscovered by the followers of Hiram Abiff. The riddle of the Egyptian Sphinx still waits for a solution, and will be revealed to none unless he becomes strong enough to discover it himself.

But the true Word still lives. The light of truth still shines deep into the interior world of man, and sends its divine influence down into the valleys, and wherever the doors and windows are open to receive it, there will it dispel the darkness, rendering men and women conscious of their own godlike attributes and guiding them on the road to perfection, until, when all their struggles have ceased and the law has been restored, they will find permanent happiness in the realisation of the highest universal ideal, their own divine self.

Chapter II - The Real and the Unreal

"Allah ! Bi' -smi' -llah ! -- God is One." – **Koran**

Form and Essence

Everywhere in the broad expanse of the universe we see an almost infinite variety of forms, belonging to different kingdoms and species, and exhibiting an endless variety of appearances. The substance of which those forms are composed may, for aught we know, consist essentially of the same primordial material, forming the basis of their constitution, although the qualities of the various bodies differ from each other, and it is far more reasonable to suppose that this one primordial eternal essence exists and appears in the course of evolution in various forms, than to believe that a number of different original substances have come into existence either by being created out of nothing or otherwise.

What this primordial essence is -- this immaterial substance *(The Aakaasa of the Brahmins or the Iliaster of Paracelsus, the Universal Proteus.)* -- we do not know, we only know of its manifestation in forms which we call things. Whatever finds expression in one form or another is called a thing, and a thing may change its form and the substance remain. Water may be frozen into solid ice, or be transformed by heat into visible vapour; and vapour may be chemically decomposed into hydrogen and oxygen; yet, if the necessary conditions are given, the energies which previously formed water will form water again; the forms and attributes change, but the elements remain the same and combine again in certain proportions, regulated by the law of mutual attraction.

As this hypothetical primordial substance or principle has no attributes which we can perceive with our senses, we do not know the real substance of a thing. We may gradually deprive a thing of some of its attributes and change its form, and yet it remains that thing as long as its character remains, and even after we destroy its form and dissolve its materials the character of the thing still remains as an idea in the subjective world, where we cannot destroy it, and we may clothe the old idea with new attributes and reproduce it under a new form on the objective plane.

A thing exists as long as its character exists, only when it changes its character it changes its essential nature. A material thing is only the symbol or the representation of an idea; we may give it a name, but idea remains hidden behind the veil. If we could on the physical plane separate a single substance from its character, and endow it with another, then one body could be transformed into another, as, for instance, base metals be transformed into gold; but unless we change the character of a thing, a mere change of its form will only affect its external appearance.

By way of illustration, let us look at a stick. It is made of wood, but this is not essential; it might be made of something else and still be a stick. We do not perceive the stick itself, we only see its attributes, its extension and colour and density; we feel its weight and we hear its sound if we strike. Each of these attributes or all of them may be changed, and it will remain a stick for all that, as long as its character is not lost, because that which essentially constitutes its character is its purpose, an idea which has not a definite form. Let us endow that formless idea with a new purpose that will change its character, and we shall have transformed our ideal stick into anything we choose to make of it.

We cannot change copper into gold on the physical plane, we cannot change a man into a physical child, but we may daily transform our desires, our aspirations, tastes, and our character, if we conceive of a new purpose of life. In doing this we make of man, even on the physical plane, a different being.

Essence of Man

Nobody ever saw a real man, we only perceive the qualities which he possesses. Man cannot see himself. He speaks of his body, his soul, his spirit; it is the combination of the three which constitutes the sum of his attributes. The real Ego, in which his character rests, is something unknown, whose nature becomes conceivable to us only when we divine the purpose of its existence.

As an idea and for a purpose he enters the world of matter, evolutes a new personality, obtains new experience and knowledge, passes through the pleasures and vicissitudes of life and through the valley of death, and enters again into that realm where in the course of ages his outward form will cease to exist, to appear again in such a form upon the scene when the hour for his reappearance strikes. His body and personality change his purpose, and therefore his Ego remains the same and yet not the same, because during life it acquires new attributes and changes its characteristics.

A true appreciation and understanding of the essential nature of man will show that the repeated reincarnation of the human monad in successive personalities is a scientific necessity. How could it be possible for a man to develop into a state of perfection, if the time of his spiritual growth were restricted to the period of one short existence upon this globe? If he could go on and develop without having a physical body, then why should it have been necessary for him to take a physical body at all? It is unreasonable to suppose that the spiritual germ of a man begins its existence at the time of the birth of the physical body, or that the physical parents of the child could be the generators of the spiritual monad. If the spiritual monad existed before the body was born, and could develop without it, what would be the use of its entering any body at all?

We see that a plant ceases to grow when its roots are torn from the soil, and when they are replaced into the soil the growth continues. Likewise the human soul, for the purpose of attaining self-knowledge, takes root in the physical organism of man, and develops a character, but when death tears out the roots, the soul rests and ceases to grow, until it finds again a physical organism to acquire new conditions for continued growth.

What can this inner ego be, which lives through death and changes during life, except a spiritual ray of Life, obtaining relative consciousness by coming in contact with matter? Is any man certain of his own existence? All the proof we have of our existence is in our own self-consciousness, in the feeling of the I Am, which is the realisation of our existence.

Every other state of consciousness is subject to change. The consciousness of one moment differs from that of another, according to the changes which take place in the conditions which surround us, and according to the variety of our impressions. We are craving for change and death; to remain always the same would be torture. Old impressions die and are replaced with new ones, and we rejoice to see the old ones die, so that the new ones may step into their places. We do not make our impressions ourselves, but we receive them from the outside world. If it were possible that two or more persons could be born and educated under exactly the same conditions, having the same character and receiving always the same impressions, they would always have the same thoughts, the same feelings and desires, their consciousness would be identical, and they might be considered as forming collectively only one person. A person, having forgotten all the mental impressions he ever received, and receiving no new ones, might exist for ages, living in eternal imbecility, with no consciousness whatever except the consciousness of the I Am, and that consciousness could not cease to exist as long as his personality were capable to recognise its existence relatively to itself.

This would be the only condition in which a person could possibly exist, if he had gained no spiritual self-knowledge and if he were to cease to receive any impressions from the external world; and similar to this may be the state of such a person after the death of his body, if during life he has not attained any higher knowledge than that which refers to perishing things. Having no spiritual consciousness, he can have no spiritual perceptions, he can bring with him into the spiritual world nothing except his own ignorance.

His sensations leave him at death, and the images received in his mind during life will fade away; the intellectual forces which have been set into motion by his scientific pursuits will be exhausted, and after that time the spirit of such a person, even if he has been during life the greatest scientist, speculator, and logician, will be nothing but an imbecile, living in darkness, and being drawn irresistibly towards reincarnation; to reimbody itself again under any circumstances whatever, to escape from nothingness into existence.

But he who acquires spiritual self-consciousness will be self-luminous and live in eternal light. He brings a light with him into the darkness, and that light will not be extinguished, for it is eternal, while the light of this world is darkness to him.

Relative Life

Under whatever form life may exist, it is only relative. A stone, a plant, an animal, a man or God, each has an existence for itself, and each exists only for the others, as long as the others are conscious of his existence. Man looks upon the existence below him as incomplete, and the incomplete beings below him know little about him. Man knows little about any superior beings, and yet there may be such, looking upon him with pity, as he would look upon an inferior animal, an ape that has not yet awakened to a realisation of its own nature.

Those who are supposed to know, inform us that there is no being in the universe superior to the man having become conscious of his own divine and immortal nature; but that there are innumerable invisible beings who are either far superior or inferior to mortal man as we know him. In other words, the highest beings in the universe are such as have once been men; but the men and women of our present civilisation may have to progress through millions of ages before they attain that state of perfection which such beings possess.

Existence is relative. There is something in me which causes me to live and to think. I may call it "I" or "God"; in either case it is intellectually incomprehensible, and it has no existence for me of which I am conscious, as long as I do not realise the relation between this unknown something and my own nature. Nevertheless it is; for if it were nothing it could not cause me to live and to think. It is the source of my being, and therefore it is existence and my nature is its manifestation. In realising my own existence, existence becomes to me a reality; to realise the nature of divine being is to enter into that state.

We are accustomed to look upon that which we perceive with our senses as real, and upon everything else as unreal, and yet our daily experience teaches us that our senses cannot be trusted if we wish to distinguish between the true and the false. We see the sun rise in the East, see him travel along the sky during the day and disappear again in the West; but every child now-a-days knows that this apparent movement is only an illusion, caused by the turning of the earth.

At night we see the "fixed" stars above our heads, they look insignificant compared with the wide expanse of the earth and the ocean, and yet we are told that they are blazing suns, in comparison with which our mother Earth is only a speck of dust. Nothing seems to us more quiet and tranquil than the solid rocks under our feet, and yet the earth whereon we live whirls with tremendous velocity through space; the mountains seem to be everlasting, but continents sink beneath the waters of the ocean and rise again above its surface. Below our feet moves, with ebbs and tides, the swelling bosom of our apparently solid mother the earth, above our head seems to be nothing tangible, and yet we live on the very bottom of the airy ocean above us, and do not know the things that may perhaps live in its currents or upon its surface.

A stream of light seems to descend from the sun to our planet, and yet darkness is said to exist between the atmosphere of the Earth and the sun, where no meteoric matter exists to cause a reflection; while again we are surrounded by an ocean of light of a higher order, which appears to us to be darkness, because the nerves of our bodies have not yet been sufficiently developed to react under the influence of the Astral Light. The image reflected in the mirror seems a reality to the unreasoning mind, the voice of an echo may be mistaken for the voice of a man. We often dream when awake, and while believing to be awake we are asleep.

"Consciousness" is a relative term. It is not scientific to say "we are asleep"; as long as we do not know who "we" are. We can only truly say that such and such functions of a physical or psychical organism, which are called our own, are asleep or inactive while others are active and awake. We may be fully awake relatively to one thing and asleep relatively to another. A somnambule's body is in a state resembling death, while his higher consciousness is fully alive and employs even far superior powers of perception than if all the activity of his life-principle were engaged in performing the functions of his lower organism.

"Matter" and "Motion" are relative terms; both referring to manifestations of something we do not know, and which we may call "Spirit." There is no motion without matter, no matter without some motion, and every power is therefore substantial. A solid mass of matter is condensed energy, representing a certain amount of latent power; every force is invisible substance in motion.

"Space," "extension," "duration" are relative. Their qualities change according to our standard of measurement and according to our mode of perception. To an animalculae in a drop of water that drop may appear as an ocean, and to an insect living on a leaf that leaf may constitute a world. If during our sleep the whole of the visible world were to shrink to the size of a walnut or expand to a thousandfold its present dimensions, on awakening we should perceive no change, provided that change had equally affected everything, including ourselves.

A child has no conception of its relation to space and tries to grasp the moon with its hands, and a person who has been born blind and is afterwards made to see, cannot judge of distances correctly. Our thoughts know of no intervening space when they travel from one part of the globe to another. Our conceptions of our relation to space are based upon experience and memory acquired in our present condition. If we were moving among entirely different conditions, our experiences, and consequently our conceptions, would be entirely different. Space relatively to form can only have three dimensions, because all forms are composed of three dimensions: length, thickness, and height.

Relative Consciousness

Consciousness in the Absolute is unconsciousness relatively to everything. A consciousness being in relation with nothing is inconceivable. A consciousness existing in relation to its own self is self-consciousness.

The Absolute is independent of its manifestations; but all manifestations depend on the presence of that which becomes manifest. God can exist in his own divine nature without revealing his presence to his creatures; but his creatures cannot exist without God. We know that space exists; but it is inconceivable to us as long as it does not become revealed to us in a form. Forms are objectified space. Without such a manifestation of three dimensional bodies we can form no conception of space. We know that God exists; but we cannot conceive of his existence unless his nature becomes revealed to us in its triunity within ourselves.

The dimensions of space exist in our own mind. We conceive of no dimensions of space in a mathematical point, and self-consciousness exists in itself without any relation to anything except its own self. This might therefore be called a one-dimensional space. As to two-dimensional space, every one knows that there is a difference between good and evil, between love and hate, &c., and the realisation of such a difference furnishes us with a conception of space in which we perceive only two dimensions. Three-dimensional space is the world of corporeal bodies; but there is also a fourth dimension of space, known only to the enlightened, who have learned how to square the circle, because four is the number of truth, and three the number of form.

As our conception of space is only relative, so is our conception of time. It is not time itself, but its measurement, of which we are conscious, and time is nothing to us unless in connection with our association of ideas. The human mind can only receive a small number of impressions per second; if we were to receive only one impression per hour, our life would seem exceedingly short, and if we were able to receive, for instance, the impression of each single undulation of a yellow ray of light, whose vibrations number 509 billions per second, a single day in our life would appear to be an eternity without end. *(Carl du Prel: "Die Planetenbewohner.")*

To a prisoner in a dungeon, who has no occupation, time may seem extremely long, while for him who is actively engaged it passes quickly. During sleep we have no conception of time, but a sleepless night passed in suffering seems very long. During a few seconds of time we may, in a dream, pass through experiences which would require a number of years in the regular course of events, while in the unconscious state time has no existence for us.

In books on mystical subjects we find often accounts of a person having dreamed in a short moment of time, things which we should suppose that it would take hours to dream them; for instance the following: "A traveller arrived late at night at a station. He was very fatigued, and as the conductor opened the door of the car, he entered, and immediately fell asleep. He dreamed that he was at home, and living with his family; that he fell in love with a girl and married her; that he lived happy until he meddled with political affairs, and was arrested on the charge of having entered into a conspiracy against the government. He was tried, and condemned to be shot, and led out to be executed. Arrived at the place of execution, the command was given, and the soldiers fired at him, and he awoke at the noise caused by the shutting of the door of the car, which the conductor had shut behind him when our friend entered. It seems probable that the noise produced by shutting that door caused the whole dream."

Persons fully in the subjective world receive no impressions from the objective world. If they are only partially in that state which occurs in dreams and insanity, the sensations carried to the half-conscious brain become mixed with the ideas born in the subjective world, and produce caricatures and distortion of images. In this state, when the experiences of the internal state mingles with the sensations of the external consciousness, the most erroneous impressions may be produced; because the intellect labours, but reason does not act sufficiently powerful to enable man to discriminate between the true and the false.

Objective and Subjective

But what is the difference between objective and subjective states of existence? We do not cease to live while we are asleep, but we have a different kind of perceptions in either state. The popular idea is that sensual objective perceptions are real and subjective ones only the products of our imagination. But a little reflection will show that all perceptions, the objective as well as the subjective ones, are results of our "imagination."

If we look at a tree, the tree does not come into our eye, but its picture appears in our mind; if we look at a form we perceive an impression made in our mind by the image of an object existing beyond the limits of our body; if we look at a subjective image of our own creation, we perceive the impression which it produces on our mind. In either case the pictures exist objectively in our mind, and we perceive the impressions.

The fact is, that everything appears either objective or subjective according to the state of consciousness of the perceiver, and what may be to him entirely subjective in one state may appear to him objectively in another. The highest ideal truths have to him who can realise them an objective existence, the grossest material forms have no existence to him who cannot perceive them.

But here the great question arises: "Who or what is this unknown One that perceives the images existing in its own mind, and the sensations that come to his consciousness? What is that which you call your "I," which knows that you know, and which also recognises your ignorance? What is that Self, which is neither the body nor the mind, but which uses these things as its instruments?" If you know that invisible being, you may throw away this book; it can teach you nothing new, because you know God and are the wisest of men.

The basis upon which all exhibition of magical power rests is a knowledge of the relations that exist between objective and subjective states of existence, and the source from which they originate.

Projected Mental Images

If we conceive in our mind of the picture of a thing we have seen before, an objective form of that thing comes into existence within our own mind, and is composed of the substance of our own mind. If by continual practice we gain sufficient power to hold on to that image and to prevent it from being driven away and dispersed by other thoughts, it will become comparatively dense, and can be projected upon the mental sphere of others, so that they may actually see objectively that which exists subjectively as an image within our own mind; but he who cannot hold on to a thought and control it at will cannot impress it upon the minds of others, and therefore such experiments fail, not on account of any absolute impossibility to perform them, but on account of the weakness of those who experiment, but have not the power to control their own thoughts, and to render them corporeal enough for transmission.

Everything is either a reality or a delusion, according to the standpoint from which we view it. The words "real" and "unreal" are only relative terms, and what may seem real in one state of existence appears unreal in another. Money, love, power, &c., appear very real to those who need them; to those who have outgrown the necessity for their possession they are only illusions.

That which we realise is real to us, however unreal it may be to another. If my imagination is powerful enough to represent to me the presence of an angel, that angel will be there, alive and real, my own creation, no matter how invisible and unreal he may be to another. If your mind can create for you a paradise in a wilderness, that paradise will have for you an objective existence. Everything that exists, exists in the universal Mind, and if the individual mind becomes conscious of his relation to a thing therein, it begins to perceive it.

No man can realise a thing beyond his experience, he cannot know anything to which he stands in no relation. For the purpose of perceiving, three facts are necessary: The perception, the perceiver, and the thing that is the object of perception. If they exist on entirely different planes, and cannot enter into relationship, no perception will be possible. If I wish to look at my face, and am not able to step out of myself, I must use a mirror to establish a relation between myself and the object of my perception. The mirror has no sensation, and I cannot see myself in the mirror, I can only see myself in my mind. The reflection of the mirror produces a reflection which is objective to my mind, and which comes to my perception.

Man's Original Nature

A consideration of this will give us the key to an understanding of man's original nature, and of the necessity of his "fall from grace." We cannot objectively see the light or the truth, as long as we are within the body of the one or the other. Only when we go beyond the sphere of the light, we can see its luminosity, only when we fall into error, will we learn to appreciate the truth.

As long as primordial man was one with the universal power from which he emanated as a spiritual ray or entity in the beginning, he could not know the divine source from which he came. The will and imagination of the Universal Mind were his own will and imagination. Only when he began to "step out of his divine self," could he begin to exist as an individual "Self"; only when he began to act against the law, did he begin to realise that there was a law.

Man's apparently separated existence from God is an illusion: but this illusion must be experienced by him, so as to enable him to outgrow it, and to realise his unity with God. A god who does not realise his own divine nature would not be able to enjoy it. When man, as a spiritual entity, having attained perfection, enters again into his source, his sense of self and separateness will be lost, but he will be in possession of knowledge. To see a thing, it must become objective. To know what love is, we must be separated from the object of our love. When we fully comprehend a thing, we become one with it, and know it by knowing ourselves.

This example is intended to illustrate the fundamental law of creation. The first great cause -- so to say -- stepping out of itself, becomes its own mirror, and thereby establishes a relation with itself. "God "sees his face reflected in Nature; the Universal Mind sees itself reflected in the individual mind of man. God comes to relative consciousness in his own nature, but when he again retires into himself the relation will cease, he will again become one with himself, there will be no more relative consciousness, and "Brahma will go to sleep" until the new day of creation begins. But man knows that he exists even after all his relation with external things has ceased, he does not need to look continually into a mirror to be reminded of that fact. Likewise the absolute self-consciousness of the great I Am is independent of the objective existence of Nature, and he will still "sit on the great white throne after the earth and the heaven fled away from his face"; (*St John: Revelations xx. 2).* which means that he will rest in his own divine self-consciousness.

Perception

The superior powers of inner perceptions are those possessed by the inner man, and they become developed after the inner man awakens to self-consciousness. They correspond to the senses of the external man, such as seeing, hearing, feeling, tasting, smelling.

External sensual perceptions are necessary to see sensual things; the internal sensual perceptions are necessary to see internal things. Physical matter is as invisible to the spiritual sight as astral bodies are to the physical eyes; but as every object in nature has its astral counterpart within the physical form, it may see, hear, feel, taste, and smell with its astral senses those astral objects, and thereby know the attributes of the physical objects as well or still better than the physical man might have been able to do with his physical senses; but neither the physical nor the astral senses will be able to perceive, unless they are permeated by the power of the spirit which endows them with life.

Men usually look upon a thing as real if it is seen alike by several persons, while if only one person professes to see it, it being invisible to others, it is called illusive; but each impression produces a certain state of the mind, and a person perceiving it must be in a condition to enter into a relation with that state which the impression produces.

All persons being in the same state of mind, and receiving the same impression, will perceive the same thing, but if their states of mind differ, their perceptions will differ. A horse or a lion may be seen alike by everyone who has his normal senses developed; but if one is excited by fear, his perception will differ from that of others, because the product of his own imagination distorts the impression received. A drunkard in a state of delirium tremens believes to see worms and snakes crawling over his body. His experience tells him that they have no external existence. Nevertheless they are realities to him. They really exist for him as the products of his own mental condition, but they do not exist for others who do not share that condition. But if others were to enter the same state they would see the same things.

Our perceptions therefore differ -- not only in proportion as the impressions coming from the objects of our perception differ -- but also according to our capacity to receive such impressions, or according to our own mental states. If we could develop a new sense of perception, we would be in a new world. If our capacity to receive impressions were restricted to only one sense, we would only be able to conceive of that which could become manifest to us through that sense.

Let us suppose the existence of a being who could enter into only one state of consciousness; for instance, that of hate. Having all his consciousness concentrated into one guiding passion, he could become aware of nothing else but of hate. Such a "god of hate," incapable of entering into any other mental state, could perceive no other states but those corresponding with his own. To such a being the whole world would be dark and void, our oceans and mountains, our forests and rivers would have no existence for him; but wherever a man or an animal would burn with hate, there would be perhaps a lurid glow perceiveable by him through the darkness, which would attract his attention and attract him, and on his approach that glow would burst into a flame in which the individual from whom it proceeded may be consumed.

Any other mental state or passion may serve for a similar illustration. Hate knows hate, Love knows love, and a person full of hate is as incapable to love as a being full of love is incapable to hate.

The Bhagavad Gita says: "Those that are born under an evil destiny" (having acquired evil tendencies by their conduct in former lives) "know not what it is to proceed in virtue or to recede from vice; nor is purity, veracity, or the practice of morality, to be found in them. They say the world is without beginning and without end, and without an Ishwar, that all things are conceived in the junction of the senses, and that attraction is the only cause." *(Bhagavad Gita, L. xvi.)*

Unity

Those who believe that everything exists in consequence of the unconscious attraction of two principles, forget that there could be no attraction if there were not some continually acting cause that produces that attraction. They are the deluded followers of a doctrine which they themselves cannot seriously believe. They agree that out of nothing nothing can come, and yet they believe that unconscious attraction can produce consciousness.

They are the followers of the absurd Two which has no real existence, because the eternal One divided into two parts would not become two Ones but the two halves of a divided One. One is the number of Unity, and Two is Division; the One divided into two ceases to exist as a One, and nothing new is thereby produced. If the plan for the construction of the world had been made according to the ideas of the followers of Dualism, nothing could have come into existence, because action and reaction would have been of equal power, annihilating each other. Neither could there be any progression under such circumstances at present. But behind all manifestations of power there is the eternal power itself, the source of all perfection that can become manifest. This is the Unity and Reality, in which no division exists; from which all things originate and to which all will return. In its aspect as being the source of perfection in everything and which all things desire to attain, it has been called "good."

Whatever this power of good may be, it is beyond the capacity of man to give it an appropriate name, or to describe it, because it is beyond the comprehension of mortal man. To give a name to that which includes everything, is to limit the whole to one of its parts. It has been called "God" and as such it has "many faces," because its aspect differs according to the standpoint from which we behold it. It is the Supreme cause, from which everything comes into existence; it must be absolute consciousness, wisdom and power, love, intelligence, and life, because these attributes exist in its manifestations and could not have come into existence without it. It is necessarily one and unlimited, and can therefore not be known to the limited intellect of man. It can only be known by itself; but if it reveals itself in our soul, our soul will partake of its knowledge. Therefore Angelus Silesius says --

*"God dwelleth in a light far out of human ken,
Become thyself that light, and thou shalt see him then."*

When Gautama Buddha was asked to describe the supreme source of all beings, he remained silent, because those who have reached a state in which they can realise what it is, have no words to describe it,*(2 Corinth, xii. 4.)* and those who cannot realise it would not be able to comprehend the description.

To describe a thing we must invest it with comprehensible attributes, and it then ceases to be unlimited and becomes limited. Therefore all theological discussions about the nature of "God" are useless, because "God" is the All and does not differ from anything; but not everything is God; because not everything is conscious of its own divine nature.

To become conscious of one's own divine nature, is to realise the presence of God. To deny the existence of God is an absurdity equivalent to denying one's own existence, while existence is its own proof. He can only be spiritually known, but not scientifically described, and the fight between so-called Deists and Atheists is a mere quarrel about words which have no definite meaning. Every man is himself a manifestation of God, and as each man's character differs from that of every other, so each man's idea of God differs from that of the rest, and each one has a God (an ideal) of his own: only when they all have the same aspirations, will they all have the same God.

To him who has not the power of God, the power of God does not exist. To him who perceives the presence of God, God exists, and to him his existence cannot be disputed away. The ignorant cannot be made to realise the existence of knowledge unless he becomes knowing; those who know cannot have their knowledge reasoned away.

The caricatures of gods set up by the various churches as representations of the only true God are merely attempts to describe that which cannot be described. As every man has a highest ideal (a god) of his own, which is a symbol of his aspirations, so every church has its peculiar god, who is an outgrowth or a product of evolution of the ideal necessities of that collective body called a church. They are all true gods to them, because they temporarily answer their needs, and as the requirements of the church change, so change their gods; old gods are discarded and new ones put into their places.

The god of the Christian differs from that of the Jews, and the Christian god of the nineteenth century is very different from the one that lived at the time of Torquemada and Peter Arbues, and was pleased with torture and Autos da Fe. As long as men are imperfect their gods will be imperfect; as they become more perfect their gods will grow in perfection, and when all men are equally perfect they will all have the same perfect "God," the same highest spiritual ideal recognised alike by science and by religion as being divinity in humanity; because there can be only one supreme ideal, one absolute Truth, whose realisation is Wisdom, whose manifestation is power expressed in Nature, and whose most perfect expression is ideal Man.

Seven Steps

There are seven steps on the ladder, representing the religious development of mankind: On the first stage man resembles an animal, conscious only of his instincts and bodily desires, without any conception of the divine element. On the second he begins to have a presentiment of the existence of something higher. On the third he begins to seek for that higher element, but his lower elements are still preponderating over the higher aspirations.

On the fourth his lower and higher desires are counterbalancing each other. At times he seeks for the higher, at other times he is again attracted to the lower. On the fifth he anxiously seeks for the divine, but seeking it in the external he cannot find it. He then begins to seek for it within himself. On the sixth he finds the divine element within himself and develops spiritual self-consciousness, which on the seventh grows into self-knowledge. Having arrived at the sixth, his spiritual senses begin to become alive and active, and he will then be able to recognise the presence of other spiritual entities, existing on the same plane.

On the seventh he finds that he himself is the God which he has been seeking. His will is free from every selfish desire, his thought is one with his will, his word becomes a creative act. Such a spiritual being may still dwell in a human body upon this planet, and not even be recognised as something superior to the rest of mankind; for his personality is not God. He lives, and yet he lives not; for it is God, his divine Self, the eternal Reality living in him.

Chapter III – Form

"The Universe is a thought of God." – **Paracelsus**

Primordial Essence

According to Plato the primordial essence is an emanation of the Demiurgic Mind, which contains from eternity the idea of the natural world within itself, and which idea is thrown into objectivity by the power of the divine self-conscious will. This doctrine seems to be almost as old as the existence of reasoning man on this globe. It contains essentially the same truth which has been taught by the ancient Rishis, and has been expressed by the deepest thinkers of all ages, apparently from the first planetary spirit, that made his appearance on this earth, down to the modern philosophers who teach that the world is a product of ideation and will. *(Schopenhauer: "Die Welt als Wille und Vorstellung.")*

The great Christian Mystic, Jacob Boehme describes the Great First Cause as a trinity of will, intelligence and action. His doctrine corresponds to that which is taught in the East, regarding the three emanations of Brahm, and of which that German shoemaker could at that time hardly have known anything, if he had not been an Illuminate. He says in his book on "The Three Principles," that by the activity of the Will-Fire at the Centre the eternal consciousness of the latter was reflected in Space as in a mirror, and from this activity Light and Life were born. He then describes, how by the action radiating from the incomprehensible centre, radiating into the element of Matter, and the subsequent reaction from the periphery toward the centre rotation was caused, and how in the Ether, the world of forms came into existence, and grew into material density. Thus through the action of the Father in the Son, the "Holy Ghost" became manifest, and its manifestation is the visible and invisible universe in one, with all its suns, stars, planets, their forms and inhabitants, with all the angels and demons, devas, elementals, men and animals, or in other words, with all the energies and powers and forms of the visible and invisible side of nature.

This trinity manifests itself on three different planes or modes of action, that have been termed Matter, Soul, and Spirit, or according to the symbolism of ancient occult science, Earth, Water, and Fire. The One becomes manifest in the Three, but the Three is a whole and does not consist of three parts, of which one comes into succession after another, it springs into existence at once. Reaction cannot exist without Action, and both are due to a co-existing Potency or Cause. Spirit or "Fire" is immaterial, formless, and universal, manifesting its power in forms. It is the "creator," the great "carpenter" of the universe, the "stepfather of Christ," whose wife is Maja (Nature), the ever immaculate virgin.

Soul or "Water" is a semi-material element, formless in its original state. It is the organising element of corporeal forms. It penetrates and surrounds the planets as it surrounds and penetrates the bodies of men and animals and all other bodies and forms, and all material forms will soon perish after the soul-principle has ceased to be active in them.

Matter or "Earth," or (as it is called in its primordial state) Aakaasa, is an invisible material element pervading all space. Condensed by the organising power of the soul, it clothes the forms of the latter and renders them visible on the physical plane.

Seven Principles

By the interaction of the three primordial elements, Spirit, Soul, and Matter, four intermediate links become manifest, and these four added to the three former represent seven principles.

These three, respectively seven principles, must not be supposed to exist separately; they are seven aspects of one element, in the same sense as the seven notes of one octave are seven modifications of one vibration producing sound.

Man is a unity; but also a trinity of expression, capable to enter four distinct states of consciousness and existence, a compound of four elements joined to the fifth One Element, making him a harmonious accord of five notes.

He may also be regarded as a manifestation of three higher and three lower powers, in which the unmanifested seventh is to become manifest. All these divisions are legitimate and not arbitrary; because they are based upon the action of natural certain laws.

A. The element of Matter, Aakaasa, represented by "Earth."

AB. A combination of Matter and Soul, known as the Astral Body, a mixture of "Earth and Water."

B. The Soul, known as the animal principle in man, represented by "Water."

ABC. The Essence of Life, a combination of Matter, Soul, and Spirit, "Earth, Water, and Fire."

AC. The Mind, a combination of Matter and Spirit, or "Earth and Fire" (the principle of Intellectuality).

BC. The Spiritual Soul, a combination of Soul and pure Spirit, or "Water and Fire" (the principle of Spiritual Intelligence).

C. Pure Spirit or "Fire."*(The Sanscrit terms for the seven principles are: 1, Pracriti; 2, Lingasarira; 3, Kamarupa; 4, Jiva; 5, Manas; 6, Buddhi; 7, Atma. -- See "Five Years of Theosophy," p. 153.)*

The divisions adopted by Paracelsus and in "Esoteric Buddhism" are nearly identical with the above: 1. The physical body. 2. Vitality (Mumia). 3. Astral Body (Sidereal body). 4. Animal Soul. 5. Intellectual Soul. 6. Spiritual Soul. (The man of the new olympus). 7. Spirit.

It is said that this division was also known to the ancient Jews, and that the Hebrew Alphabet, consisting of 22 letters, was made with reference to it; because the three in seven states produces twelve symbols, and $3 + 7 + 12 = 22$.

This sevenfold division of principles, representing the constitution of man as well as that of the universe as a whole, was also known to the ancient Egyptians, and described as follows --

I. chat. The material body.
II. bas. (heart) and nif. (breath) Physical life.
III. Ka. The astral body (Personality).
IV. ab. Will. (Kama) The centre.
V. ba. Soul (Manas).
VI. chaib. The shadow of the spirit (Buddhi).
VII. chu. The spirit (Atma).

The ancient Alchemists represented the same ideas by the symbols of the seven planets --

[saturn] Saturn. The material element.
[jupiter] Jupiter. Power or Life.
[mars] Mars. Will, Strength.
[sun] Sun. The centre; the source of all planets.
[venus] Venus. Love. In its lower aspect desire.
[mercury] Mercury. Mind, Intelligence.
[moon] Moon. Spirituality.

The qualities of these powers differ in their combination according to the preponderating influence of one over another; and this causes their aspects to be either good or evil. Thus these aspects are bad as follows --

If spirituality [moon] is overruled by materiality [saturn].
If the mind [mercury] is dominated by blind force [jupiter].
If love [venus] overruled by passion [mars].
If the contrary is the case, their aspects are good.
The sun [sun] occupies the centre of these planets; it is their parent, and not dominated by any of them.

Jane Leade also adopts a sevenfold division of principles; but in a reversed order
Spirit. The word. The creator.
Wind. The breath or the life.
Water. Coagulated wind (soul).
Light. Intelligence.
Heaven. The astral world.
Air. Physical life.
Earth. The matrix or centre.
To these seven principles correspond four planes of existence or states of consciousness; namely --

I. The physical world.
II. The astral world.
III. The spiritual world.
IV. The divine plane of existence.

Each of these worlds has its own state of being, and each form in either of them contains all the above-named seven principles, which are fundamentally one and inseparable; only with this difference, that according to the plane in which a form exists, some of these principles are active while others are latent.

Thus in a stone or a tree the higher principles are entirely latent and as if non-existent, while in one of the higher plane the higher principles are alone manifest while the lower ones have ceased to manifest any activity.

The following table may give an approximate illustration of this theory. The prominently active principles are printed in larger, and the less active ones in smaller, type; while those that are still latent, or have become so, are enclosed in brackets.

Physical Nature	Astral Plane	Devachan
PHYSICAL MATTER	(Physical Matter)	(Physical Matter)
PHYSICAL LIFE	(Physical Life)	(Physical Life)
Astral Life	ASTRAL LIFE	(Astral Life)
Kama Life	KAMA LIFE	(Kama Life)
{ Lower Manas	Lower Manas	(Lower Manas)
(Higher Manas) }	(Higher Manas)	HIGHER MANAS
(Buddhi)	(Buddhi)	BUDDHI
(Atma)	(Atma)	Atma

Upon this earth all the seven principles may become manifested in man; he may live alternatively or successively, in either one of these four states of consciousness; his spirit belongs to God, his mind to heaven, his desires to the soul of the world, and his body to earth. After death the lower principles become inactive and he moves upwards on the scale of being in proportion as he has become attuned to it during his life.

Divine State of Being

What are the conditions of the divine state of being, we do not know nor care to speculate about it. Our object ought to be to attain it rather than to worry our brains in seeking to gratify our scientific curiosity in regard to it. It might be supposed that in this plane only the Buddhi, Atma, and the highest essence of the Manas is active; but Jacob Boehme tells us, that "all the Seven Spirits of God are born one in another; one gives birth to the other and there is neither first nor last.

They are all seven equally eternal";*("The life and doctrines of Jacob Boehme," p. 73.)* and furthermore he describes that the third principle reappears in the seventh; and that therein consists the "resurrection of the flesh,"*(Ibid. p. 84.)* which causes a divine being to be -- not an unsubstantial spirit -- but possessing the "Body of God." "In the seventh form all the other forms of nature manifest their activity"; the element of earth therefore manifests itself again on a higher octave, and this will give us a key to the understanding of the meaning of the words of St Paul, when he speaks of a body "that has been sowed in corruption and is raised in glory"; but which is surely not the astral form of a ghost. *(1 Cor. 15:42-44.)*

Bodily Spheres

All forms are the expression of either one or more of these elementary principles, and exist as long as their respective powers are active in them. They are not necessarily visible, because their visibility depends on their power to reflect light. Invisible gases may be solidified by pressure and cold, and rendered visible and tangible, and the most solid substances may be made invisible and intangible by the application of heat. The products of cosmic thought are not all visible to the physical eye, we see only those which are on our plane of existence.

All bodies have their invisible spheres. Their visible spheres are limited by the periphery of their visible forms; their invisible spheres extend farther into space. Their spheres cannot be always detected by physical instruments, but they nevertheless exist, and under certain conditions their existence can be proved to the senses. The sphere of an odoriferous body can be perceived by the organ of smell, the sphere of a magnet by the approach of iron, the sphere of a man or an animal by that most delicate of all instruments, the sensitive soul.

These spheres are the magnetic, caloric, odic, luminous auras and other emanations belonging to every object in space. Such an emanation may sometimes be seen as the Aurora Borealis in the polar regions of our planet, or as the photosphere of the sun during an eclipse. The "glory" around the head of a saint is no poetical fiction, no more than the sphere of life radiating from a precious stone.

As each sun has its system of planets revolving around it, so each body is surrounded by smaller centres of energy evolving from the common centre, and partaking of the attributes of that centre. Copper, Carbon, and Arsenic, for instance, send out auras of red; Lead and Sulphur emit blue colours; Gold, Silver, and Antimony, green; and Iron emits all the colours of the rainbow.

Plants, animals, and men emit similar colours according to their characteristics; persons of a high and spiritual character have beautiful auras of white and blue, gold and green, in various tints; while low natures emit principally dark red emanations, which in brutal and vulgar or villainous persons darken almost to black, and the collective auras of bodies of men or plants or animals, of cities and countries, correspond to their predominant characteristics, so that a person whose sense of perception is sufficiently developed may see the state of the intellectual and moral development of a place or a country by observing the sphere of its emanations.

These spheres expand from the centre, and their periphery grows in proportion to the intensity of the energy acting within the centre. We know the sphere of a rose by the odour that proceeds from the latter if we have the power to smell, we know the character of the mind of a man if we enter the sphere of his thoughts. The quality of psychic emanations depends on the state of activity of the centre from which they originate. They are symbols of the states of the soul of each form, they indicate the state of the emotions. Each emotion corresponds to a certain colour. Love corresponds to blue, Desire to red, Benevolence to green, and these colours may induce corresponding emotions in other souls. Blue has a soothing effect, and may tranquillise a maniac or subdue a fever; Red excites to passion, a steer will become furious at the sight of a red cloth, and an unreasoning mob become infuriated at the sight of blood. This chemistry of the soul is not any more wonderful than the facts known in physical chemistry, and these processes take place according to the same law which causes Chloride of Silver to turn from white into black if exposed to light.

Ethereal Forms

The thoughts of the Universal Mind expressed in matter on the physical plane comprise all the forms of the mineral, vegetable, and animal kingdoms on Earth, described by physical science. Each material form contains within itself its ethereal counterpart, which will, under certain conditions, separate itself from the more material part, or be extracted therefrom by the hands of an Adept. These astral parts may be reclothed with condensed Aakaasa and be rendered visible, and in this way an object can be duplicated by him who knows how to manipulate these invisible forces. *(A. P. Sinnett: "The Occult World.")*

Such astral forms exist after their material forms have decayed; the astral forms of the dead may be seen by the clairvoyant hovering over the graves, bearing the resemblance of the once living man. They may be artificially infused with life and with a borrowed consciousness, and made use of in the practices of Necromancy and Black Magic, or be attracted to "spiritual seances" to represent the spirits of the dead.

There are persons in whom this principle -- either in consequence of constitutional peculiarities or in consequence of disease -- is not very firmly united with the physical body, and may become separated from it for a short period. *(This intimate relation of the astral form and the physical body is often illustrated at so-called exposures of "spiritual mediums." If a materialised form is soiled by ink or soot, the colouring matter will afterwards be found on the corresponding part of the medium's body, because, when the astral form re-enters that body, it will leave the soiling matter on the corresponding parts of the latter.)* Such persons are suitable "mediums" for so-called spirit-materialisations, their ethereal counterparts appear separated from their bodies and assume the visible form of some person either living or dead. It receives its new mask by the unconscious or conscious thoughts of the persons present, by the reflections thrown out from their memories and minds, or it may be made to represent other characters by influences invisible to the physical eye.

As the brain is the central organ for the circulation of nerve-fluid, and as the heart is the organ for the circulation of the blood, so the spleen is the organ from which the astral elements draw their vitality, and in certain diseases, where the action of the spleen is impeded, this "double" of a. person may involuntarily separate itself from the body. It is nothing very unusual that a sick person feels "as if he were not himself," or as if another person was lying in the same bed with him, and that he himself were that other. Such cases of "Doppel-gaengers," Wraiths, Apparitions, Ghosts, &c., caused by the separation of the Lingasarira from the physical form can be found in many works treating of mystic phenomena occurring in nature.*(Adolphe D'Assier; "L'humanite posthume.")* Usually these astral forms are without consciousness and without any life of their own; but they may be made to be the seat of life and consciousness, by withdrawing life from the material form and concentrating it into the astral body. A person who has succeeded in doing this may step out of his physical form and live independent of the latter, and an Adept even entirely remain outside his physical body and continue to live in his ethereal and invisible form.

The stories of fakirs who have been buried alive for months and resurrected afterwards might here be used as illustration. They are too well known to need repetition in this place. Moreover, phenomena, however well attested they may be. can never stand in the place of knowledge; they furnish no explanation of the mysterious laws of nature. The occurrence of phenomena proves nothing but that they occur. Real knowledge is never attained by the observation of external phenomena, it can only be attained by understanding the law.

Invisible Beings

But there are also many forms whose natural home is the astral plane, of which physical science does not know, because they can be seen only by means of the astral perception, a faculty which is at present in possession of only comparatively few persons. The astral plane has, like the physical plane, its mineral, vegetable, and animal kingdom, its four elements; and as in our world the earth, the air, and the sea have their inhabitants, so in the astral world there are inhabitants, the Spirits of Nature, to be found in the elements of the earth, air, water, and fire. They are all the product of originally shapeless ideas, existing in the Universal Mind, condensed into organised forms by the creative power of nature; visible and objective to each other as long as they exist on the same plane.

Individual forms on that plane often make their presence felt to men or animals, but under ordinary circumstances they cannot be seen. They may, however, be seen by the clairvoyant, and under certain conditions, even assume visible and tangible shapes. Their bodies are of an elastic semi-material essence, ethereal enough so as not to be detected by the physical sight, and they change their forms according to certain laws.

Bulwer Lytton says: "Life is one all-pervading principle, and even the thing that seems to die and putrefy but engenders new life and changes to new forms of matter. Reasoning then by analogy -- if not a leaf, if not a drop of water, but is no less than yonder star -- a habitable and breathing world -- common sense would suffice to teach that the circumfluent Infinite, which you call space -- the boundless Impalpable which divides the earth from the moon and stars -- is filled also with its correspondent and appropriate life."

And further on he says: "In the drop of water you see animalculae vary; how vast and terrible are some of these monster-mites as compared with others. Equally so with the inhabitants of the atmosphere. Some of surpassing wisdom, some of horrible malignity; some hostile as fiends to man; others gentle as messengers between Earth and Heaven."*(Bulwer Lytton: "Zanoni.")*

Our ignorant and therefore sceptical age is accustomed to admire in such descriptions the fancy of the writer, never suspecting that they were intended to convey a truth; but there are many witnesses to testify that such invisible but substantial and variously shaped beings exist, and that they, by the educated will of man, can be made conscious, intelligent, visible, and even useful to man. This assertion is supported by the testimony found in the writings of Rosicrucians, Cabbalists, Alchemists, and Adepts, as well as in the ancient books of wisdom of the East and in the Bible of the Christians.

Such existences are, however, not necessarily personal beings. They may be impersonal forces, acquiring form, and life, and consciousness by their contact with man. The Gnomes and Sylphes, the Undines and Salamanders, do not entirely belong to the realm of fable, although they are something very different of what the ignorant believe them to be. How insignificant and little appears individual man in the infinity of the universe ! and yet there is only a comparatively insignificant part of the universe revealed to him by the senses. Could he see the worlds within worlds above, beneath, and everywhere, swarming with beings whose existence he does not suspect, while they, perhaps, know nothing of his existence, he would be overwhelmed with terror and seek for a god to protect him; and yet there are none of these beings higher or as powerful as the spiritual man who has learned to know his powers.*(See "Theophrastus Paracelsus," chap. v. [6])*

The beings of the spiritual plane are such as have once been men, their constitution is beyond the comprehension of those that are not their equals, and their ethereal forms in a state of perfection we cannot conceive. Still higher beings, having outgrown the necessity of manifesting themselves in a form, enter the state of the formless. We may look upon a personal man as a single note in the great orchestra composing the world, and upon a Dhyan Chohan*(Son of*

Wisdom (Planetary spirit).) as a full accord or a compound of notes in the symphony of the gods. There may be unharmonious compositions of notes in music, and there are evil spiritualities as there is darkness in contradistinction to light.

Realm of the Soul

The surface realm of the Soul is the realm of the emotions. Emotions are not merely the results of physiological processes depending on causes coming from the physical plane, but they belong to a form of life on the astral plane, they come and go without any known cause. The state of the weather, or circumstances over which we have no control, cause certain emotions. A person entering a room where every one is laughing is liable to participate in the laughter without knowing the cause of the hilarity; a whole crowd may be swayed by the intense emotion of a speaker, although they may not even understand what he says; one hysterical woman may create an epidemic of hysteria among other women, and a whole congregation may become excited by the harangue of an emotional exhorter, no matter whether his language is foolish or wise.

A sudden accumulation of emotion or energy on the astral plane can kill a person as quickly as a sudden explosion of powder. We hear of persons who were "transfixed by terror" or "paralysed by fear." In such cases the astral consciousness having become abnormally active at the expense of the consciousness on the physical plane, the activity of life on the physical plane ceases when the affected person faints or dies.

All forms come into existence according to certain laws. The solar microscope shows how, in a solution of salt, a centre of matter is formed, and how to that centre its kindred forces are attracted, crystallising around it, and becoming solid and firm. Each kind of salt produces the peculiar crystals that belong to its class and no other, however often the process may be repeated. In the vegetable kingdom the seed of one plant attracts to itself those forces which it requires to produce a plant resembling its parent; the seed of an apple-tree can produce nothing else but an apple-tree, and an acorn can grow into nothing else but an oak. The principal characteristics of an animal will be those that belong to its parents, and the external appearance of a man will correspond more or less to that of the race and family in which he was born.

As every mathematical point in space may develop into a living and conscious and visible being, after once a certain centre of energy (a germ) has been formed, so in the invisible realm of the soul astral forms may come into existence, wherever the necessary conditions for their growth exist. In the same manner as a living germ on the physical plane attracts matter for its growth, a psychic germ on the astral plane causes to crystallise around a thought an invisible but nevertheless substantial entity. As the forms on the physical plane correspond to the characters of the germs, so the forms on the astral plane are expressions of the characteristics of the prevailing emotions on that plane. They manifest themselves either in beautiful or in horrible shapes, because every form is only

the symbol or the expression of the character which it represents.
The animal forms are expressions of forces acting on the animal plane. Some have a consciousness of their own and realise their existence, but under ordinary circumstances they have no more intelligence than animals, and cannot act intelligently. They follow their blind attraction, as iron is attracted to a magnet, and wherever they find suitable conditions for their development, they are attracted thither. We therefore see that if an emotion is not controlled in the beginning it grows and becomes uncontrollable. Some people have died of grief and some others of joy.

Elemental Forms

But if these unintelligent forms are infused with the principle of intelligence proceeding from man, they become intelligent and act in accordance with the dictates of the master from which they receive their will and intelligence, and who may employ them for good or for evil. Every emotion that arises in man may combine with the astral forces of nature and create a being, which may be perceived, by persons possessing higher faculties of perception, as an active and living entity. Every sentiment which finds expression in word or action calls into existence a living entity on the astral plane. Some of these forms are very enduring, according to the intensity and duration of the thought that created them, while others are the creations of one moment and vanish in the next. There are numerous cases on record in which some person or other having committed some crime is described as having been persecuted for years by some avenging demon, who would appear objectively and disappear again. Such demons are the products of the involuntary action of the imagination of their victims; but they are nevertheless real to them.*(A person in Paris became insane and was removed to an insane asylum in Italy, where he raged and had to be confined to a solitary cell. After a while he became suddenly well and was permitted to return to Paris. Some months afterwards a report reached him, that the cell which he had occupied in the asylum was still haunted by his "ghost," which continued raving and making a noise, and that this ghost had been seen by many persons. Curious to see his own "ghost" the man returned to Italy, went to the asylum, saw his ghost, and becoming again obsessed with it, remained insane to the end of his life.)*
They may be called into existence by memory and remorse, and their images existing in the mind, become objective by fear, because fear is a repulsive function; it instinctively repulses the object of which a man is afraid, and by repelling the image from the centre towards the periphery of the sphere of mind, that image is rendered objective.
Instances are known in which persons have been driven to suicide, hoping thereby to escape these persecuting demons. Such demons are said to have in some cases taken even a tangible form. But whether tangible or intangible, the substance of which they are formed is merely a projection of substance of the person to whom they thus appear. They are, so to say, that person himself.

In the "Lives of the Saints," and in the history of witchcraft, we often find instances of the appearance of "doubles" in visible and even tangible forms. Such phenomena take place in medium-istic persons, if by contrary emotions the Will becomes divided, acting in two different directions, and projecting thereby two forms; for it is the Will of man that creates subjective forms, consciously or unconsciously, and under certain conditions they become objective and visible. As an illustration of this law we may cite from the Acta Sanctorum an episode in the life of Saint Dominic. He was once called to the bedside of a sick person, who told him that Christ had appeared to him. The saint answered that this was impossible, and that the apparition had been produced by the devil, because only holy persons could have an apparition of Christ. As he said so, a doubt as to whether the apparition seen may not have been a true one after all, entered his mind, and immediately a division of consciousness was produced, which caused the double of Dominic to appear at the other side of the patient's bed. The two Dominies were seen by the patient, and heard to dispute with each other, and while one Dominic asserted that the apparition had been the work of the devil, the other one maintained that it was the true Christ. The two Dominics were so exactly identical, that the patient did not know which of them was the true saint and which one his image, and he could not make up his mind what to believe; until at last the saint called upon God to assist him, -- that is to say. he concentrated his willpower again within himself; his consciousness became again a unity, and the "double" disappeared from view.

Absurd as such stories may appear to our "enlightened age," their absurdity ceases when the occult laws of nature, and the fact of the possibilities of a double consciousness are understood.

An Adept in a letter to Mr Sinnett says: "Every thought of man upon being evolved passes into another world and becomes an active entity by associating itself -- coalescing, we might term it -- with an Elemental -- that is to say, with one of the semi-intelligent forces of the kingdoms. It survives as an active intelligence -- a creature of the mind's begetting -- for a longer or shorter period, proportionate with the original intensity of the cerebral action which generated it. Thus, a good thought is perpetuated as an active, beneficent power, an evil one as a maleficent demon. And so man is continually peopling his current in space with the offspring of his fancies, desires, impulses, and passions; a current which re-acts upon any sensitive or nervous organisation which comes in contact with it, in proportion to its dynamic intensity.... The Adept evolves these shapes consciously, other men throw them off unconsciously." *(A. P. Sinnett: "The Occult World,")*

This testimony is corroborated by one coming from another source, and proving that to create subjective forms it is not necessary to give a distinct shape to our thoughts by the power of imagination, but that each state of feeling or sentiment may find expression in subjective forms, whether or not we may be conscious of their existence. A form is a state of mind, and a sentiment is a state of mind; a sentiment expressed will be represented by a corresponding form.

Mr Whitworth, a clairvoyant, describes how in his youth, while seeing a German professor perform on an organ, he noticed a host of appearances moving about the keyboard -- veritable Lilliputian sprites, fairies, and gnomes, astonishingly minute in size, yet as perfect in form and features as any of the larger people in the room. He described them as being divided into sexes and clothed in a most fantastic manner; in form, appearance, and movement they were in perfect accord with the theme:

"In the quick measures, how madly they danced, waving their plumed hats and fans in very ecstasy, and darting to and fro in inconceivable rapidity, with feet beating time in rain-like patter of accord ! Quick as a flash, when the music changed to the solemn cadence of a march for the dead, the airy things vanished, and in their place came black-robed gnomes, dressed like cowled monks, sour-faced Puritans, or mutes in the black garb of a funeral procession ! Strangest of all, on every tiny face was expressed the sentiment of the music, so that I could instantly understand the thought and feeling that was intended to be conveyed. In a wild burst of sounding grief came a rush of mothers, tear-eyed and with dishevelled hair, beating their breasts and wailing pious lamentations over their dead loved ones. These would be followed by plumed knights with shield and spear, and host of fiery troops, mounted or foot, red-handed in the fiery strife of bloody battle, as the clang of martial music came leaping from the keyboard, and ever, as each change brought its new set of sprites, the old ones would vanish into the air as suddenly as they had come. Whenever a discord was struck, the tiny sprite that appeared was some misshappen creature, with limbs and dress awry, usually a humpbacked dwarf, whose voice was guttural and rasping, and his every movement ungainly and disagreeable."

He then describes how in his riper age he saw such fairy-like beings coming from the lips of persons talking, and which seemed in every action the very counterpart of the feeling conveyed in the uttered speech. If the words were inspired by good sentiments, these figures were transcendentally beautiful; bad sentiments produced horrid-looking creatures; hate was expressed by hissing snakes and dark, fiery devils; treacherous words produced figures beautiful in front and disgusting and horrid behind; while love produced forms silvery, white, and full of beauty and harmony.

"On one never-to-be-forgotten occasion I was a pained witness to a scene of living faithlessness on one side and a double-faced, treacherous duplicity on the other. A fair young girl and her departing lover had met to exchange greetings ere he went on a distant journey. Each word of hers gave forth beautiful, radiant fairies; but while the front half of each that was turned to the girl was equally fair to look upon, and smiled with all the radiant seeming of undying affection, the rear half of each was black and devilish, with fiery snakes and red forked tongues protruding from their cruel lips, as gleams of wicked cunning danced in sneaking, side-long glances from the corners of the half-closed eyes. These dark backgrounds of the little figures were horrible to look at, ever shifting, dodging, and seeming to shut up within themselves, as they sought to keep only bright and honest toward the trusting girl, and hold the black deception out of sight. And it was noticeable that while a halo of cloudless radiance surrounded the good outside seeming, a pall of thick vapour hung like a canopy of unbroken gloom above the other." *(Religio-Philosophical Journal.)*

All forms are manifestations of life, they have no life of their own; for life is a universal power. They are the creations of thought-power, acting upon the Aakaasa. The creations of man are kept alive by the life-power that radiates into them from the life-centre in man who is a god in that world which he creates in his mind; his creatures are like shadows, vanishing when the fountain of light from which they drink is exhausted. When the psychical action of man, that gave them life, ceases to act, or acts in another direction, they will disappear sooner or later, and in the same way the forms of men disappear, when the life coming from God is withdrawn.

However, as the corpse of a man does not dissolve immediately as soon as the principle of life is departed, but decays slowly or rapidly according to their molecular density and cohesion, likewise the astral forms and memories created by the thoughts and sentiments of man require time for their dissolution. They continue to exist as long as man infuses life and consciousness into them by his thought and his will, and if they have once gained a certain amount of power, they may still cling to him, although he may not desire their companionship. They depend on him for their life, and the struggle for existence forces them to remain with the source from which they draw their vitality. If they depart from that fountain they die; they are therefore forced to remain, and, like the phantom created by "Frankenstein," they persecute their creators with their unwelcome presence.

To rid oneself of such a presence, he who is persecuted should direct the full power of his aspirations and thoughts into another and higher direction, and thereby starve them to death. In this way the spiritual priniciple of every man becomes his special Redeemer, who by the transformation of character saves him from the effects of his sin, and before whose pure light the illusions created by the lower attractions will melt like the snow under the influence of the sun.

Thought Projection

Elemental forms being the servants of their creator -- in fact, his own self -- may be used by him for good or for evil purposes. Love and hate creates subjective forms of beautiful or of horrid shapes, and being infused with consciousness, obtain life, and they may be sent on some errand for good or for evil. Through them the magician blends his own life and consciousness with the person he desires to affect.

A lock of hair, a piece of clothing, or some object that has been worn by the person he desires to affect, forms a connecting link. The same object can be attained if that person is put into possession of an article belonging to the magician, because wherever a portion of anything with which the magician was connected exists, there will a part of his own elements exist, which will form a magnetic link between him and the person whom he wishes to affect. If he projects his astral form at a distance, his personality will be present with his victim, although the latter may not be able to see it. *(Lord Lytton, "Zanoni" and "Strange Story.")*

The astral image of a person may be projected consciously or unconsciously to a distance. If he intensely thinks of a certain place, his thought will be there, and if his thought is spiritual and Consequently self-conscious he will be there himself. Wherever a man's consciousness is, there is the man himself, no matter whether his physical body is there or not.

The history of spiritualism and somnambulism furnishes abundant evidence that a person may be consciously and knowingly in one place, while his physical body lies dormant in another. Franciscus Xavier was thus seen in two different places at one and the same time. Likewise Apollonius of Tyana, and innumerable others mentioned in ancient and modern history.

The Elemental sent by a magician is a constituting part of the magician himself, and if the victim is vulnerable or mediumistic, the latter may be injured by the former, But the astral form of the magician may also be injured by physical force, and as the astral form re-enters the physical body, the latter will partake of the injuries inflicted upon the former.

The magician, who, by the power of his will, has obtained control over the semi-intelligent forces of Nature, can make use of these forces for the purposes of good or evil. The helpless medium, through whom manifestations of occult power take place, can neither cause nor control such manifestations. He cannot control the elementals, but is controlled by them. The elements of his body serve as instruments through which these astral existences act, after the Medium has surrendered his will and given up the supreme command over his soul. He sits passively and waits for what these elementals may do; he unconsciously furnishes them with his life and power to think, and his thoughts and the thoughts of those that are present become reflected in these astral forms, enabling them to manifest apparently an intelligence of their own.

A medium for spirit-manifestations is merely an instrument for the manifestation of invisible forces over which he has no control. The best of such mediums have been very unjustly blamed for "cheating." The thoughts of the person visiting a Medium, are reflected by him. It is therefore not the Medium's person that cheats purposely, but his visitors are cheating themselves through his instrumentality. A mirror that would not reflect all the objects that are brought before it, would be a very unnatural and deceptive thing; a Medium who would only reflect such thoughts as he or she chooses to reflect would be an impostor, for exercising an intelligence of his own, he would not be in that passive condition which constitutes his mediumship.

The Adept in Magic is not the slave of these forces, but controls them by the power of his will. He consciously infuses life and consciousness and intelligence into them, and makes them act as he pleases; they obey his command, because they are a part of himself. The spiritualists do this unconsciously; they sing at their seances, thinking that the more the conditions are harmonious the better will be the manifestations. The true reason for this is, that the more the thoughts of the sitters are in a state of abstraction, the more they are "absent-minded," the easier it will be for the Elementals to take possession of them.

The astral elements used by the Elementals in spiritual seances for the purpose of producing physical phenomena, are not only taken from the medium, but from all present, whose constitution is not strong, and who may therefore be easily vampirized for the purpose of furnishing the required elements. In seances for materialisations, they are also taken from the clothing of those present, and furnish material for the drapery of the "spirits," and it has been observed, that the clothing worn by people who frequently attend to such seances, wears out sooner than usual.

To bring fresh-spilled blood into such "spiritual seances," increases the strength of the "materialisations" very much, and a knowledge of such facts has given rise to some abominable practices of black magic, which are still going on in many parts of the world, although secretly and unknown to the public. This knowledge has also undoubtedly given rise to the sacrifice of animals in the performance of religious ceremonies. A certain executioner was unfortunately gifted with clairvoyance, and every time after having decapitated a person he could see the "spirits" of dead people -- sometimes even his friends and relatives -- pounce upon the fresh-spilled blood of the criminal, and feed on its emanation and aura. It is also a fact that, at a time when the blood-drinking mania in Europe was started by medical ignorance, some people who practised it became insane, and many became demoralised by it.

One of the favourite aids for the materialism of spooks is the aura seminalis, which increases the power of ghosts, elementals and vampires for assuming a substantial form. There are many curious practices going on at such seances, which we must forbear to describe. See "The Life and Doctrines of Theophrastus Paracelsus," pp. 66 and 90.

Apparitions

The astral remnant of man is without judgment and reason, it goes wherever his instincts attract it, or wherever any unsatisfied craving impels it to go. If you wish to be haunted by the "ghost" of a man, attract him by the power of desire. Leave some promise you made to him unfulfilled, and instinctively the astral form of the deceased will be attracted to you to seek its fulfilment, drawn to you by its own unsatisfied desire.

It is not his fault if you do not perceive his presence and hear his voice, it is because your astral senses are asleep and unconscious; you may feel his presence and it may cause a feeling of depression in your mind; he speaks to you, but in a language which you have not yet learned to understand. In those elementary remnants remains that which constituted the lower nature of man, and if they are temporarily infused with life, they will manifest the lower characteristics of the deceased, such as have not been sufficiently refined to join his immortal part.

If a music-box is set to play a certain melody and made to start, it will produce that same melody and no other, although it has no consciousness of its own. The remnant of emotional and intellectual powers in the astral remnant of man will, if this remnant is made to speak, become manifest in the same kind of language which the man during his life used to speak.

The fresh corpse of a person who has suddenly been killed, may be galvanised into a semblance of life by the application of a galvanic battery. Likewise the astral corpse of a person may be brought back into an artificial life by being infused with a part of the life principle of the medium. If that corpse is one of a very intellectual person, it may talk very intellectually; and if it was that of a fool, it will talk like a fool. The intellectual action resembles mechanical motion in so far, that if it is once set into action, it will continue without any special effort of the will, until impulse is exhausted.

We often see this in daily life. There are old and young people frequently seen, who are in the habit of telling some favourite story, which they have already told many times, and which they repeat on every occasion. It may be noticed, that when such an one begins to tell his story, it is of no use to tell him that one knows it already. He has to finish the story nevertheless.

An orator or a preacher does not need to think and reason about each word he utters. When the stream of ideas once flows, it flows without any effort of will. If life from a medium flows into the astral brain of a deceased person, that brain will elaborate its latent ideas in the same way it was accustomed to do during life. We also reason while we dream; we draw logical conclusions during our sleep; but reason is absent, and although, while we dream, our logic seems to be reasonable, nevertheless we often see that it was foolish, when we awake and our reason returns.

The mental organism of man resembles a clockwork, which if it is once set into operation will continue to run until its force is exhausted; but there is no clockwork which winds itself up without extraneous assistance, and there is no mental organism able to think without a power that causes it to begin the process of intellectuation.

But here we must draw the attention to one of the many dangers of that amusement called the practice of spiritism.

In a departed soul the attraction of good and evil still continues to act, until the final separation of the higher and the lower takes place. It may follow the attraction of the higher principles and be attracted to "heaven," or again come into contact with matter through the instrumentality of mediumship, take again part in the whirling dance of life, though by vicarious organs; follow once more the seduction of the senses, and lose entirely sight of the immortal self.

Necromancy

It is therefore not merely dangerous to a person to hold intercourse with the "spirits of the departed"; but it is especially injurious to the latter, -- as long as the final separation of their lower principles from the higher ones has not yet taken place. Necromancy is a vile art, and so has therefore always been abhorred. It may disturb the blissful dreams of the sleeping soul, which aspires to a higher state of existence. It is like disturbing the peace of a saint during his hours of meditation, or to seduce a child. It is a step towards degradation; and as every impulse has a tendency to repeat itself, the most terrible consequences may follow after what seemed to be at first merely some innocent amusement.

These astral remnants are used by the black magician and by the elemental forces in nature for the purpose of evil. If they are unconscious, they will only serve as the blind instruments of the latter; if they are conscious he may enter into an alliance and co-operate with them.

Such alliance, either consciously or unconsciously on the part of him who enters into such an unspiritual intercourse, may take place between an evil-disposed person and a very evil inhabitant of the spiritual plane.

Many people who are in actual possession of powers to work black magic work evil unconsciously; that is to say, they are unconscious of the effects which their will produces, and of the mode in which it acts. The spiritual force created by hate enters the organism of another, and the person from whom the evil power proceeds may be entirely ignorant of it. Such black magicians unconsciously furnish the elements by which their own evil spirit acts. If the will of a black magician is not strong enough to effect his evil purpose, the force will return and kill the magician. This is undoubtedly true, and the grossest illustration of it is, if a person by a fit of rage or jealousy is induced to kill himself. It is the reaction following an unfulfilled desire, which induces the rash act; the act is merely a result of his previous mental state.

Strength of Character

The surest protection against all the practices of black magic, whether they are caused consciously or unconsciously, is to acquire strength of character -- in other words, faith in the divine power within one's own soul.

As man becomes ennobled, the lower elements in his constitution are thrown off and replaced by higher ones, and in a similar manner a transformation takes place in the opposite way if he degrades himself by his thoughts and acts. Sensual man attracts from the Aakaasa those elements that his sensuality requires, for gross pleasures can only be felt by gross matter. A man with brutal instincts growing and increasing degrades himself into a brute in character, if not in external form. But as the form is only an expression of character, even that form may come to approach an animal in resemblance.

The proof of this assertion is seen every day, for we meet every day in the streets brutish men, whose animal instincts are only too well expressed in their external forms. We meet with human snakes, hogs, wolves, and those upon whom alcohol has stamped his seal, and it does not need the instructions given in book on physiognomy to enable almost anybody to read the character of certain persons more or less correctly expressed in their exterior forms.

In the physical plane the inertia of matter is greater than in the astral plane, and consequently its changes are slow. Astral matter is more active, and changes its form more rapidly. The astral body of a man whose character resembled an animal will therefore appear to the seer as an animal in its outward expression. *(E. Swedenborg: "Heaven and Hell.")*

The astral form of an evil person may appear in an animal shape if it is so filled with brutish instincts as to become identified with the image of that animal which is the expression of such instincts. It may even enter the form of an animal and obsess it, and it sometimes happens that it enters such forms for its own protection against immediate decomposition and death.

It would be easy to give anecdotes illustrating instances in which such things took place. *(For examples, see Goerres: "Christian Mysticism"; Maxi-millian Perty: "Mystic phenomena in Nature"; D'Assier: "Post-humus Humanity"; Catharina Crowe: "Nightside of Nature"; Hardinge Britten: "History of Spritualism"; H. P. Blavatsky: "Isis Unveiled," &c., &c.)*

The principal object of the reader should be to learn to know the nature of his own constitution and the law which rules in all forms. If he once understands the modes in which the law acts, it will be a matter of little importance to know in what particular cases it has manifested itself in such modes. Accounts of phenomena can never supply the place of the understanding of the law.

Chapter IV - Life

"I never was not, nor shall I hereafter cease to be." - **Bhagawat Gita**

One Life

The universe of forms may be compared to a kaleidoscope in which the various forms of the original energy manifest themselves in an endless variety, appearing, disappearing, and re-appearing again. As in a kaleidoscope the pieces of variously-coloured glass do not change their substance, but only change their positions, and, through the delusive reflections of mirrors at each turn of the instrument, are made to appear in new constellations and figures, so the One Life manifesting itself appears in an infinite number of forms unconscious or conscious, blind or intelligent, voluntary or involuntary, from the atom, whose auras and ethers rush through a common vortex, *(Babbitt: "Principles of Light and Colour." [1878])* up to the blazing suns whose photospheres extend over millions of miles, and from the microscopic Amoeba, up to perfect Man, whose intelligence conquers the gods.

Forms are materialised thoughts. If you can control thought you can control life and call into existence a form; but few persons are able to hold on to one thought even for one minute of time, because their minds are wavering and their will is divided.

If a form comes into existence on the physical plane, its growth is simply a process by which something that already exists in thought becomes visible and material. This something is the character of the form, and as each character is individual and a whole, it becomes expressed in all parts of the form. A human being -- for instance -- will not have the body of a man, and the head of an animal, but its human character will be expressed in all its parts, and as the character constituting humanity is expressed in all human individuals, so is the character of an individual expressed in all its parts.

This is a truth upon which the doctrines of Astrology, Phrenology, Chiromancy, Physiognomy, &c., are based, which are necessarily true, because Nature is a Unity. An animal, a plant, or a man, is a unity, and is therefore expressed in all the parts of the forms. It can be scientifically demonstrated that each component part of an organism is a microcosm, in which are represented the principles composing that organism. We may by examining a part of a leaf know that it comes from a plant, and by looking at an animal substance see that it came from an animal, or by testing even the most minute part of a mineral or metal know that it belongs to the mineral kingdom. Likewise we may read a man's character in his hands or face or feet or in any other part of his body, if we have acquired the art how to read it correctly.

Psychometry

Upon this law is based the science of Psychometry *(Prof. W. Denton: "Soul of Things." J. K. Buchanan: "Manual of Psychometry.")* By this science we may obtain a true history of past events. By psychometrically examining a stone taken from a house we may obtain correct information in regard to the former or present inhabitants of that house, or a fossil may give us a true description of antediluvian scenery and of the mode of life of prehistoric animals or men. By the psychometrical examination of a letter we may obtain information about the person who wrote the letter and also of the place in which the letter was written.*(By submitting a letter which I had received in an occult manner from a "Master" in Tibet, to a German peasant woman, for the purpose of having it examined psychometrically, I received a correct description of a certain temple in Tibet, and of certain persons with whom I afterwards became acquainted. -- H.)*
If this art were universally known and practised, criminals could be detected by examining psychometrically a piece of the wall, the floor, or the furniture of the room in which a murder or robbery was committed; it would make an end to convicting of innocent persons on circumstantial evidence, or to letting the guilty escape for want of proof; for the psychometer would, by the superior powers of his perception with the spiritual eye, see the murderer or robber or counterfeiter as plain as if he had seen them with his external eyes while the deed was committed.

Character

Each form is the external expression of a certain character which it represents, and as such it has certain peculiar attributes, which distinguish it from other forms. A change of its character is followed by a gradual change of the form. An individual who becomes degraded in morals will, in the course of time, show his degradation in his external appearance; persons of a different appearance and different characters may, in the course of time, as their characters harmonise, resemble each other to a certain extent in appearance. Forms of life, belonging to the same class and species, resemble each other, and each nationality has certain characteristics expressed in the individuals belonging to it.
A full-blooded Irishman will not easily be mistaken for a full-blooded Spaniard, although the two may be dressed alike, but, if they emigrate, they or their children will in time lose the national character which they possessed. Change of character changes the form; but a change of form does not necessarily change the character. A man may lose a leg and become a cripple, and still his character may remain the same as before; a child may grow into a man, and still his character remain that of a child unless modified by education.
These facts are incontrovertible proofs that the character of a being is more essential than his external form. If the character of an individual were to depend on his inherited form, children born of the same parents and educated under the same circumstances would always manifest the same moral characteristics, but it

is well known that the characters of such children often differ widely from each other, and possess characteristics which their parents do not possess.

If, as it frequently happens, children show the same or similar talents and intellectual capacities as their parents, such a fact is by no means a proof that the parents of the child's physical body are also the parents or producers of its intellectual germ; but it may be taken as an additional evidence of the truth of the doctrine of reincarnation, because the spiritual monad of the child would be naturally attracted, in its efforts to reincarnate, to the bodies of parents, whose mental and intellectual constitution would correspond nearest to its own talents and inclinations, developed during a previous earthly life.

"Character" means "individuality." It is that which distinguishes one individual from another. That which represents the true character of something is its individual being, and not its corporeal form, and this individuality exists after the corporeal body, which was the expression of its qualities which has been dissolved. This individuality, called the "soul," is not seen with our physical eyes, neither during the life of the form nor after its death. The life of the body may depart; but the life of the individuality is independent from that of the form or personality.

The individuality may belong either to a class as a whole, or to separate isolated beings. In the lower kingdoms no differentiation of character or soul exists; there is only a differentiation of form; they have one common soul; but in intelligent beings a distinct individuality belongs to each form; each self-conscious being has its own individual soul as soon as it has attained an individual character, and its individuality is independent of the existence of its personality. Forms perish; but the individuality remains unchanged after their death.

Seen from this standpoint, "death" is life, because, during the time that death lasts, that which is essential does not change; life is death, because only during life in the form the character is changed, and old tendencies and inclinations die and are replaced by others. Our passions and vices may die while we live; if they survive us they will be born again.

The character of an oak exists before the acorn begins to grow, but the growing germ attracts from earth and air such elements as it needs to produce an oak; the soul of a child exists as such before the physical form of the child is born into the world, and during its life in the form it may attract from the spiritual atmosphere the elements to which its aspirations and tendencies reach.

Each seed will grow best in the soil that is best adapted to its constitution, each human monad existing in the subjective state will be attracted at the time of its incarnation to parents whose qualities furnish the best soil for its own tendencies and inclinations, and whose moral and mental attributes correspond to its own.

The physical parents cannot be the progenitors of the spiritual germ of the child; that germ is the product of a previous spiritual evolution, through which it has passed in connection with former objective lives. In the present existence of a being the character of the being that will be its successor is prepared. Therefore every man may be truly said to be his own father; for he is the incarnated result of the personality which he evolved in his last life upon the planet, and the next personality which he will represent in his next visit upon this globe, is evolved by him during his present life.

Spiritual Development

The development of a plant reaches its climax in the development of the seed; the development of the animal body reaches its climax in the capacity to reproduce its form, but the intellectual and spiritual development of a man goes on long after he has acquired the power of reproduction, and it may not have reached its climax when the physical form is on the downward path, and ceases to live. The condition of the physical body undoubtedly furnish facilities for the development of character in the same sense as a good soil will furnish facilities for the growth of a tree; but the best soil cannot transform a thistle into a rose-bush, and the son of a good and intellectual man may be a villain or a dunce.
As the primordial essence proceeds to manifest itself in forms, it descends from the universal condition to general, special, and finally individual states. As it ascends again to the formless, the scale is reversed, and the individual units expand, to mingle again with the whole.
Life on the lowest planes manifests itself in an undifferentiated condition; air has no strictly defined shape; one drop of water in the ocean shares an existence common to all other drops; one piece of clay is essentially the same as another. In the vegetable and animal kingdom the universal principle of life manifests itself in individual forms; still there is little difference between individual plants, trees, animals, and men belonging to the same species, and the peculiar attributes which distinguish one individual form from another cease to exist when the form disappears.
That which essentially distinguishes one individual from another is independent of form. Distinctions of form disappear after the forms have dissolved; distinctions of character remain. Those attributes which raise their possessors eminently above the common level begin at a state where external appearances cease to be of great consequence. Socrates was deformed and yet a great genius; the size of Napoleon's body was not at all in proportion with the greatness of his intellect. Spirituality rises above the grave of the form, and the influence of great minds often grows stronger after the bodies that served them have turned to dust. Strong minds exert a power far beyond their physical form while they live; that power remains what it is when they die. They do not die when the form disappears.
All characters may become reincarnated or reim-bodied after they have left the form, but if an individual has no specific character of its own the common character belonging to its species or class will be all that, after leaving the old body, can enter the new. If an individual has developed a specific character of its own, that distinguishes it from its fellows, that individual character will individually survive the dissolution of its form, because the law that applies to the whole, or to the class, will also apply to the part.

Individuality

A drop of water mixed in a body of water will become dispersed in the mass, it may be evaporated and condensed again, but it will never again be the same drop; but if a drop of some ethereal oil is mixed with the water, and the whole is evaporated in a retort, it will, after being condensed, form again the same individual drop in the mass. A character may lose its individuality during life and sink to the common level, but if it has established a distinction from others, its individuality will survive the death of the form. To build up a character an individual form is required; to build up an individual form a character must exist. If we wish to produce a form we must first decide upon its character. A sculptor who would aimlessly cut a stone, without making up his mind as to what form he desired to produce, would not accomplish anything great. The form is a temple of learning for the character, in which the latter gains experience by passing through the struggles of life. The harder the struggle the faster may the character of the individual become developed; an easy life may increase the size of the form, but leave the character weak; a hard struggle may weaken the form, but strengthens the spirit.

If we wish to make a new form out of old clay, we must first of all determine what that form shall be which we are about to create. The clay is passive, we may mould it into a thing of beauty or make it to represent something vile. If we wish to change our character for the better during our life, we must first of all learn to know a higher purpose of life, and reach up for a higher ideal, to be realised within our own self. After this nothing else needs to be done but to keep away everything that will prevent this ideal to realise itself in us.

If we only protect it in its work, it will accomplish that work alone and without our active co-operation. We need not run after, catch, invent, create or manufacture our ideal, we only need to let that which already exists become a reality in us. We cannot even grow a cabbage; we can only prepare the conditions under which a cabbage can grow. We cannot grow an ideal in us; the ideal grows itself, if we furnish the soil, and that soil is our life.

If our soul is to expand its consciousness beyond the narrow limits of this world and realise the glory of an universal existence, then must we let a high and universal ideal realise itself in us. Dreaming and talking of some ideal is to no purpose, we must let it nourish itself by our life. Wisdom and Power, Love and Truth, Justice and Knowledge, are no objects for dreaming or for scientific research; they must become our life and nourish us by our living in harmony with these universal principles, otherwise we cannot rise above the limitation of form, which is the cause of the delusion of separation and personality.

Selfishness

From the illusion of separatedness caused by the realisation of form arises this delusion of self. From this delusion arise innumerable others. From the sense of self arises the love of self, the desire for continuance of personality, greed, avarice, envy, jealousy, fear, doubt and sorrow, pain and death, and the whole range of sufferings which render life miserable and afford no permanent happiness. If a person is miserable and can find no happiness in himself, the surest and quickest way for him to be contented is to forget his own personality. A person living in a continual state of isolation of the heart, cares for nothing but for his own personality. He passes away his life in dreaming of that which he does not possess, and thus he loses his spiritual substance and power, becoming himself like a vapoury dream.

Isolation on the physical plane produces starvation. He who is not nourished by the spirit of universal love starves his soul. An organism upon a low scale of existence, a stone, endures isolation; a scrub pine may live in a place where no higher plant can exist. An idiot may live alone in a cave and not trouble himself, because he has no spiritual aspirations requiring nourishment; but one who desires to attain life and strength in the spirit, must be nourished by that spirit, whose name is universal spiritual love.

As on the physical plane, so on the astral plane, isolation produces starvation. A desire locked up in the heart feeds on the life of him who harbours it; stored up anger seeks for some object upon which to spend itself; passions are never contented, they always clamour for more. The forces of the astral plane are conscious, even if not intelligent; they refuse to be "killed out," they cry for life, and follow the currents of life's attractions. The astral soul of a drunkard will be attracted to drunkards; the astral spook of the lewd seek enjoyment in a brothel through the organs of another; the ghost of the miser is hovering over his buried treasures until the force which put him there is exhausted. There are spooks, ghosts, vampires incubi, succubi, and elementals of various kinds, all thirsting for life.

An isolated desire does not die, but grows into a passion; passions grow stronger at one's expense by being imprisoned. Accumulated energy cannot be annihilated, it must be transferred to other forms, or be transformed into other modes of motion; it cannot remain for ever inactive.

It is useless to attempt to resist a passion which one cannot control. If its accumulating energy is not led into other channels it will grow until it becomes stronger than reason. To control it, it should be led into another and higher channel. Thus a love for something vulgar may be changed by turning it into a love for something high, and vice may be turned into virtue by changing its aim. Passion is blind, it goes where it is led to, and requires reason to guide it. Love for a form disappears with the death of the form, or soon after; love of character remains even after the form in which that character was embodied ceased to exist.

The ancients said that Nature suffers no vacuum. We cannot destroy or annihilate a passion. If one passion is driven away another will take its place. We should therefore not attempt to destroy the low, but displace the low by the high; vice by virtue, and superstition by knowledge.

There are some persons who live in perfect isolation on the intellectual plane. They are such whose thoughts are entirely absorbed by intellectual speculation, having no time or inclination to attend to the claims of their character. They feed their brains while their hearts are made to starve. They live in dreams and scientific illusions, in the smoke of the speculations arising from their vapoury brains. They are like misers, filling the mind with what they believe to be immortal treasures, consisting of collections of theories, dogmas, hypotheses, suppositions, inferences, and sophistry, while they have no room for the development of spirituality or the divine knowledge of self.

This class is constituted of the very learned, the great dogmatists, rationalists, material philosophers, and "sceptical" scientists of our age, with overgrown brains and petrified hearts. They argue about immortality or deny its existence, instead of seeking to attain it; they sometimes become criminals for the sake of gratifying their scientific curiosity. Their astral corpses will continue to exist for a while after the death of the body, until their life is exhausted, and having attained no spirituality during terrestrial life, they will, after their borrowed treasures have departed, be spiritual idiots.

No Isolation in God

There exists no isolation on the spiritual plane, nor can we speak of isolation in God; for if God is self-existent, self-conscious, self-knowing, and self-sufficient, his self, his existence, his knowledge encloses the All with all of his creatures. Well may he who has gained the knowledge of his own divine self be satisfied to live in a tomb; for what other company should be desired by one who enjoys the presence of God; what comfort should be given to one who lives in divine peace; what could be offered to one who possesses the All?

Life itself never perishes; only the forms perish, if life ceases to manifest itself in them.

Life is universally present in nature, it is contained in every particle of matter, and only when the last particle of life has departed the form ceases to exist. Life in a stone does not appear to exist, and yet without life there would be no cohesion of its atoms. If the life-principle were extracted from a mineral its form would be annihilated.

A seed taken from the tomb of an Egyptian mummy began to germinate and grow after it was planted in the earth, having kept its life-principle during a sleep of many centuries. If the activity of animal life could be correspondingly arrested, an animal or a man might prolong individual existence to an indefinite period. Stones may live from the beginning of a Manvantara unto its end; some forms reach a very old age, but if the life-impulse is once given it is difficult to arrest it without destroying the form.

If the life of a person could be suspended by arresting its activity for some years (as has been actually done in the well-known instances of buried fakirs), we might preserve all our great statesmen and politicians for ages, and wake them up only on occasions when their advice would be required.

Love, Will and Life

Life may be transferred from one form upon another, and the power by which it may be transferred is the power of Love, because Love, Will and Life are essentially the same power, or different aspects of one, in the same sense as heat and life are modifications of motion. The power of hate may kill, and the power of love has been known to call the apparently dead back to life. Spiritual Love is Life, a spiritual power more powerful than all the drugs of the Pharmacopoeia. A person may actually give his life to another and die himself, so that another may live. This transfer can be made and sick persons restored to health, by the power of love.

The fountain of this universal love is also the source of the life of all things; it is divine self-consciousness, the power by which God recognises himself in everything; in other words, it is divine wisdom, the Light. *("In him was the life, and the life was the light of all men." -- St John i. 4.)* It is everywhere present, and manifests itself in every form capable to correspond to its living vibrations. It cannot be found by vivisection nor by means of the microscope, telescope, or chemical analysis, and modern science knows nothing about it. Nevertheless it is a principle or power, in and through which we all live and have our being, and if it were withdrawn from us for one moment, we would be immediately annihilated.

"He is the light in all luminous things. He is the Knower, the Knowledge, and the object of Knowledge." -- **Bhagavad Gita xiii. 17.**

To be blind to the universal presence of this Light is to be blind to the fact that grasses and trees, men and animals, live and grow, and that every form strives to be initiated into a higher degree according to the law of evolution. The building of the "Temple of Solomon" goes on unceasingly. Invisibly act the elements of nature, the master builders of the universe, and no sound of a hammer is heard. Life inhabits a form, and when the form is decayed it gathers the elements and builds itself a new house. A rock, exposed to the action of wind and rain, begins to decay on its surface the elements gather again and appear in a new form. Minute plants and mosses grow on the surface, living and dying and being reborn, until the soil accumulates and higher forms come into existence. Centuries may pass away before this part of the work is completed; but finally grasses will grow, and the life that was formally dormant in a rock now manifests itself in forms capable to enter the animal kingdom.

A worm eats a plant, and the life of the plant becomes active and conscious in a worm; a bird eats the worm, and the life that was chained to a form crawling in darkness and filth, now partakes of the joys of an inhabitant of the air. At each step on the ladder of progression life acquires new means to manifest its activity, and the death of its previous form enables it to step into a higher one.

But a time arrives in the process of its evolution when its activity becomes so high and its sphere so expanded, that no physical organism, no form of which we can conceive, will be able to serve as an instrument in which its attributes could find an appropriate expression. Then will the mortal frame be too insignificant to serve the immortal genius, and the freed Eagle will arise from the form.

Forms are nothing but symbols of life, and the higher the life expresses itself the higher will be the form. An acorn is an insignificant thing compared with the oak, but it has a character, and through the magic action of life it may develop into an oak. The germ of its individual life is incarnated in the acorn, and forms the point of attraction for the universal principle of life. Its character is already formed, and if it grows it can become nothing else but an oak.

Buried in the earth it grows and develops from a lower into a higher state through the influence of the highest, because the principle of life is present in it. But however great its potency for growth may be, still it cannot germinate without the life-giving influence of the universal fountain of life reaching it through the power of the sun, and the sun could not make it grow unless the same principle of life were contained within the germ.

The rays of the sun penetrate from their airy regions to the earth; their light cannot enter the solid earth, which protects the tender seed of a plant from the fiery rays, whose activity would destroy its inherent vitality. But the seed is touched by the heat that radiates into the earth, and a special mode of life manifests itself in the seed. The seed begins to sprout, and the germ struggles towards the source of the life-giving influence, and strives towards the light. The roots have no desire for light, they only crave for nutriment, which they find in the dark caverns of matter. They penetrate deeper into the earth, and may even absorb the activity of the higher parts of the plant. But if these parts belong to a species whose character it is to grow towards the light, its nobler portions will enter its sphere, and ultimately bear flowers and fruits.

The soul of man being buried in matter, feels the life-giving influence of the supreme spiritual sun, while at the same time it is attracted by matter. If man's whole attention is attracted to the claims of his body, if all his aspirations and desires are directed to satisfy the desires of his "self," he will himself remain a thing of earth, incapable to become conscious of the existence of Light. But if he strives for Light and opens his soul to its divine influence, he will enter its sphere and become conscious of its existence.

The true Elixir of Life can only be found at the eternal fountain of life. It springs from the seventh principle, manifesting itself as spiritual power in the sixth and shedding its light down into the fifth, illuminating the mind. In the fifth it is manifest as the intellectual power in man, radiating down into the fourth it creates desires, by calling forth instincts in the lower triad, and thereby enabling the forms to draw the elements which they need from the storehouse of nature. It for ever calls men to life by the voice of truth, whose echo is the power of intuition crying in the wilderness of our hearts, baptising the souls with the water of truth, and pointing out to them the true path to the realisation of their own immortality.

Chapter V - Harmony

"Let no one enter here who is not well versed in mathematics and music."
– Pythagoras

Laws of Harmony

"To listen to the music of the spheres" is a poetical expression, but it expresses a great truth; because the Universe is filled with harmony, and a soul who is in full harmony with the soul of the universe may listen to that music and understand it. The world as well as man resemble musical instruments, in which every string should be in perfect order, so that no discordant notes may be sounded. We may look upon matter on the physical plane as a state of low vibration and upon spirit as the highest vibration of life, and between the two poles are the intermediary states constituting the grand octave called Man. Plato is said to have written over the door of his academy: "Let no one enter here, unless he is versed in mathematics," and Pythagoras demanded of his disciples an additional "knowledge of music"; meaning the capacity to keep their soul attuned to the harmonies of the divine law of being, so as to be able to realise the beauty of truth. For without such an elevation of soul and without spirituality, all desire for a knowledge of that which transcends the realm of the sensual is merely an outcome of vanity, an insane craving for gratifying curiosity, which defeats its own end; because the more one seeks to examine objectively the One which includes the All, the more does he recede from it and separate himself from the realisation of that truth which is one, eternal, omnipresent and infinite. It is not the personality of man that can grasp the impersonal. If man wants to know God, he must die to himself, and enter God's nature; which means that he must overcome the disharmony caused by the delusion of division, separation and self, and again realise the unity of the whole.

The foundation of nature is Unity. God is only One. He is the Law, and requires no "law-giver"; being Himself omnipresent within the All of his nature; self-sufficient, self-existent and absolute. The Law is everywhere, and everything exists in the Law, and without the law of existence no existence is to be found. But as by the act of creation and subsequent evolution a variety of forms comes into existence, with innumerable beings capable to will, and to think, and to use the law contrary to divine wisdom, many disharmonies are caused in what ought to be a harmonious whole.

Thus the law is still the same; but its action may be misapplied and its use perverted. It is still the foundation of every individual being, and the sooner each individual will become able to recognise the highest and fundamental law of its own nature, which is identical with the law that rules the All, the sooner will the original harmony be restored.

Man is himself an outcome of the action of law, and that law is in him. It is the centre and fountain of his own being; he is an expression of it, and it is his true self. He is himself the law, and will recognise himself as the law when he learns to know his true self. All the elements in his nature which do not recognise this one universal law, and act in accordance with it, do not belong to man's divine nature; they are not his real self, but produce the disharmony which exist in his world. Only when all the inhabitants of his kingdom will bow before the superiority of that law, will there be perfect harmony.

Cause and Effect

In every department of nature every effect depends on a corresponding cause, and every cause will produce a certain effect according to the conditions in which it becomes manifest. If we knew the causes we could easily calculate their effects. Each thought, each word, each act creates a cause, which acts directly on the plane to which it belongs, creating there new causes, which react again upon the other planes.

A motive or thought which finds no expression in an act will have no direct result on the physical plane, but it may cause great emotions in the sphere of mind, and these may again react on the physical plane. The best intention will produce no visible effect unless it is put into execution; but intentions produce certain mental states, that may be productive of actions at some time in the future.

The performance of an act will have an effect, no matter whether it was premeditated or not, but an act without a motive will not directly affect the planes of thought. Such an act imposes no moral responsibility upon the performer, but it will, nevertheless, have its effects on the physical plane that may react upon the mind.

From the causes created on the physical, astral, and spiritual planes innumerable combinations of effects come into existence, creating new causes, that are again followed by effects, and every force that is put into action on either plane continues to act until it is exhausted by transformations into other modes of action, when its vibrations will be changed into others, and the previous effects will cease to exist.

By the threefold action of that law as thought, will, and performance on the physical, emotional, intellectual and spiritual planes a great many conditions ensue which give rise to endless modifications and varieties, and again produce innumerable secondary causes, which again produce effects, and at last the actions of the law of Karma will become so complicated, that it is impossible to follow it into its details.

The law of Karma is the law of justice for the purpose of restoring harmony; it includes retribution in the shape of "punishment" and "reward." It knows nothing of "revenge," neither does it recognise any personal merits; it is the Law itself, and acts according to its own nature and not in accordance to this or that consideration. It is the law according to which the sum of the causes created by one individual in one incarnation will produce certain effects in his next incarnation, and cause him to either enjoy or suffer that which he has either willingly, and with determination, or ignorantly created himself.

Every being in nature having attained individuality has its own individual Karma, determining the course of its future career; each of the individual elements in the constitution of man has its own Karma, and man being identified with his nature, partakes of the Karma of the principles which constitute his own nature; but as God is superior to nature and therefore not subject to it, so the individual man who conquers his nature, rises above it, and becoming one with the law, becomes free of the Karma affecting his terrestrial nature. "Giving his nature away," and sacrificing himself wholly to the law of divine being, he also "forgives" his sins.

Unity

The discords in nature, caused by the action of the deluded self-will and the perverted desires of individual entities, cannot cease in any other way than by the restoration of the unity of the individual will with the will of the fundamental law of the whole. This unity exists; it does not need to be created by man; he is only required to recognise it. If he recognises it practically, it will become realised in him. Personal man cannot recognise himself as being this Unity, because he is divided against himself; his "self" is an illusion, and an illusion cannot become a realisation of truth. If the truth becomes realised, the illusion ceases to be.

All numbers are the outcome of one; in all numbers the one is contained, and without the one at the bottom no numbers could come into existence. This number one remains always the same; whether divided or multiplied by itself, it does not change. All mathematics is based upon the faith into the immutability of number one. We have no positive proof that it never changes; our knowledge about it is only negative; because it has never been known to change. In the same way our intellectual knowledge of God is only negative; we cannot prove his eternal immutability scientifically; we only believe in it; the only proof we have of it is, that our own inner self-consciousness, if we have once attained it, remains ever the same. This proof is sufficient for the wise; but it will go for nought with the fool.

The foundation of nature is one; but the numbers of its manifestation appear to be infinite. Nevertheless, all things in nature are related to each other, owing to their relation to the one, which is at the bottom of their existence.

Everything has its number, measure, and weight, and there is nothing in nature which is not ruled by mathematical laws. Suns and stars have their periodical revolutions. The molecules of bodies combine in certain proportions, known to chemistry, and in all events on the physical plane as well as in the realm of the emotions a certain regularity and periodicity has been observed. There are regular hours for the appearance of day and night, fixed intervals for spring and summer, autumn and winter, for ebbs and tides in the ocean and in the waters constituting the soul. The physiological and anatomical changes in animal forms occur at fixed periods, and even the events of life take place according to certain occult laws; because, although man's will seems to be free, nevertheless his actions are controlled by certain circumstances, and even the comparative freedom of his will is a result of the action of the law of his evolution.

Magic Numbers

The followers of Pythagoras believed every process in nature to be regulated by certain numbers, which are as follows:

3	9	15	45
4	16	34	136
5	25	65	325
6	36	111	666
7	49	175	1225
8	64	260	2080
9	81	369	3321

This table represents a succession of numbers, which are obtained by the construction of Tetragrams or magic squares, and it was believed that by the use of these numbers every effect could be calculated if the original number referring to the cause were known. If everything has a certain number of vibrations, and if these vibrations increase or diminish at a certain ratio and in regular periods, a knowledge of these numbers will enable us to predict a future event.

The magic squares of odd numbers are formed as described below: by writing down the numbers of their squares in regular succession, cutting out their "heart" and transposing the numbers that are left to their opposite places. The following is the process in forming the magic square of the number III. The square of 3 is 9:

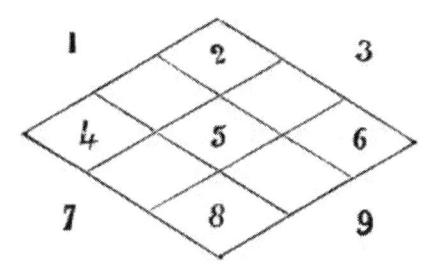

We see here the numbers 1, 3, 7, 9, left on the outside of the square. If they are inserted in a certain order into the blank spaces at the opposite sides of the square, the following figure will be the result:

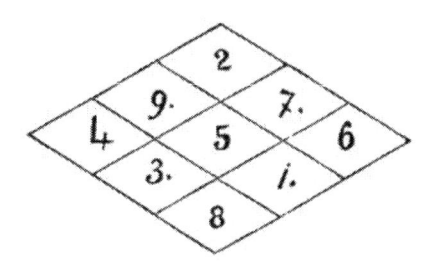

These numbers, if added in any column of three, will always produce 15.

The following will make still clearer the order in which the numbers are to be inserted, with the figure drawn in an upright position.

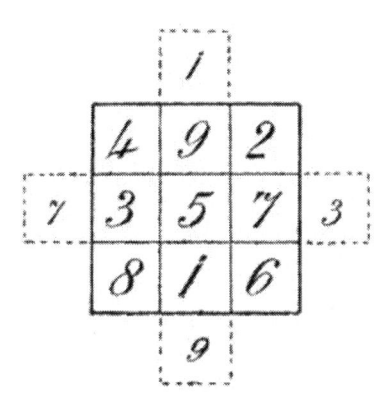

According to this principle all the other magic squares of odd numbers are made.

The following is the tetragram of the number seven:

VII.

22	47	16	41	10	35	4
5	23	48	17	42	11	29
30	6	24	49	18	36	12
13	31	7	25	43	19	37
38	14	32	1	26	44	20
21	39	8	33	2	27	45
46	15	40	9	34	3	28

Each column added together produces 175.

IX.

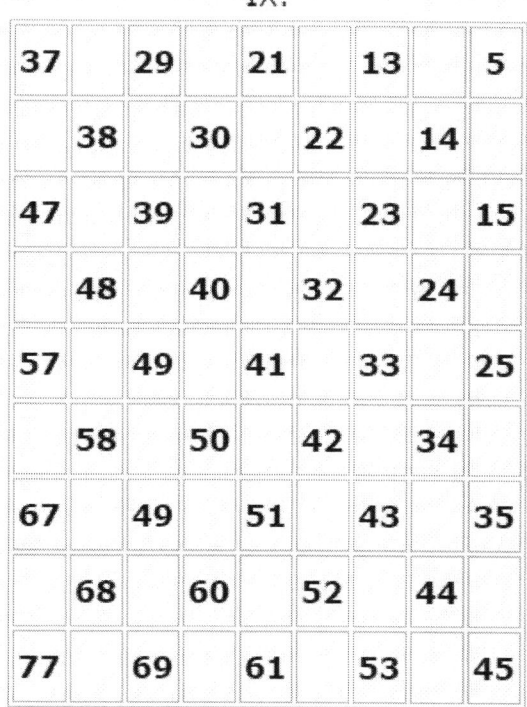

37		29		21		13		5
	38		30		22		14	
47		39		31		23		15
	48		40		32		24	
57		49		41		33		25
	58		50		42		34	
67		49		51		43		35
	68		60		52		44	
77		69		61		53		45

N.B. -- The numbers omitted here may be inserted by the student.

The construction of tetragrams of even numbers is more complicated, but the following examples will show the principles after which they are constructed:

VI.

6	(32)	(3)	(43)	(35)	1
(7)	11	(27)	(28)	8	(30)
(24)	(14)	16	15	(23)	(19)
(13)	(20)	22	21	(17)	(18)
(25)	29	(10)	(9)	26	(12)
36	(5)	(33)	(4)	(2)	31

Summa = 111.

VIII.

8	(58)	(62)	(4)	(5)	(59)	(63)	1
(9)	15	(51)	(53)	(52)	(54)	10	(16)
(48)	(18)	22	(44)	(45)	19	(23)	(41)
(25)	(39)	(35)	29	28	(38)	(34)	(32)
(33)	(31)	(27)	37	36	(30)	(26)	(40)
(24)	(42)	46	(20)	(21)	43	(47)	(17)
(49)	55	(11)	(13)	(12)	(14)	50	(56)
64	(2)	(6)	(60)	(61)	(3)	(7)	57

Summa = 260.

Every person has a certain number that expresses his character and if we know that number, we may, by the use of the magic squares, calculate certain periodical changes in his mental and emotional states, which induce him to make certain changes in his outward conditions, and in this way calculate approximately the time when some important changes may take place in his career.

The Number Seven

Periodicity is a manifestation of universal law, and an attention to it may lead to some important discoveries Its actions have long ago been known to exist in the vibrations producing light and sound, and it has recently been recognised in chemistry by experiments tending to prove that all so-called simple elements are only various states of vibrations of one primordial element, manifesting itself in seven principal modes of action, each of which to be sub-divided into seven again. The difference which exists between so-called single substances is, therefore, no difference of substance or matter, but only a difference of the function of matter or in the ratio of its atomic vibration.

This periodicity is also known to exist in the macrocosm of the universe; the tide of civilisation rises and sinks according to certain laws, and ages of spiritual ignorance are followed by eras of spiritual enlightenment; upon the Kali Yuga follows the Satya Yuga (the era of wisdom), as sure as day follows the night. This periodicity is stated to be as follows:

Satya Yuga = 4,800 divine years.
Treta Yuga = 3,600 divine years.
Dwapara Yuga = 2,400 divine years.
Kali Yuga = 1,200 divine years.
Each divine year being equal to 360 years of mortal men.
(See also H. P. Blavatsky: "Theosophical Glossary.")

The number Seven represents the scale of nature, it is represented in all departments of nature, from the radiant sun, whose light is broken by a dewdrop into the seven colours of the rainbow, down to the snowflake crystallising in six-pointed stars around the invisible centre. The law of seven has been found to rule in the development and growth of vegetable and animal organisms, in the constitution of the universe, and in the constitution of Man.

Seven is the rule by which the totality of existence is measured, but Five is the number of Harmony. If the fifth note in the musical scale is in accord with the first and the third, harmony will be the result. There are other accords which are harmonious, but the most perfect accord is caused by the harmony of the first, the third, and the fifth. Two sounds may be harmonious, but to attain a perfect accord a third one is required.

The same law rules in the constitution of Man. If his body (his first principle) is in accord with his instincts (the third), he experiences pleasant sensations, but full harmony and happiness is only attained when his fifth principle (his intelligence) fully assents in the union of the first and the third. Other parallels may be drawn between the musical scale and the scale of principles in man, and it will be found that both have their accords in moll [minor] and in dur [major] that correspond to each other. Each man's life is a symphony, in which either harmonious or discordant tunes may prevail.

Love

The power by which harmony is produced is the power of Love. Love produces union and harmony, hate causes dissension and discord. Love is the power of mutual recognition; recognition is a manifestation of consciousness, consciousness is a manifestation of life. Life, Love, Consciousness, Harmony, are essentially one. Love is the power by which a being existing in one form recognises itself in the form of another being. Why do some notes, if sounded together, produce harmony, if not on account of the similarity of the elements that compose them coming to the consciousness of our own mind? Mutual recognition among friends causes joy, and joy means harmony, happiness, and content.

If two or more notes of exactly the same kind are sounded together, they produce neither harmony nor discord, they simply increase their own strength. They are already one, in form and in spirit; but if different notes are struck, each containing an element also contained in the other, each sees its own counterpart represented in the mirror held by the other, and this recognition is joy. If we listen to beautiful music the air seems filled with life. If the principle of harmony exists within ourselves we recognise it in music; it becomes alive in our soul. A discordant being may listen to the most beautiful music and will experience no pleasure because there is no harmony within his own soul.

If a principle becomes conscious of its own existence in another form and recognises its beauty in that form in its purity, and unalloyed by any adulteration, perfect harmony is the result. If two or more things contain the same element, these elements are justly adapted to each other, and seek to unite, because they are constituted alike, they vibrate together as one.

This tendency to unite is Attraction, which manifests itself on all planes of existence. The planets are attracted to the sun and to each other, because they all contain the same elements, seeking to reunite, and the power of gravitation is nothing else but the power exercised by love. Man is attracted to woman and woman to man, because if they realise in each other the presence of the elements of their own ideal, they will love each other and be fully contented. Man and woman can only truly love each other if they are both attracted by the same ideal. This ideal may be high or low, but the higher it is the more permanent will it be, and the greater will be their mutual happiness.

Original man was a Unity; an ethereal being, in whom will and thought were one. Being misled by the allurements of sensual existence he began to dream, and while he dreamed he forgot his own divine nature and became a worm of the earth. When he opened his eyes, he found the woman before him. He, the original unity had become divided in two; which means that his will and his reason had become divided; they were no longer in harmony with each other and no longer in harmony with the law.

Man represents the imagination, woman the will. If they had both separated themselves from the law as they did from each other, woman would have no intelligence and man would have no will; but fortunately some of the original nature that constituted original man remained with them; they still are both to a certain extent embodiments of the law, and by entering again into harmony with the law, will and intelligence will become united in wisdom; the heart one with the head; the true man and the true woman one being. This is the celestial marriage of the soul with the spirit, of beauty with strength, of which all external marriages are at best symbols but usually caricatures.

Mankind is only one, but it appears in many millions of various masks. This mask is the personality of each man, the instrument through which his humanity acts, and which is full of imperfections. He, in whom humanity has become conscious, sees in every man and woman not only his brother or sister, but his own self. A person who injures another, injures himself, for each man constitutes a power which acts upon all the elements constituting humanity and the good or evil he does will return to himself; because whatever takes place in humanity, takes place within his own nature; for his true nature is that of humanity and the body of humanity belongs to it as a whole.

Love is self-recognition. You cannot love a thing or recognise yourself in it, if you are not related to it. You cannot love humanity if you have not the principle of humanity alive in you; you cannot love God and still remain Mr Smith or Mrs Jones; only God can love God. To love God you must outgrow yourself and become truly divine. He who claims to love God without having any spiritual knowledge of Him is a hypocrite or a fool.

Love is self-knowledge, God. It is a spiritual, self-existent, and self-sufficient principle, requiring for its own being only its own self; but without some object it cannot become manifest, and the quality of its manifestation depends on the quality of that object. A person in love with himself loves a nothing. Love in the high acts high, in the degraded, low. The more universal the object, the more will the power of love in a person expand the mind; but the mind, to be so expanded, must be strong, a weak mind has no power.

Love, to be strong, must be pure, intelligent, and unalloyed with selfish considerations. If we love a thing on account of the use we can make of it, we do not in reality love that thing, but ourselves. Pure love has only the well-being of its object in view, it does not calculate profits, and is not afraid of disadvantages that may grow out of its love. The intellect calculates, but love is its own law. Impure love is weak and does not enter into its object; it may cause a ruffle on the soul of another, but does not penetrate to the centre. Pure love penetrates and cannot be resisted. The most potent love potion a person can give to another is to love that person without any selfish object in view.

If you wish to progress on the road to perfection, take lessons in love. Learn to love the highest, and you will be attracted by it. Love in every man not the person, but his humanity. If you despise another you despise your own self, because he who prominently notices the faults of another has the elements of those faults in himself. A vain person is repulsed by the vanity of another, a liar expects from others the truth, a thief does not wish to have his own property taken away.

Each man is a mirror in which every other man may see his own image reflected, either as he is or as he may become in the future, for in every human soul exist the same elements, although in different states of development, and there development often depends on external conditions over which man has but little control.

Love is the most necessary element for the continuance of life; there is no life without love, and if man were to cease to love life he would cease to live. A love for a higher life will lead men to a higher condition, a love for a lower state will drag them down to the low. It often happens that if a person's love for a high ideal does not meet the object which it desires, it transfers its love upon something that is low. Old females without any offspring often transfer their parental affection upon some favourite cat or dog, and there are men who buy the semblance of love when no genuine love can be had.

Vibration

Whenever a lower vibration is not entirely out of harmony with a higher one, the higher vibration accelerates the action of the lower one and brings it up to its own level, in the same manner as a bar of iron, surrounded by an insulated electric wire, may have electricity induced in it, and through a long-continued and powerful action of the higher vibrations upon the lower ones, even the involuntary actions of the body, such as the movements of the heart, may become subject to individual will.

Two strings of a musical instrument which sound not entirely out of harmony, by being sounded together for a certain length of time, at last become harmonious; a man living in more refined society, which is not too far above his moral or intellectual level, will become more refined, servants will ape their masters, and animals take some of the lower characteristics of those that attend to them, and friends or married couples being continually in each other's company may finally resemble each other to a certain extent.

If the respective rates of the vibrations of two substances are entirely out of harmony, they may repel each other, and abnormal activity or excitement follows. The animal body, for instance, can be exposed without danger to a comparatively high degree of heat, if the temperature is gradually raised; while an even lower degree of heat may be very injurious if applied suddenly. It is not without reasons that the occultist abstains from alcohol and from animal food. "What may be one man's food, will be another man's poison"; in the sphere of matter as well as in the sphere of the emotions. Strong constitutions can bear strong food, weak minds will get frightened at unwelcome truths. No man has ever become an Adept merely because he lived on vegetables; a vegetable diet is however preferable to meat-eating for various reasons. Apart from the self-evident fact that it is entirely opposed to the divine law of justice that he who strives after the attainment of a higher state of existence should destroy animal life, or cause others to destroy it for the purpose of gratifying his appetite. Those who desire to become more spiritual and refined should avoid supplying their bodies with that which is gross; those who desire to master their passions should not feed them with substances in which the elements of such passions reside.

A great variety of different kinds of food produces impurities of the blood; a struggle ensues between the different auras, and excitement, fever, and disease is the result. The same law explains the origin of venereal and cutaneous diseases, and in the astral plane, a great variety of emotions, called into existence within a short space of time, may render a person insane.

If two forces of a character different from each other meet, disharmony will be the result. Everybody has his own peculiar emanations and auras and transmits them to others, so every one receives the magnetic auras of others or of the locality by which he is surrounded, and these emanations may be either wholesome or pestiferous; men and women may either cure or poison each other by them, and it is therefore well to follow the advice which Gautama Buddha gave to his disciples, and eat and sleep alone.

Vice and Virtue

Many people are very careful to have their food well prepared, so that no unhealthy food enters the body; while at the same time they are very careless as to what thoughts enter their mind; but the quality of the thoughts that dwell in the mind, and of the emotions which nourish the soul, is of far more importance than the quality of the food which enters the body. The mind and the will of man, no less than his body, may be poisoned; the food which the mind requires comes from the highest planes of thought; the food for the soul from the light of divine wisdom. Only that which has descended from heaven can rise to heaven again. There is no such thing as "sin" in the usual acceptation of this term and there is no one to punish it. Our mistakes are our teachers; our vices are often the basis of our virtues, our passions are the steps which furnish material for the steps that lead us to heaven. Vice and virtue are manifestations of one energy, which we may employ according to the degree of our wisdom; but he who has no power for evil has also no power for good.

We may spend the treasure which nature has lent us either for a high or for a low purpose, it concerns only ourselves; but we cannot expend the same sum again after it has been expended. A purely animal life will produce happiness if the possessor is contented with it. If a person has no higher object in view than to eat and drink, sleep, and propagate his species, he may be thereby rendered happy; there can be nothing wrong; but he who desires to become an immortal being, must take care not to waste his strength.

Only that which is pure can be harmonious.

Singleness of purpose renders a motive pure, but a variety of purposes causes impurity. If a person devotes himself to a certain mode of life, because all his desires are directed towards that end, his motive will be pure; but if he has besides other objects in view, his motive will be impure, and may defeat his aim. The word "asceticism" is continually misunderstood. A man who lives in a convent, or as an hermit in the wilderness, is not an "ascetic," if he has no desire for a life in the world; for it is no act of self-denial to avoid that which we do not want. "Asceticism" means discipline, and a person who is disgusted with the ways of the world undergoes a much more severe discipline, if he remains in the world, than if he runs away, and goes where he may enjoy his peace.

The real ascetic is therefore he who lives in the midst of the society whose manners displease him, and whose tastes are not his own, and who, in spite of all the temptations by which he may be surrounded, still maintains his integrity of character. Strength only grows by resistance. Our enemies are our friends, if we know how to use them. A hermit living in the woods, where he has no temptations, gains no strength. Isolation is only suitable for an Adept; the Neophite must go throughout the ordeal of life.

A tiger does not sin if he kills a man, he only follows the law of his nature. He who follows the dictates of his nature commits no crime. But what is virtue in an animal may become vice in a man; because he has two natures, an animal and a spiritual nature. If he knows his own higher nature, he will follow it, and for the purpose of obtaining knowledge of it he must sin and suffer the consequences. Real sin is the wilful rejection of the manifestation of divine truth.

The saintly Eckhart says: "God has made great sinners of those who were to become the performers of great works; so that they could attain a superior wisdom by means of his love. If God found it necessary that I should have sinned and suffered for the purpose of gaining experience, I do not wish that I had not sinned, nor do I regret having sinned; for thus his will is done on earth as it is in heaven. A truly honest man will also not wish that he should have no desire for sinning; because without the power to sin he would have no means to overcome it. There can be no victory without a battle, and no true knowledge of good without the experience of evil."

Suffering

Suffering is an absolutely necessary condition for man as long as he has not attained perfection. To believe in the presence of suffering is as necessary for his terrestrial nature as it is necessary for his spiritual nature to realise the presence of God. There is no other Redeemer of Mankind except Self-knowledge attained by experience. If all the poverty in the world could be artificially abolished at once, men and women would perish in indolence. Nothing can be truly enjoyed which has not been gained by one's own exertions. If there were one teacher supposed to be infallible, whose dictates would be accepted by everybody, the whole world would be satisfied in believing his theories; there would be no incitement for anyone to seek himself for the' truth. If we support a lazy beggar in his idleness, we rob him of the opportunity to gain by experience that knowledge which he can rightfully claim.

Metals are purified by fire, and the heart gains knowledge by suffering. The lower desires must starve to nourish the higher; the animal passions must be crucified and die; but the angel of Love removes the stone from the sepulchre, and liberates the higher energies from the sphere of selfishness and darkness; and the resurrected virtues live and become active in a new world of light and harmony.

If you wish to represent to your mind the process of spiritual purification, seek to understand that you are a world created by a dream, filled with the product of the imagination of nature, and thrown into disorder by the absence of the light of divine wisdom, which is the recognition of divine law, the true inner self-consciousness, which you do not possess. You are comparable to an empty nothing, an evanescent soap-bubble, upon whose glittering surface various colours play; but in which there is no true life and no substance as long as the truth has not become a living power in you.

In this world as in a mirror the invisible image of the divine Adonai is for ever reflected and his power is latent within you. If, by the strength of obedience and the knowledge which you have already received, you can subdue the turbulent elements in your world and restore order in Chaos by ceasing to give life and strength to your desires and dreams, then will the image of the Lord of All, whose presence is everywhere, become visible in yourself and his power awaken within you.

In this principle will and thought and the law are as one without any division. If you know the law, it will lead you to unity and restoration of harmony; the divine ideal will become realised within you, and as it becomes a reality in you, you will recognise it as being your own immortal self.

Bones, muscles, nerves, &c., are the elements of the physical constitution of man; illusions, delusions, dreams, theories, opinions, and dogmas are the inhabitants of his mind; truth, love, justice, purity, self-knowledge, freedom, harmony, and happiness are the elements and attributes of his spiritual organism, and the more these principles manifest their universality in him, the more will he himself approach the divine state.

To recognise the divinity in humanity is to become divine; to behold the realisation of the highest ideal within one's own soul is divine adoration; to desire not the possession of any creature, but to adore the Creator within them all, including oneself, is worship; to recognise and enjoy the harmonies of the universe manifested in nature is divine praise; to let the unity of will, thought, and law be restored within one's soul is true meditation; to rise above the illusion of self and sacrifice oneself to the God of All is true prayer; to realise the truth within one's own heart is to dispel the clouds of error; to become nothing oneself is to enter into that higher self-consciousness which constitutes man's divine state.

There is not a single instance known in history in which true prayer has not been efficacious. If any man has not obtained that which he asked, it only proves that he did not know how to pray. True prayer does not consist in words, but in actions, and the gods help him who helps himself; but he who expects that the gods should do for him that which he ought to accomplish himself, does not know how to pray, and will be disappointed. Prayer means the rising up in our thoughts and aspirations to the highest ideal; if we do not rise up to it, we do not pray. If we expect our highest ideal to come down to us, we expect an absurdity and impossibility.

To attain the highest the spirit should be the master, the passions the servants. A helpless cripple is the slave of his servant; a man who depends on ignorant servants to do work which he can do himself, has to submit to their whims and imperfections, and if he changes his servants, that does not change his position. A person who has vulgar desires and tastes becomes their servant; they dictate to him, and he has to exert himself to attain the means to gratify their claims; but he who has no ignoble desires to serve, is free. Having conquered the world of which he himself is the creator and which belongs to him, his strife with the astral elements ceases. For him discord no longer exists, and resting with his heart at the centre, he is himself the sun illuminating his world and enjoys the harmonies which he created in his own divine nature.

Chapter VI - Illusions

"Reason dissipates the illusions and visionary interpretations of things, in which the imagination runs riot." - **Dr Caird**

Power of Imagination

The first power that meets us at the threshold of soul's dominion is the power of imagination: it is the plastic and creative power of the mind. Man is conscious of being able to receive ideas and to put them into forms. He lives not entirely in the objective world, but possesses an interior world of his own. It is in his power to be the sole autocrat in that world, the master of its creations and lord over all it contains.

He may govern there by the supreme power of his will, and if ideas intrude, which have no legitimate right to exist in it, it is in his power either to drive them away or suffer them to remain and to grow. His reason is the supreme ruler in that world, its ministers are the emotions. If man's reason, misled by the treacherous advice of evil emotions, suffers evil ideas to grow, they may become powerful and dethrone reason.

This interior world, like the outer world, is a world of its own. It is sometimes dark, sometimes illumined; its space and the things it contains are as real to its inhabitants as the physical world is real to the physical senses; its horizon may be either narrow or expanded, limited in some and without limits in others; it has its beautiful scenery and its dismal localities, its sunshine and storms, its forms of beauty and horrible shapes. It is the privilege of man to retire to that world whenever he chooses; physical enemies do not persecute him there; bodily pain cannot enter. The vexations of material life remain behind, only that which moves his soul enters with him.

In this interior realm is the Temple of Man wherein he can lock the door against the intrusion of sensual impressions. On the entrance of that temple are the Dwellers of the Threshold, made of desires and passions, which are our own creations, and which must be conquered before we can enter. Within that temple exists a world, as big and illimitable as the unbounded universe. In this inner realm is the God whose spirit floats over the waters of the deep, and whose fiat calls into existence the creatures which inhabit the kingdom of mind.

In the air surrounding the centre of that interior world is the battle ground of the gods. There the gods of love and hate, the daemons of lust and pride, and anger, the devils of malice, cruelty, and revenge, vanity, envy, and jealousy, hold high carnival, they stir up the emotions, and, unless subdued by Reason, grow strong enough to dethrone it.

Reason rests upon the recognition of Truth. Wherever truth is disregarded illusions appear. If we lose sight of the highest, the low will appear, and an illusion will be created. One is the number of Truth, Six is the number of illusion, because the Six have no existence without the Seventh, they are the visible products of the one, manifesting itself as six around an invisible centre. Wherever they are six, there must be the seventh. The six cannot know the seventh if the seventh does not become manifest. God knows himself; but we cannot know his presence unless that presence becomes manifested in us. One is the number of life, and six the number of shadows, having no life of their own.

Animal Forms

Forms without life are illusive, and he who mistakes the form for the life or principle of which it is an expression is haunted by an illusion. Forms perish, but the principle that causes their existence remains. The object of forms is to represent principles, and as long as a form is a true representation of a principle the principle gives it life; but if a form is made to serve another principle than the one which called it into existence, degradation will be the result.

The irrational forms produced by nature are perfect expressions of the principles they are intended to represent; rational beings only are the dissemblers. Each animal is a true expression of the character represented by its form, only at the point where intellectuality begins deception commences. Each animal form is a symbol of the mental state which characterises its soul, because it is not itself the arbitrary originator of its form. But rational man has it in his power to create, and if he prostitutes one principle in a form for another, the form will gradually adopt that shape which characterises the prostituted principle, of which, in the course of time, it becomes a true expression.

Therefore we find that a man of noble appearance, by becoming a miser, gradually adopts the sneaking look and the stealthy gait of an animal going in search of its prey; the lascivious may acquire the habits, and perhaps the appearance, of a monkey or goat, the sly one the features of a fox, and the conceited the looks of a donkey.

If our bodies were formed of a more ethereal and plastic material than of muscles and bones, each change of our character would produce quickly a corresponding change of our form; but gross matter is inert and follows only slowly the impressions made upon the soul. The material of which astral forms are made are more plastic, and the soul of a villainous person may actually resemble a pool filled with vipers and scorpions, the true symbol of his moral characteristics, mirrored in his mind. A generation of saints would, in the course of time, produce a nation of Apollos and Dianas, a generation of villains would grow into monsters and dwarfs. To keep the form in its original beauty the principle must be kept pure and without any adulteration.

Purity

One fundamental colour of the solar spectrum, if unmixed, is as pure as another; one element, if free from another, is pure. Unmixed copper is as pure as unalloyed gold, and emotions are pure if free from extraneous mixture. Forms are pure if they represent their principles in their purity; a villain who shows himself what he is is pure and true to his nature, a saint who dissembles is impure and false. Fashions are the external expressions of the mental states of a country, and if men and women degenerate in their character, their fashions will become absurd.

The want of power to discriminate between the true and the illusive, between the form and the principle, and the consequent error of apprehending the low for the high, is the cause of suffering. Man's material interests are generally considered to be of supreme importance, and the interests of the highest elements in his constitution are forgotten. The power that should be expended to feed the high is eaten up by the low. Instead of the low serving the high, the high is made to serve the low, and instead of the form being used as an instrument of action for a high principle, a low principle is substituted for a higher one, for the purpose of serving the form.

Such a prostitution of principle in favour of form is found in all spheres of social life. We find it among the rich and the poor, the educated and the ignorant, in the forum, the press, and the pulpit, no less than in the halls of the merchant and in the daily transactions of life. The prostitution of principle is worse than the prostitution of the body. He who uses his intellectual powers for selfish and villainous purposes is more to be pitied than she who carries on a trade with her bodily charms to gain the means by which she may keep that body alive. The prostitution of universal human rights for the benefit of a few individuals is the most dangerous form of prostitution on Earth.

The difference between vulgar prostitution of the body and the more refined prostitution of the intellectual faculties for the purpose of accomplishing selfish ends, is merely that in the first class merely the grossest parts of the human organisation are misused, while in the other class the higher and nobler elements are prostituted. There are few women in the world who have become degraded from an inclination to be so; in the great majority of cases they are the victims of circumstances which they had not the power to resist; but intellectual prostitutes belong to the higher classes, where want and poverty are unknown.

To employ the intellectual powers for selfish purposes is the beginning of intellectual prostitution. Blessed are they who are able to gain their bread by the honest work of their hands, for an employment which requires little intellectual attention will leave them free to employ their powers for the purpose of spiritual unfoldment; while those who spend all their energy upon the lower planes of the mind are selling their immortal birthright for a worthless mess of potage which will nourish the impermanent intellect while it starves the soul.

The soul no less than the body requires to be nourished. The heart starves if the brain is overfed. The nutriment of the soul comes from the action of the spirit in the body, and this food is as "material" and necessary for it as physical food for the physical body. The existing of the emotions is no nutriment for the soul. The emotions belong to the astral form. The nutriment of the soul is drawn out of the material body by the power of the divine light of the spirit within the heart.

Illusion of Self

The greatest of all illusions is the illusion of Self. Material man looks upon himself as something existing apart from every other existence. The shape of his form creates the illusion of being a separate part of the whole.

Still, experience shows that there is not a single element in his body, in the constitution of his soul, or in the mechanism of his intellect, that is not continually departing, and is replaced by others. What belongs to him to-day belonged yesterday to another, and will belong to another to-morrow. In his physical form there is a continual change. In the bodies of organised beings tissues disappear slowly or quickly, according to the nature of their affinities, and new ones take their places, to be replaced in their turn by others. The human body changes in size, shape, and density as age advances, presenting successively the symbols of the buoyant health in youth, the vigorous constitution of manhood, or the grace and beauty of womanhood, up to the attributes indicating old age, the forerunner of decay and cessation of activity in that individual form. No less is the change in the mind. Sensation and desires change, consciousness changes, memories grow dim. No man has the same opinions he had when he was a child; knowledge increases, intellect grows weak, and on the mental as well as on the physical plane the special activity ceases when the accumulated energy is exhausted by transformation into other modes of action or is transferred into other forms.

The lower material elements in the constitution of man change rapidly, the higher ones change slowly, but only the highest elements are enduring. Nothing can be said to belong essentially to man but his character. He who cares a great deal for his lower nature, cares for that which is not his own, but which he has only borrowed from nature. While he enjoys its possession an illusion is created, making it appear to be an essential part of himself. But man's terrestrial nature is not more an essential part of himself than the clothes which a man wears, a constituent part of the man. His only true self is his character, and he who loses the purity and strength of his character loses all his possessions.

Illusion of Money

One of the kings of illusions is Money, the king of the world. Money represents the principle of equity, and it should be employed to enable everyone to obtain the just equivalent for his labour. If we desire more money than we can rightfully claim, we wish for something that does not belong to us but to another. If we obtain labour without paying for it its proper equivalent, we deprive others of justice, and therefore deprive ourselves of the truth, which is a more serious loss to ourselves than the loss of money to the defrauded.

Money as such is a symbol, only the principle which it represents has a real existence. Nevertheless we see the world lie at the feet of the illusion. The poor clamour for it, and the rich crave for more, and the general desire is to obtain the greatest amount of reward by giving the least possible equivalent. Clergymen save souls, and doctors cure bodies for the purpose of making money; law is sold to him who is able and willing to pay, fame and reputation and the semblance of love can be obtained for money, and the worth of a man is expressed in the sum of shillings or pounds which he may call his own.

Starvation threatens the poor, and the consequences of superabundance the rich, and the rich take advantage of the distress of the poor to enrich themselves more. Science exerts her powers to increase the amount of the material comforts of man. It vanquishes the impediments presented by time and space, and turns night into day. New engines are invented, and the work whose performance in former times required the use of a thousand arms, may now be accomplished by a child.

An immense amount of personal suffering and labour is thereby saved. But as the means to satisfy the craving for comfort increase a craving arises for more. Things that formerly were considered luxuries now become indispensable needs. Illusions create illusions, and desires give rise to desires. The sight of the principle is lost, and the golden calf is put into its place. Production is followed by over production, the supply exceeds the demand, the price of labour comes down to starvation rates, and on the rotten soil the mushrooms of monopoly grow. The more the facilities increase to sustain the battle of life, the more increases its fury.

The noblest power of man, his intellect, whose destiny it is to form a solid basis for the highest spiritual knowledge of man, is forced to labour for the satisfaction of the animal instincts of man; the body flourishes while the soul starves and becomes a beggar in the kingdom of truth.

Illusion of Love

From the love of self arises the love of possession. It is the hydra-headed monster whose cravings can never be stilled. Nearest to the illusion of self stands the illusion of so-called Love. True love is not an illusion, it is the power that unites the worlds and an attribute of the spirit; but the illusion of love is not love, but only love's shadow. True love is sacrifice, but false love cares for itself, and seeks for enjoyment. True love exists, even if the form is dissolved; false love dies, when the form to which it was attached decays.

Ideal women is the crown of creation, and has a right to be loved by man. A man who does not love beauty has no element of beauty in him. Man loves beauty and woman loves strength. A man who is the slave of his desires is weak, and cannot command the respect of woman. If she sees him squirm under the lash of his animal passions, she will see an animal and will not be able to look upon him as her protector and god.

Marital love is a law of nature and a necessity for the propagation of man. But however beautiful the relations between husband and wife may be, sexual intercourse belongs to the animal kingdom and not to the spiritual nature of man. Mutual attraction between animals is not less beautiful and usually more pure than among mankind; the birds of the air do not marry for money, and often animals die on account of their grief over the death of their mates.

A person who has not yet outgrown his terrestrial nature will yearn for terrestrial love; a celibacy enforced by law is a crime against nature: a celibacy enforced by circumstances is a misfortune; but for the spiritually unfolded soul there exists a higher attraction; the true divine requires no law to teach him celibacy; he is already a natural celibat, and inhabitant of that kingdom (coelum), where terrestrial marriage does not exist.

Illusion of Life

Another illusion is the craving for physical life, and well may he crave for it who has no individual character of his own, because, if he loses his life, he loses his all. Men and women cling to the illusion of life because they do not know what life is. They will submit to indignity, dishonour, and suffering rather than die. But why should animal life be so desirable as to sacrifice character for it? One life is only one temporary condition among a thousand similar ones through which the individuality of man passes in its travels on the road to perfection, and whether he remains a longer or a shorter interval at one station, cannot be of any very serious importance to him. Man can make no better use of his life than to sacrifice it, if necessary, for a high purpose; because this act will strengthen his own individuality, in which rests the power by which he is enabled to reappear in a new form.

On the other band, he who sneaks away from the battle of life for selfish purposes, or because he is afraid to continue its struggles, will not escape. He may wish to step out of life and destroy his body, but the law cannot be cheated. Life will remain with him until his natural days would have ended. He cannot destroy it, he can only deprive himself of the instrument through which he can act. He resembles a man who has to perform some work and throws away the instrument which would have enabled him to perform it. Vain will be his regrets.

Another illusion is a great deal of what is called "science." True knowledge makes a man free, but false science renders him a slave to the opinions of others. Many men waste their lives to learn that which is foolish and neglect that which is true, mistaking that which is evanescent and perishing for the eternal. Often learning is not the aim but the means to the aim of the student, while his real objects are the attainment of wealth, position, and fame, or the gratification of ambition or curiosity. The true wealth of a nation or a man does not rest in its collected opinions, but in moral and spiritual possessions, which alone will remain permanent.

There is nothing more productive of a tendency to the development of an extreme degree of selfishness than the development of a high degree of intellectuality, without any accompanying growth of spirituality. A high degree of intellectuality enables a person to take personal advantages over others who are less clever, and unless he possesses great moral powers he will not be able to resist the temptations that are put in his way. The greatest villains and criminals have been persons of great intellectual qualifications.

That which a man really needs to know, and without whose knowledge he cannot obtain the consciousness of his own true and immortal nature, is not taught in our colleges. The most favoured student is he who is taught by his God. "Blessed is he whom wisdom teaches, not by perishable emblems and words, but by its own inherent power; not what it appears to be, but as it is."

The desire for power and fame are other illusions.

True power is an attribute of the spirit. If I am obeyed because I am rich, it is not myself who commands obedience, but my riches. If I am called powerful because I enjoy authority, it is not myself who is powerful, but it is the authority vested in me. Riches and authority are illusions thrown around men, which often vanish as quickly as they have been acquired. Fame is often enjoyed by him who does not deserve it. The most honoured man is he who has cause to respect himself.

Place of birth and condition of life are circumstances which are usually not matters of choice, and no one has a right to despise another on account of his nationality, religious belief, colour of skin, or the act he may play on this planet. Whether an actor plays the part of a king or a servant, the actor is, therefore, not despised, provided he plays his part well.

"Honour and shame from no conditions rise;
Act well your part, there all the honour lies."
-- Alexander Pope

Religion

One of the greatest illusions is much of what goes today by the name of "religion," not religion itself, but its mask in the shape of clericalism, priestcraft, and orthodoxy. Each religious system represents an expression of truth, but it requires the possession of truth to find truth therein.

As a man's spirit cannot exist upon this earth and express itself except in and through the material body, so each church, however spiritual its soul may be, has an external, physical, animal, and mental organism, represented by the members composing the church or society and by its doctrines, creeds, theories, and speculations; neither can the spiritual organism be separated from the lower principles; such a separation would be death to the visible church.

Thus the lower self of the church battles for life and is founded upon selfishness, while its spires reach up to heaven. All that can be hoped for reasonably is that the spirituality at the top may gradually descend to the foundations, and that each member may find the truth contained in his religious system, not by the candle light of blind speculation and foolish belief, but by its own light; for the truth requires no other light but itself.

There are other illusions which come without being asked, and remain, although their stay is not wanted. They are the unwelcome visitors -- Fear, Doubt, and Remorse. Their father is "selfishness," and "cowardice" is the name of the mother. Born from the kingdom of darkness, their substance is ignorance, which only the magic of true knowledge can dissolve.

Men live in fear of a revengeful power which has no existence, and die from fear of an evil that does not exist. They are afraid of the effects of causes which they, nevertheless, continue to create; and not daring to face their natural consequences, they seek to escape from the creatures which they themselves have created.

Every act creates a cause, and the cause is followed by an effect which reacts on him who created the cause, whether he may experience that effect in this life or in another. To escape the effect of the cause which has been created, he who created the cause must try to transform himself into another being. If the elements composing his lower nature have led him into making mistakes they will suffer, but if he succeeds in living in his higher nature he changes himself into a superior being.

Only in this sense is the Christ in every human nature the "Lamb" taking upon himself the sins of the world. The lamb is the symbol of obedience to divine law; this obedience is wisdom; wisdom is self-knowledge; divine self-knowledge is divine being, and he who has entered the state of Divinity is one with the law and has ceased to sin.

Such is the only rational philosophy of the "forgiveness of sins," and priests could forgive sins if they were able to change the sinner into a saint. This can, however, only be done by the individual exertions of the "sinner," who may be instructed by one who is wise. To become sufficiently wise to instruct another about the laws of his nature it is of the utmost importance that the instructor should know these laws, and be acquainted with the true constitution of man.

Power of Reason

The truth is the saviour of man, ignorance is his perdition. Reason is the power of the mind to recognise the truth, and in the light of truth the shadows of doubt and fear and remorse cannot exist.

Illusions are dispersed through the power of true knowledge. When the will is held in abeyance the imagination is rendered passive, and the mind takes in the reflections of pictures stored up in the Astral Light without choice or discrimination. When reason does not guide the imagination the mind creates disorderly fancies and hallucinations.

The passive seer dreams while awake, and to him his dreams are realities, they are impressions caused by foreign ideas taking possession of the unresisting mind, and, according to the scource from which such impressions come, they may be either true or false. Various means have been adopted to suspend the discriminating power of reason and render the imagination abnormally passive, and all such practices are injurious, in proportion as they are efficacious. The ancient Pythoness attempted to heighten her already abnormal receptivity by the inhalation of noxious vapours; some whirl in a dance until the action of reason is temporarily suspended; others use opium, Indian hemp, and other narcotics, which render their mind a blank, and induce morbid fancies and illusions.

The fumigations which were used at former times for the purpose of rendering reason inactive, and allowing the products of a passive imagination to appear in an objective state, were usually narcotic substances. Blood was only used for the purpose of furnishing substance to Elementals and Elementaries, by the aid of which they might render their bodies more dense and visible.

Cornelius Agrippa gives the following prescription: Make a powder of spermaceti, aloe wood, musk, saffron, and thyme, sprinkle it with the blood of a hoopop. If this powder is burnt upon the graves of the dead, the ethereal forms of the latter will approach, and may become visible.

Eckartshausen made successful experiments with the following prescription: Mix powdered frankincense and flour with an egg, add milk, honey, and rosewater, make a paste, and throw some of it upon burning coals.

Another prescription given by the same author consists of hemlock, saffron, aloes, opium, mandragora henbane, poppy-flowers, and some other poisonous plants. After undergoing a certain preparation, which he describes, he attempted the experiment, and saw the ghost of the person which he desired to see; but he came very near poisoning himself. Dr Horst repeated the experiment with the same result, and for years afterwards whenever he looked upon a dark object, he saw the apparition again.

Chemistry has advanced since that time, and those who desire to make such experiments at the risk of their health, may now accomplish this in a more comfortable and easy manner by inhaling some of the stupefying gases known to chemical science.

Fortune-tellers and clairvoyants employ various means to fix their attention, for the purpose of suspending thought and rendering their minds passive; others stare at mirrors or crystals, water or ink,* but the enlightened renders his imagination passive by maintaining, under all circumstances, tranquillity of the mind.

There are numerous prescriptions for the preparation of magic mirrors; but the best magic mirror will be useless to him who is not able to see clairvoyantly; while the natural clairvoyant calls that faculty into action by concentrating his mind on any particular spot, a glass of water, ink, a crystal, or anything; for it is not in the mirror where such things are seen, but in the mind; the mirror merely serves to assist in the entering of that mental state which is necessary to produce clairvoyant sight. The best of all magic mirrors is the soul, and it should always be kept pure, and be protected against dust and dampness and rust, so that it may not become tarnished, and remain perfectly clear, and able to reflect the light of the divine spirit in its original purity.

The surface of a lake whose water is in motion reflects only distorted reproductions of images projected upon it, and if the elements in the interior world are in a state of confusion, if emotion fights with emotion and the uproar of the passions troubles the mind, if the heaven of the soul is clouded by prejudices, darkened by ignorance, hallucinated by insane desires, the true images of things seen will be equally distorted.

The divine principle in man remains in itself unaltered and undisturbed, like the image of a star reflected in water; but unless its dwelling is rendered clear and transparent, it cannot send its rays through the surrounding walls. The more the emotions rage, the more will the mind become disturbed and the spiritual soul be forced to retreat into its interior prison; or if it loses entirely its hold over the mind, it may be driven away by the forces which it cannot control, burst the door of its dungeon, return to the source from whence it came. *(See H. P. Blavatsky: "Isis Unveiled.")* But as long as this Christ is one of the passengers in the boat tossed by the waves of the inner life, he will always be ready to come forth, stretch out his hand (manifest his power), bidding the turbulent waters to be still. Then will the storms cease to rage and the soul be restored to calmness.

The author says: "Such a catastrophe may happen long before the final separation of the life-principle from the body. When death arrives, its iron and clammy grasp finds work with life as usual; but there is no more soul to liberate. The whole essence of the latter has already been absorbed by the vital system of the physical man. Grim death frees but a spiritual corpse, at best an idiot. Unable either to soar higher or awaken from lethargy, it is soon dissolved in the elements of the terrestrial atmosphere."

If a person suffers his reason to give up the control over his imagination he surrenders one of the greatest prerogatives of man. True meditation does not consist in rendering the mind passive for the influences of the astral plane, nor does it consist in dreaming. It is a state in which the mind does not roam in the realms of the imagination, but is held still by the soul so as to receive the light of the spirit.

"Yoga is the exercise of the power to hold in abeyance the transformations of the thinking principle," says the Patanjali, and the Bhagavad Gita teaches: "Whenever the wavering and unsteadfast heart wanders away, let him subdue it and bring it back to the control of the soul."*(Bhagavad Gita, vi. 2 b.)*

This cannot be accomplished by means of the imagination (which ought to be at rest); neither can the mind control its own self; but it is done by means of the spiritual power of spiritually awakened man.

A person who dreams does not control the actions which he performs in his dream, although he may dream that he is exercising his will. The things seen in his dream are to him realities, and he does not doubt their substantiality, while external physical objects have no existence for him, and not even the possibility of their existence comes to his consciousness. He may see before him a ditch and dream that he wills to jump over it, but he does not actually exert his will, he only dreams that he wills.

Hypnotism

A person in a magnetic trance has no active will of his own, and is led by the will of the operator. What he sees is real to him, and if the operator creates a precipice in his imagination, the subject will, on approaching it, experience and manifest the same terror as he would in his normal state if a precipice were yawning under his feet. A glass of water transformed into imaginary wine by the will of the "mesmeriser" makes the subject intoxicated, and if that water has been transformed into imaginary poison it may injure or kill the sensitive. *(Mrs Chandos Leigh Hunt of London, in her "Private Instructions in Organic Magnetism," informs us, that imaginary intoxicants, emetics, &c., have a powerful effect upon subjects.)* A powerful "hypnotiser" can form either a beautiful or a horrible picture in his mind, and by transferring it by his will upon the mental sphere of a sensitive, he may cause him either pleasure or suffering.

Eliphas Levi (Abbe Constant) cites a case in which some sceptics submitted a poor girl to magnetic experiments, to gratify their curiosity, and to see whether "magnetism was true." They succeeded in putting her to sleep, and commanded her to look into hell. She became terribly agitated, and begged for mercy, but they insisted that she should go there.

"The features of the subject became frightful to see; her hair stood upright on her head; her eyes were wide open, and showed nothing but the white; her bosom heaved, and a kind of death-rattle came from her breast."

"'Go there! I will it!' repeated the magnetist."

"'I am there,' said the wretched subject, between her closed teeth, and fell exhausted. Then she spoke no more; her head rests on her shoulder; her arms hang motionless down. They approach her and touch her. They wish to awaken her; but the crime has been done; the woman was dead, and the authors of this sacrilegious experiment were safe from prosecution on account of the public's incredulity in regard to such things."

Such states may be induced not merely during the "hypnotic" sleep, but also during the normal condition, and without any conscious desire on the part of a magnetiser. If the audience sheds tears during the performance of a tragedy, although they all know that it is merely a play, they are in a state of partial "hypnotisation." Hundreds of similar occurrences take place every day in every country, and there is sufficient material everywhere in every-day life for the student of psychology to investigate and explain, without seeking for cases of an abnormal character.

All these things are classified as illusions, because the power of reason, the power of discriminating between the true and the false has been suspended, which causes a person to mistake things for realities which only exist in his own imagination, but if this definition is applied to every-day existence, it appears that the whole world is in a state of hypnotic sleep, for there are few that are capable of seeing the truth or to discriminate between the true and the false, and few who act always according to reason.

Whenever the external form of a thing is examined carefully, it will always be found to constitute an illusion. The illusion does not exist in those things, it exists in ourselves. God did not create the world for the purpose of deluding mankind. The illusions are caused by our own misconceptions of truth, which hinder us to see that which is real. If we were to see that which is real, we would be knowing the truth. If we had always known the truth we would not have needed to come into the world. Our existence upon this planet is a certificate of our ignorance, and the fact of having been born a proof of our folly.

That which distinguishes a man from an animal is the use of his reason. If a "Medium" submits the control over his imagination to another being he surrenders his reason. This other being may be another person, or an invisible power. It may be an elemental, an astral corpse, or a malicious influence, and the Medium become an epileptic, a maniac, or a criminal. A person who surrenders his will to an unknown power is not less insane than he who would entrust his money and valuables to the first stranger or vagabond that would ask him for it. If a crime is committed in consequence of "hypnotic suggestions," it is the hypnotiser and not the sensitive person who is responsible for it. Such cases occur every day; for it is not necessary that a very sensitive person should be put to sleep for to become capable of being influenced by the will of another. All individual minds act upon each other; each influences the other or becomes influenced by others without knowing the source of the influence. Thoughts and impulses come and go, and their source is not known. No man creates his own thoughts out of nothing, and he who has no self-knowledge cannot even know who or what it is that is thinking or willing in him.

How many murders and crimes are committed every year through sensitive persons, who have been influenced, "hypnotised," or "mesmerised" by invisible powers to commit them, and who had not sufficient will-power to resist, it is impossible to determine. In such cases we hang or punish the instrument, but the real culprit escapes. Such a "justice" is equivalent to punishing a stick with which a murder has been committed, and to let the man who used the stick go free. Verily the coming generations will have as much cause to laugh at the ignorance of their ancestors as we now laugh at the ignorance of those who preceded us.

Mental Imagery

We take not things for what they are, but for what we imagine them to be. The savage sees in the sculptured Minerva only a curious piece of rock, and a beautiful painting is to him only a piece of cloth daubed over with colours. The greedy miser, looking at the beauties of nature, thinks only of the money-value they represent, while for the poet the forest swarms with fairies and the water with sprites.

The artist finds beautiful forms in the wandering clouds and in the projecting rocks of the mountains, and to him whose mind is poetic every symbol in nature becomes a poem and suggests to him new ideas; but the coward wanders through life with a scowl upon his face; he sees in every corner an enemy, and for him the world has nothing attractive except his own little self. The world is a mirror wherein every man may see his own face. To him whose soul is beautiful, the world will look beautiful; to him whose soul is deformed, everything will seem to be evil.

The power of the imagination, if rendered strong by the will and made alive by the spirit, is little known. The impressions made on the mind by the effects of such an imagination may be powerful and lasting upon the person. They change or distort the features, they render the hair white in a single hour; they mark, kill, disfigure, or break the bones of the unborn child, and make the effects of injuries received by one person visible upon the body of another with whom that person is in sympathy. They act more powerfully than drugs; they cause and cure diseases, produce hallucinations, and stigmata.

Imagination performs its miracles, either consciously or unconsciously. By altering the surroundings of animals the colour of their offspring can be changed at will. The tiger's stripes correspond to the long jungle grass, and the leopard's spots resemble the speckled light falling through the leaves.*(Sir John Lubbock: "Proceedings of the British Association.")*

The forces of nature, influenced by the imagination of man, act on the imagination of nature, and create tendencies on the astral plane, which, in the course of evolution, find expression through material forms. In this way man's vices or virtues become objective realities, and as man's imagination becomes purified, the earth becomes more beautiful and refined, while his vices find their expression in poisonous reptiles and noxious plants.

The Elementals in the soul of man are the products of the action of the thought in the individual mind of man; the elemental forms in the soul of the world are the products of the collective thoughts of all beings. These elemental powers are attracted to the germs of animals, and may grow into objective visible animal forms, and modify the characters and also the outward appearance of the animals of our globe. We therefore see that as the imagination of the Universal Mind changes during the course of ages, old forms disappear and new ones come into existence. Perhaps if there were no snakes in human forms, the snakes of the animal kingdom would cease to exist.

But the impressions made on the mind do not end with the life of the individual on the physical plane. A cause which produces a sudden terror, or otherwise acts strongly on the imagination, can produce an impression that not only lasts through life but beyond it.

A person, for instance, who during his life has strongly believed in the existence of eternal damnation and hell-fire, may at his entrance into the subjective state after death, actually behold all the terrors of hell which his imagination during life has conjured up; the terrified soul, seeing before it all the horrors of its own vivid imagination, rushes back again into the deserted body, and clings to it in despair, seeking protection. Personal consciousness returns, and it finds itself alive in the grave, where it passes a second time through the pangs of death, or, by sending out its astral form in search of sustenance from the living, it becomes a vampire, and prolongs for a while its horrible existence. *(Maximilian Perty: "Die mystischen Erscheinungen in der Natur.")* Such misfortunes in orthodox countries are by no means rare, and the best remedy for it is knowledge and the cremation of the body soon after death.

On the other hand, the convicted murderer who, before stepping on the gallows, has been fully "converted" and "prepared" by the attending clergyman, and made to believe firmly that his sins have been forgiven, and that the angels will stand ready to receive him with open arms, may, on his entrance to the subjective state, see the creations of his own imaginations before him until the delusion fades away.

In the state after death and in the devachanic condition the imagination neither creates new and original forms nor is it capable of receiving new impressions; it lives on the sum of the impressions accumulated during life, which evolute innumerable variations of mental states, symbolised in their corresponding subjective forms, and lasting until their forces are exhausted.

These mental states may be called illusive in the same sense as events of the physical life may be called illusive, and life in "heaven" or "hell" may be called a dream, as life on this earth is called a dream. The dream of life only differs from the dream after death, that, during the one, we are able to make use of our will to guide and control our imagination and acts, while during the latter that guidance is wanting, and we earn that which we have sown. No effort, whether for good or for evil, is ever lost. Those who have reached out in their aspirations towards a high ideal on earth will find it in heaven; those whose desires have dragged them down will sink to the level of their desires.

It is generally supposed that this world in which we live is the most dense and "material," and the astral world the land of vapoury ghosts; but the terms "materiality," "density," &c., are merely relative terms. What appear to us dense and material now, will appear ethereal or vaporous if we are in another state, and things which are invisible to us now may appear grossly material then. There are worlds more dense and material to its inhabitants than our physical world is to us; for it is the light of the spirit that enlivens matter, and the more matter is gathered up by sensuality and concentrated by selfishness, the less penetrable to the spirit will it become, and the more dense and hard will it grow, although it may for all that not be perceptible to our physical senses, they being adapted merely to our present state of existence.

There is no heaven or hell but that which man creates in his imagination; nevertheless, the state in which he lives is real to him. If we wish to secure happiness after death in our next life upon this planet, we must secure it before we die by controlling our impulses for evil, and by cultivating a pure and exalted imagination.

Light of the Spirit

We should enter the higher life now, instead of waiting for it to come to us in the hereafter. The term "heaven" means a state of spiritual consciousness and enjoyment of spiritual truths; but how can he who has evolved no spiritual consciousness and no spiritual power of perception enjoy the perception of spiritual things which he has not the spiritual power to perceive? A man without spiritual power entering a heaven would be like a man blind and deaf and without the power to feel. Man can only enjoy that which he is able to realise, that which he cannot realise does not exist for him.

The surest way to be happy is to rise above "self." People crave for amusements and pastimes; but to forget one's time is to forget one's self; by forgetting themselves they are rendered happy. The charm of music consists in the temporary absorption it causes to the personality in the harmony of sound. If we witness a theatrical performance and enter into the spirit of the play, we forget our personal sorrows and live in the actor. An orator who is in full accord with his audience becomes inspired with the sentiments of his audience; it is his audience that gives expressions of his feelings through him. There are no "spirits" required to inspire an inspirational speaker. If he is impressible the thoughts of those that are present will be sufficient to inspire him.

If we enter a cathedral or a temple, whose architecture inspires sublimity and solemnity, expanding the soul; where the language of music speaks to the heart, drawing it away from the attachment to the earth; and the beauty and odour of flowers lull the senses into a forget-fulness of self, such amusements render us temporarily happy to an extent proportionate to the degree in which they succeed in destroying our consciousness of personality and self.

Illusions as such do not exist; their existence is an illusion. Nature is not an illusion, but a manifestation of truth. Every form in nature is an expression of truth; but it requires the eye of truth to find the truth in those forms. If we cling to forms, we cling to illusions, having no real existence; if we cling to the truth we have the reality. If our happiness depends on the possession of a cherished form, our happiness will perish when that form disappears.

To attain real knowledge is to make the mind free of its illusions; this freedom is attained only by a love for the truth; for the truth is the life and the foundation of our existence, which will remain after all the illusions constituting our lower nature have passed away; when we will possess nothing but that which we are, and being ourselves the light and the truth we will be in possession of truth.

Chapter VII - Consciousness

"I am that I am." – **Bible**

Universal Mind

Everything in the universe is a manifestation of the Universal Mind. Everything is therefore mind itself, and exists in absolute consciousness; but relative consciousness begins when it becomes manifest in the form. The term consciousness signifies realisation of existence.
Consciousness in the absolute is unconsciousness in relation to things.
Consciousness means knowledge and life; unconsciousness is ignorance and death. An imperfect knowledge is a state of imperfect consciousness; the highest possible state of consciousness is the full realisation of the truth.
A thing has no existence relatively to ourselves before we become conscious of its existence. A person who does not realise his own existence is unconscious, and, for the time being, to all practical purposes dead.
We cannot actually realise the existence of a power which we do not possess. We see the effects produced by electricity and realise that such effects take place; but we do not realise the existence or the nature of what is called "electricity" if we are not conscious of that same power existing in our own constitution.
In the same sense we can realise the effect of the manifestation of divine wisdom within the universe; we behold the expression of beauty, justice, and truth; but we cannot realise the existence of these principles, unless we become conscious of their presence in us. God's works exist and we see the products of the action of his spirit in nature; but God himself is to us a nonentity if we are not rendered divine by his presence in us; we cannot realise the nature of God, unless his divine nature is present in us and comes to our own consciousness.
A state of existence is incomprehensible unless it is experienced and realised, and it begins to exist from the moment that it is realised. If a person were the legal possessor of millions of money and did not know it, he would have no means to dispose of it or enjoy it. A man is present at the delivery of the most eloquent speech, and, unless he hears what is said, that speech will have no existence for him. Every man is endowed with reason and conscience, but if he never listens to its voice, the relation between him and the voice of wisdom will cease to exist, and it will die for him in proportion as he dies to the power to hear it.
A man may be alive and conscious in relation to one thing, and dead and unconscious relatively to another. One set of his faculties may be active and conscious, while another set is unconscious and its activity suspended. A person who listens attentively to music is conscious of nothing but sound; one who is

wrapt in the admiration of form is only conscious of seeing; another, who suffers from pain, may be conscious of nothing but the relation that exists between him and the sensation of pain. A man absorbed in thought believes himself alone in the midst of a crowd. He may be threatened by destruction and be unconscious of the danger. If he has the strength of a lion, it will avail him nothing unless he becomes conscious of it; he cannot be immortal unless he becomes conscious of his own immortal life.

The more a person learns to realise the true state of his existence the more will he become conscious of real existence. If he does not realise his true state he does not know himself. If he fully knows himself, he will be conscious of his own powers, he will know how to exercise them and become strong.

To become conscious of the existence of a thing is to possess it. To perceive its existence means to enter into relation with it, and to realise the existence of that relation. Consciousness begins, therefore, wherever sensation begins, but sensation and perception of a form are only followed by a recognition of the truth if the principle that exists in that form is a conscious power in our own constitution.

If a stranger is introduced to us we perceive his exterior form and see the clothes which he wears, we realise his existence as a living form, but we know nothing of his true character. His appearance may be prepossessing and still he may be untruthful, his clothing may be new and elegant and still his character bad. His body may be healthy, but his soul may be diseased. His certificates and testimonials may be excellent, and yet they may deceive us.

If we want to know the true character of the man, we must be able to realise the nature of his character in ourselves. We may look into his eyes, and when soul speaks to soul, the two will enter into conscious relation with each other, and there will be no deception possible. This recognition of the truth by direct perception is one of the faculties which at the present state of evolution are not yet fully developed in man. It is a sixth sense that as yet exists only as a bud in the tree of life, while the other five senses have been fully developed. Still it exists, and therefore the first impression we receive of a stranger is usually correct, but not always believed, because speculation comes in to mislead. Perception is the entering into a relation to the object of one's perception. Such a relation is only possible if the perceiver and the object of his perception exist upon the same plane of existence. For this reason physical objects are perceived by the physical senses; the things of the soul by the soul, and that which belongs to the spirit can only be perceived by the power of the self-conscious spirit in man.

Everything that exists, exists within the Universal Mind, and nothing can exist outside of it, because the Universal Mind includes all. Perception is a faculty by which mind learns to know what is going on within itself. To see a thing is to perceive the existence of its appearance within one's own mind; to feel the presence of an invisible power within the soul is to become conscious of its presence by means of the sense of touch that belongs to the mind.

Relative Consciousness

Man can know nothing but what exists within his own mind. Even the most ardent lover has never seen his beloved one, he merely sees the image which the form of the latter produces in his mind. If we pass through the streets of a city the images of men and women pass review in our mind while their bodies meet our own; but for the images which they produce within our consciousness we would know nothing about their existence.

The images produced in the mind come to the consciousness whose workshop is the brain; if man's consciousness were centered in some other part of his body, he would become conscious in that part of the sensations which he receives. He might for instance see with his stomach or hear with his fingers, as has often been proved by scientifically conducted experiments, and the reason of it is that sensation is not a quality belonging to the physical body; but belongs to the astral form, whose senses are not so localised; but which penetrates the physical body and whose senses become localised therein.

A self-conscious power, being universally diffused through space, would have the faculty to realise all that takes place in any portion of it, because it would be in conscious relation with everything. A conscious power being bound to a material form, can only realise that which enters into relationship with that form. All self-consciousness and all perception cannot belong to a limited form; it belongs to the divine nature of man, which is not limited by the limitations of form.

From the influence of the universal power of Mind, and the resistance of the form, physical senses came into existence. If man had originally remained in perfect harmony with the Universal Mind, he would never have become clothed in a material form. There could be no perception without resistance. If our bodies were perfectly transparent to light we could not perceive the light, because light cannot illuminate itself. The Astral Light penetrates our bodies, but we are not able to see it, because the physical body offers no resistance to it.

At the time when we fall asleep, consciousness gradually leaves its seat in the brain and merges into the consciousness of the "inner man." We then begin to realise another state of existence; and if a part of the consciousness still remains with the brain, the perception of the interior consciousness comes to the cognisance of the personal self. It is therefore possible in that half-conscious state, between sleeping and waking, when consciousness is oscillating between two states of existence, to receive important revelations from the higher state and retain them in the personal memory.

The more our consciousness merges in that higher state, the better will we realise the higher existence, but the impressions upon our external self will become dim and not be remembered; but as long as the greatest part of our consciousness is active within the material brain, the perceptions of a higher state will only be dim and mixed up with memories and sensations of the lower state of existence.

Astral Light

There probably was a time in the development of the body of man, when his form was -- so to say -- all eye, and his whole surface sensitive to the power of light. The resistance of his form to the influence of light created the eye. Fishes have been found in subterranean lakes which have no eyes; there being no light, they needed no organs to receive it and none to resist it. In tropical countries the intensity of light is stronger. Tropical man needs the dark pigment in his skin to protect his nude body from the influence of the tropical sun.

There are semi-material existences (Elementals) which have no teguments sufficiently solid to protect them from terrestrial light. Such natures are very sensitive to the action of light, they can only continue to live in darkness, and only manifest their powers at night.

Adolphe d'Assier, who spent much time in the investigation of occult phenomena, tells of a case, where a person slept in a "haunted house," for the purpose of investigating the spook. He went to bed and left the light burning. At once a dark shadow seemed to rush through the door into his room and went under his bed. Soon a long arm extended from under the bed, reached up to the table and extinguished the light, and immediately the rampage began. Furniture was overthrown and broken, and the noise was so great that it attracted the neighbours, who came with a light, when the dark shadow fled through the door.

If the astral body of man were exposed to the full influence of the astral light, without having acquired the power to resist it, it would be destroyed slowly or quickly according to the intensity of that light. The myths of "hell" and "purgatory" are suggestive of that action of the destructive action of the Astral Light. But this destruction is not necessarily accompanied by sensation, unless that body is conscious. A corpse from which the spirit has withdrawn may be cremated and cannot feel it, an astral corpse may dissolve into its elements and feel no pain. Only when a form becomes associated with spirit, in whatever plane of existence, there will sensation become manifest.

Some of the practices of black magic and necromancy are based upon this fact, and it does not appear impossible that the astral bodies of the dead may be tormented by the living, if they knew how to endow them with spirit, and to reawaken consciousness by infusing some of their own life within these forms.

If our bodies were sufficiently ethereal to pass through others without experiencing any resistance, we would not feel their presence. If the keyboard of the ear were not present to receive the vibrations of sound, hearing would be defective. The power to resist produces sensation.

Man suffers because he resists. If he were to obey the laws of his nature under all circumstances, he would know no bodily disease; if he were to execute in all things the divine will of God, he would incur no suffering.

Life, sensation, perception, and consciousness may be withdrawn from the physical body and become active in the astral body of man. The astral man then becomes conscious of his existence independent of the physical body and can develop faculties of sense. He may then see sights which have no existence for the physical eye, hear sounds that the physical ear cannot hear, feel, taste, and smell things whose existence the physical senses cannot realise, and which consequently have no existence to them.

What an astonishing sight would meet the eyes of a mortal, if the veil that mercifully hides the astral world from his sight were to be suddenly removed ! He would see the space which he inhabits occupied by a different world full of inhabitants, of whose existence he knew nothing. What before appeared to him dense and solid would now seem to be shadowy, and what seemed to him like empty space he would find peopled with life.

Scientifically conducted researches have brought to light many instances of cases in which the astral senses have been rendered more or less active. The Seeress of Prevorst, for instance, perceived many things which for other persons had no existence; the history of the saints gives numerous similar examples, and modern "mediumship" proves the existence of such inner senses by facts which occur every day. If the astral senses of a person are fully alive and active, he is able to perceive things without the use of his physical senses. He will be clairvoyant and clairaudient, he will be able to see, hear, feel, taste, and smell the astral attributes of things existing in or out of corporeal forms.

All houses are "haunted," but not all persons are equally able to see the ghosts that haunt them, because to perceive things on the astral plane requires the development of a sense adapted to such perceptions. Thoughts are "ghosts," and only those that can see images formed of thought can see "ghosts," unless the latter are sufficiently materialised to refract the light and to become visible to the eye.

We may feel the presence of an astral form without being able to see it, and be just as certain of its presence as if we did behold it with our eyes; for the sense of touch is not less reliable than the sense of sight. The presence of a holy, high, and exalted idea that enters the mind fills it with a feeling of happiness, with an exhilarating influence whose vibrations may be perceived long after that thought has gone.

Seeing

The explanation which material science gives in regard to the process of seeing only explains the formation of a picture on the retina of the physical eye, but gives no explanation whatever how these pictures come to the consciousness of the mind. If the mind of man were enclosed in the physical body of man he could not perceive the size of any exterior thing. In such a case he could at best see the minute picture formed on his retina, and the outside world would appear to him like the microscopic object seen through a reversed telescope.

But the reflections formed in the physical eye only serve to call the attention of the mind to the objects of its perception, or awaken the interior sense of feeling which the mind possesses to a consciousness of its relation to the objects of its perception, which exist within its own sphere. Visible man is the kernel of the invisible man, the sphere of his mind surrounds him in all sides like an invisible pulp, extending far into space, and he can become conscious of the objects existing within that sphere if he recognises his relation with them.

This invisible and ethereal sphere is as essential to constitute a man as the pulp of a peach is essential to constitute a peach, but material science knows only the kernel, and knows nothing about the pulp. Still this soul sphere exists, and intermingles with the spheres of others, producing sympathies, or antipathies, according to the harmony, or disharmony, of their respective elements. A great many events may take place within one's mind and we may not perceive them, unless our attention is attracted to them, and they come to our consciousness.

The mind perceives what is going on in the physical plane by being awakened by physical means to a consciousness of his relationship with physical things; it perceives what is going on in the realm of the soul by being awakened to a consciousness of his relationship with the realm of the soul by influences coming from that realm, and it perceives spiritual truth by being awakened to a recognition of its relationship to truth by the power proceeding from it.

The physical body may be dormant and perceive no external objects; the astral senses are undeveloped; the spiritual power of perception in the majority of mankind is still inactive, and feels the presence of the spirit only by the uncertain reflex of its light, like a man in a semi-conscious condition may see the reflex of light shining through the closed lids and not know what it is. This is the power of intuition that precedes an awakening to spiritual knowledge.

Mental Perception

Mind has no conceivable limits, and distance is therefore no impediment to mental perception, because a mind being in solidarity with the whole stands in relation to every part of the whole, and as soon as man recognises his relation to an object in space he becomes conscious of its presence.

The reason why the mind of man does not perceive everything and requires the aid of the physical senses, is that Adam is still sleeping the sleep which came over him while he was an inhabitant of the paradise. He is still unconscious of the fact that his real nature comprises the all; his consciousness has become bound to a material form, and he is now the prisoner of that form.

To see a thing is identical with touching it with the mind. The individual mind of man being one with the universal mind, extends through space; it is therefore not merely the images of things, but the things themselves that exist within the periphery of our mind, however distant from the centre of our consciousness they may be, and if we were able to shift that centre from one place to another within the sphere of the mind, we might in a moment of time approach to the object of our perception.

The mind substance is everywhere, but its consciousness is limited. If the whole sphere of the mind of a man were self-conscious, he would be omnipresent and all-knowing. As the sphere of perception of an individual mind expands, so expands the sphere of his conscious being.

The centre of consciousness in man is located in the brain, and if the mind touches an object the impressions have to travel all the way to the brain. If we look at a distant star our mind is actually there and in contact with it, and if we could transfer our consciousness to that place of contact, we would be ourselves upon that star and perceive the objects thereon as if we were standing personally upon its surface.

This however is an impossibility as long as the centre of our consciousness is in the brain; because that consciousness is an illusion itself, it enables us to roam through space by means of our imagination, but does not reveal the truth. The consciousness of the brain is in regard to our true self-consciousness what the false light of the moon is to the light of the sun. Our true self-consciousness rests in the heart, and therefore the heart can expand in that universal love, which is not imaginary, through the whole of creation. If that love becomes self-conscious in our heart, all the mysteries of the universe will be open before us.

Perception is passive imagination, because if we perceive an object, the relation which it bears to us comes to our consciousness without any active exertion on our part. But there is an active imagination by which we may enter into relation with a distant object in space by a transfer of consciousness. By this power we may act upon a distant object if we succeed in forming a true image of it in our own consciousness. By concentrating our consciousness upon such an object we become conscious in that place of the sphere of our mind where that object exists. Thus we establish a conscious relation between such an object and ourselves, but this requires that spiritual power which resides in the heart.

States of Consciousness

Consciousness is existence, and there are as many states of consciousness as there are states of existence. Every living being has a consciousness of its own, and the state of its consciousness changes every moment of time, as fast as the impressions which it receives change; because its consciousness is the perception of the relation it bears to things, and as this relation changes, consciousness changes its character.

If our whole attention is taken up by animal pleasure, we exist in an animal state of consciousness; if we are aware of the presence of spiritual principles, such as hope, faith, charity, justice, truth, &c., we live in our spiritual consciousness, and between these two extremes there are a great variety of gradations.

Consciousness itself does not change, it only moves up and down on the scale of existence.

There is only one kind of consciousness which never changes its place because it is independent of all relation to things. It is the self-consciousness of self-existence, the realisation of the I am. It can be ignored, but once attained it cannot change, because God never changes; its change would involve non-existence or the annihilation of all.

He who has not attained that true self-consciousness, the realisation of the existence of his own real self does not exist. He may be highly developed physically and intellectually; nevertheless he is nothing else but a compound of physical and intellectual elements and his sense of self an ever-changing illusion. He cannot die, because he has never come to life; he does not truly exist, because he does not realise his true existence. There is no one truly alive, except he who can realise his own true divine life.

When Life manifests itself in a form it begins to live relatively to form; but the degree of consciousness of the form depends on the state of its organisation. In a low organised form there is sensation, but no intelligence. An oyster has consciousness, but no intelligence. A man may have a great deal of intellect and no consciousness of spirituality, sublimity, justice, beauty, or truth.

Wisdom

The lowest existences follow implicitly the laws of nature or of Universal Reason; because in them exists no differentiation of mind; they have no will and reason of their own. The highest spiritual beings follow their own reason; but their will and reason is in harmony with the universal law. The difference between the lowest beings and the highest ones is, therefore, that the lowest ones perform the will of "God" unconsciously and unknowingly; while the highest ones do the same thing knowingly and consciously. It is only the reasoning beings who imagine that they are their own law-givers, and may do what they please. All evil is caused by reasoning; the enlightened does not reason; he has Reason itself for his guide.

The muscular system exercises its habitual movements in the act of walking, eating, &c., without being especially guided by a superintending intellect, like a clockwork that, after being once set in motion, continues to run; and a man who is in the habit of doing that which is right and just, will act in accordance with the law of wisdom and justice instinctively, and without any consideration or doubt. Each state of mind has its own mode of perception, sensation, instinct, and consciousness, and the activity of one may overpower and suppress that of the other. A person being only conscious of the sensations created by some physical act, is at that time unconscious of spiritual influences. One who is under the influence of chloroform loses his external sensation. One in a state of trance is awake on a higher plane of existence, and unconscious of what happens on the physical plane.

Lower Consciousness

The unintelligent muscular system is conscious of nothing else but the attraction of Earth. In it the element of Earth predominates, and unless it is upheld by reason, it acts according to the impulse created in it by that attraction. The astral body is unintelligent, and unless infused with the intelligence coming from the higher principles, it follows the attractions of the astral plane. These attractions are its desires.

As the physical body, if unguided by reason, follows the law of gravitation, so the astral body follows the attractions of desire. The animal consciousness of man is that unreasoning attraction which impels him to seek for the gratification of his instincts.

Correctly speaking, there is no such thing as animal reason, animal intellect, animal consciousness, &c. Consciousness, reason, intelligence, &c., in the absolute, have no qualifications; they are universal principles, that is to say, functions of the Universal One Life, manifesting themselves on various planes in various forms.

The condition of a person whose consciousness is no more illumined by reason, is seen in emotional mania and obsession. In such cases the person acts entirely according to the impulses acting in him, and when he recovers his reason, he is unconscious of his actions during that state. Such states manifest themselves sometimes in only one person, or they affect several persons simultaneously, and even whole countries, as has been experienced in some wholesale "obsessions" occurring during the Middle Ages.*("Histoire des diables de Loudin.")*

Cases of obsession are by no means unfrequent, and many cases of insanity are merely cases of obsession. It is extremely desirable in the interests of humanity that our superintendents and doctors of insane asylums should study the occult laws of nature, and learn to know the causes of insanity, instead of merely studying their external effects.

They are often observed in cases of hysteria, may be witnessed at religious meetings, during theatrical performances, during the attack upon an enemy, or at any other occasion, where the passions of the multitude are excited, inducing them to acts of folly or bravery, and enabling people to perform acts which they would be neither willing nor able to perform if they were guided only by the calculations of their intellect. All such states are the manifestation of unseen powers, acting in and through different forms.

Transfer of Consciousness

There are persons in whom the astral body has become the centre of consciousness, and they may acquire the power to transfer that consciousness to a distant locality. Mind is everywhere, and capable of receiving impressions. If we steadily concentrate our thoughts upon a distant person or a place, a current of mind is created. Our thoughts go to the desired locality, for that locality, however far it may be, is still within the sphere of mind. If we have been there before, or if there is something to attract us, it will not be difficult to find it. Under ordinary circumstances consciousness remains with the body. But if our astral elements are sufficiently alive, so as not to cling to the body, but to accompany our thoughts, then our consciousness may go with them, being projected there by the power of the will, and the more the will is intense the easier will this be accomplished. We shall then visit the chosen place consciously and know what we are doing, and our astral elements carry the memory back and impress them upon our physical brain.

This is the secret how the thought body may be projected to a distance by those who have acquired that power. It is a power that may be acquired by birth or learned by practice. There are persons in whom, in consequence of either an inherited peculiarity of the constitution or from sickness, such a separation between the physical and astral elements may either voluntarily or involuntarily take place, and the astral form either consciously or unconsciously travel to distant places or persons, and by the assistance of the odic and magnetic emanations even "materialise" into a visible and even tangible form.*

* Adolphe d'Assier cites several instances in which the "double" of a person was seen simultaneously with the physical form. A young lady at college was seen by her mates in the parlour of the school, while at the same time her double was in the garden. The stronger the "double" grew, the more faint became her corporeal form. When she recovered her strength, the double disappeared from sight. In this case, the consciousness of the lady was evidently divided between the room and the garden, and as her thoughts went to the flowers they formed a body there. In studying the law according to which such apparently mysterious things occur, it will be advisable to remember that all forms, whether material or ethereal, consist merely of certain vibrations of primordial matter, manifesting themselves according to the character impressed upon them.

The Kama-rupa is sometimes attracted unconsciously to places while the physical body is asleep. It has been seen by impressible persons on such occasions, but it shows no signs of intelligence or life; it only acts like an automaton and returns when the physical body requires its presence. At the time of death, when the cohesion between the lower and higher principles is loosened, such a projection is of not unfrequent occurrence; it may then be for a short time, conscious, alive, and intelligent, and represent the true man. *(Numerous instances of such occurrences may be found in E, Gurney, "Phantasms of the Living.")*

There are a great number of cases on record where, in consequence of a sudden and intense emotion, for instance, the desire to see a certain person, the thought body projecting itself from the physical body has become conscious and visible at a distance. In cases of home-sickness we find some approach to an instance of this. The person separated from home and friends, having an intense yearning to see his native place again, projects his thoughts to that place. He lives -- so to say -- in that place, while his physical body vegetates in another. He becomes weaker, and finally dies; that is to say, he goes where his thoughts already are, although his gradual going is imperceptible and unrecognisable to physical senses.

Separation

In cases of sickness or death a similar process of separation takes place. When, from whatever cause, the union between the physical form and the astral body becomes weakened, the astral form separates itself for a while or permanently from the physical form.

The symptoms of such a beginning of separation is often observed in severe sickness, when the patient has the sensation as if another person were lying in the same bed with him. As recovery takes place, the principles whose cohesion has been loosened become reunited and that sensation disappears.

According to the plane of existence, where a person lives is the state of his consciousness, and each of these planes has its own sensations, perceptions, and memories. What is seen and perceived and remembered in one state, is not remembered in another state, and it is therefore not improbable that a person, entering into a higher state of consciousness after the death of his body, will remember nothing about the conditions of his terrestrial life.

A case is cited in Dr Hammond's book on insanity, in which a servant, while in a state of intoxication, carried a package with which he had been entrusted to the wrong house. Having become sober, he could not remember the place, and the package was supposed to be lost; but after he got drunk again he remembered the place, he went there and recovered the package. This goes to show that when he was drunk he was another person than when he was sober; man's individuality continually changes according to the conditions in which he exists, and as his con-ciousness changes he becomes another individual, although he still retains the same outward form.

In the state of intoxication the person is only conscious of his animal existence and entirely unconscious of his higher existence. A somnambule in the lucid condition looks upon her body as a being distinct from her own self, who is, to a certain extent, under her care. She speaks of that being in the third person, prescribes sometimes for it as a physician prescribes for his patient and often shows tastes, inclinations, and opinions entirely opposed to those which she possesses in her normal condition. Persons while in a trance may love another person intensely, because they are then capable to perceive his good interior qualities, and detest him when they are in their normal condition, when they merely behold his external attributes. *(H. Zschokke: "Verklaerungen" (Transfigurations).)*

In the state of trance the body is entirely unconscious and unable to realise any physical sensation. It may be burnt or buried. Such a proceeding would not affect the inner man otherwise than to prevent his return to that body. But while his earthly form is unconscious, his spiritual self is conscious, and may be engaged in duties beyond our comprehension, among scenes from which it must be painful to return to the bonds of Earth.

Even while physical consciousness is active the consciousness of the higher principles may be so exalted as to render the body little conscious of pain. History speaks of men and women whose souls rejoiced while their earthly tabernacles were undergoing the tortures of the rack, or devoured by flames at the stake.

Double Consciousness

Man leads essentially two lives, one while he is fully awake, another while he is fully asleep. Each has its own perceptions, consciousness, and experiences, but the experiences during sleep are not remembered when we are fully "awake." At the borderland between sleep and waking, where the impressions of each state meet and mingle, is the realm of confused dreams, which seldom contain any truth.

This state is, however, favourable to receive impressions from the inner self. The inner man may use symbolical forms and allegorical images to convey ideas to the lower self, and to give it admonitions, forebodings, and warnings in regard to future events.

There are various kinds of dreams. Many a difficult problem has been solved during sleep, and the terrestrial world is not always without any reflex of the light from above. The mind of the sleeper during the sleep of the body comes into contact with other minds, and passes through experiences which one does not remember when awake. Man, in his waking condition, often has experiences which he afterwards does not remember, but which he, nevertheless, enjoyed at the time when they occurred, and which at that time were real to him.

One extraordinary case is mentioned in A. P. Sinnett's "Incidents in the Life of Madame Blavatsky." Speaking of her sickness in Tiflis, Madame Blavatsky says, that she had the sensation as if she were two different persons, one being the Madame Blavatsky, whose body was lying sick in bed, the other person an entirely different and superior being. "When I was in my lower state," she says, "I knew who that other person was and what she (or he) had been doing; but when I was that other being myself, I did not know nor care who was that Madame Blavatsky." It is therefore very well possible that Madame Blavatsky's "transcendental Ego," with all its consciousness, faculties, and powers of perception, in fact, her real self, was consciously and really undergoing certain mysterious experiences in Tibet, while the physical instrument, which we call "Madame Blavatsky," was sick at Tiflis.

Man feels in himself at least two sets of attractions that come to his consciousness. One set drags him down to earth and makes him cling to material necessities and enjoyments, the other set, lifting him up into the region of the unknown, makes him forget the allurements of matter, and brings him nearer to the realm of immortal beauty. The greatest poets and philosophers have recognised this fact of double consciousness, or the two poles of one, and between those two poles ebbs and floods the normal consciousness of the average human being.

Goethe expresses this in his "Faust" in about the following terms:

"Two souls, alas! are conscious in my breast,
One from the other seeks to separate.
One clings to earth, where all its life is rooted,
The other rises upwards to the gods."

One attraction arises from Wisdom, another from folly. By the power of Knowledge, Man is enabled to choose which way he will follow, and by the power of obedience he is enabled to proceed. He may live on the lower planes of consciousness and become dead to spirituality and immortal life; or in the highest spheres of thought, where his mind expands and where he ultimately will find that spiritual self-consciousness, which is Divine Wisdom, the realisation of eternal truth.

Few may be able to reach such a state, and few will be able to comprehend its possibility; but there have been men who, on the threshold of Nirwana, and while their physical bodies continued to live on this planet, could consciously roam through the interplanetary spaces and see the wonders of the material and spiritual worlds. This is the highest form of Adeptship attainable on Earth, and to him who accomplishes it the mysteries of the Universe will be like an open book. Divine Wisdom for the purpose of manifesting itself requires an organism. In the mineral kingdom it manifests itself as attraction, in plants as life, in animals as instinct, in human beings as reason, in Divine natures as self-knowledge; on every plane the character of its manifestation depends on the character of the organism through which it acts. Without a human organism, even the most intelligent animal cannot become a man; without a spiritual organism even the most pious Christian will be only a dreamer.

Every state of consciousness requires for its expression a suitable organism, and the greater the realm of its manifestation, the more expanded must be the sphere of its activity. There is no realisation of physical existence without a physical body; there is no emotional nature without an organised astral form; no ideation without an organised mind, and no divine existence without an incorruptible body. Without that spiritual organisation, whose elements are self-conscious immortality, divine justice, eternal beauty and harmony, universal justice and love, knowledge and power, purity and perfection, freedom and glory, even the most devout worshipper can only feel.

Even the most devout worshipper, as long as the divine spirit has not awakened within his soul, will merely feel the beauties of the spiritual realm in the same sense as a blind man may enjoy the warm rays of the sunshine without being able to see the light; only when the process of spiritual regeneration has been accomplished will he be able to see the sun of divine glory within his own soul, and know that he exists as an eternal, self-existent and immortal power in God. To become a magician requires a perfect man and not merely a being born of a dream; the exercise of spiritual power requires a substantial body as its foundation; to attain true knowledge of all the mysteries of the universe requires an organisation as large as the world. This spiritual body grows out of the elements of the corruptible material body. Without that organism there can be no realisation of one's own divine nature: "Unless a man is reborn in the Spirit, he cannot enter the Kingdom of God."

Chapter VIII – Unconsciousness

"Omne bonum a Deo, imperfectum a Diabalo." – **Paracelsus**

Consciousness & Unconsciousness

Consciousness is knowledge and life; unconsciousness is ignorance and death. If we are conscious of the existence of a thing, we know that a relation exists between ourselves and that thing. If we become unconscious of its existence, neither we nor that object ceases to exist, but we fail to recognise its relation to us.

As soon as we begin to realise that relation, the character of the object perceived in the sphere of our mind becomes a part of our mental constitution, and we begin to live in relation to it. We then possess it in our consciousness, and may retain it there by the power of our Will. If it disappears, we may recall it by the power of recollection and memory. To know an object is to live relatively to it, to forget it is to cease to exist in relation to it.

Unconsciousness, ignorance, and death are therefore synonymous terms, and everyone is dead in proportion as he is ignorant. If he is ignorant of a fact, he is dead relatively to it, although he may be fully alive relatively to other things. We cannot be conscious of everything at once, and therefore, as our impressions and thoughts change, our consciousness and relation to certain things change, and we continually die relatively to some things and live relatively to others.

There can be no absolute unconsciousness; because the One Life is self-existent and independent of its manifestations. It manifests itself in our forms, and even if our forms dissolve, Life continues to be and to evolve other forms.

There can be no cessation of absolute consciousness as long as there is absolute being, because the "Absolute" never ceases to be in relation to itself. Relative death and unconsciousness occurs every moment, and we are not aware of its occurrence. We meet hundreds of corpses in the streets, which are entirely dead and unconscious in regard to certain things of which we are alive; and we are dead in regard to many things to which others are alive and conscious.

Only simultaneously occurring omniscience in regard to everything that exists would be absolute life without any admixture of death, but such a state is an impossibility as long as man is bound to a personality and limited form, and has therefore only a limited existence and consciousness.

Each principle in man has a certain sphere of activity, and its perceptions can only extend to the limits of that sphere. Each is dead to such modes of activity as are in no relation with it. Minerals are unconscious of the action of intelligence, but not of the attraction of Earth; the spirit is dead to earthly attraction and mechanical pressure, but not to love. If we can change the mode of activity in a form, we call into existence a new state of consciousness, because we establish new relations of a different order; the old activity dies and a new one begins to live.

Higher States

If the energy which we are now using for the purpose of digesting food, for performing intellectual labour and for enjoying sensual pleasures, were used for the purpose of developing the spiritual germs contained within the constitution of man, we would be in a comparatively short time rewarded for our labour by becoming superior beings, of a state so far above our present condition, that we can at present not even conceive of it, because we have no experience about it. All we know about such states is that which has been told to us by those who have entered it, and in moments of tranquillity and exaltation the soul of even not highly spiritually developed people may occasionally pass by the temple of divine wisdom, when the door is left ajar, and from the glance caught of the interior light that streams through the Gates of Gold it may form a conception about the beauties contained therein.

In the constitution of average man life is especially active in the physical body, and he clings to the life of that body as if it were the only possible mode of existence. He knows of no other mode of life, and is, therefore, afraid to die. A person who has concentrated his life and consciousness into his astral body will be conscious of another existence, and his physical body will be only so far of value to him, as by its instrumentality he can act on the physical plane. Physical death is a continuation of the activity of life in other principles. If we, by an occult process, concentrate all our life into our higher principles before our body ceases to live, we master death, and live independent of our physical body.

Such beings exist and are called "Nirmaanakaayas." See H. P. Blavatsky, "The Voice of the Silence," Part III. They are not to be confounded with the so-called "Theosophical Mahatmas," who are terrestrial men and Adepts; but who have been represented by some fanatical admirers as "spirits" or ghosts.

Eternal Principles

Such a transfer of life and consciousness is not beyond possibility. It has been accomplished by many, and will be accomplished by others. The material elements of the physical body are continually subject to elimination and renewal. By permitting the physical body gradually to die, while the spiritual organism becomes developed, the astral body assumes the functions of the physical form. No one would be willing to look upon such a change as death, and nevertheless it would be nothing else but a mode of dying slow as far as the physical body is concerned, while at the same time it is a raising of the real man into a superior form of existence. Death -- whether slow or quick -- is nothing but a process of purification, by which the imperfect is eliminated and rendered unconscious. Nothing perishes but that which is not able to live. Principles cannot die, only their manifestations cease in one plane, to appear in another.

Only that which is perfect can remain without being changed. God does not redeem the personal man by the process of death; he redeems himself by freeing himself from the personality of the man. Truth, wisdom, justice, beauty, goodness, &c., cannot be exterminated; it is merely the forms in which they become manifest that can be destroyed.

If all the wise men in the world were to die, the principle of Wisdom would nevertheless continue to exist, and manifest in due time in other receptive forms; if Love were to leave the hearts of all human beings, it would thereby not be annihilated, it would merely cease to exist relatively to men, and men would cease to live, while love would continue to be. Eternal principles are self-existent, and therefore independent of forms, and not subject to change; but forms are changeable, and cannot continue without the presence of the principles whose instruments for manifestation they represent.

Death

The human body is an instrument for the manifestation of life, the soul is an instrument for the manifestation of spirit. When life leaves the body, the body disintegrates; if the spirit leaves the astral form, the latter dissolves. A person in whom the spiritual principle has become entirely inactive is morally dead, although his body may be full of life and his earthly soul full of animal desires. Such spiritless living corpses or shells are often seen in fashionable society as well as in the crowds where the vulgar assemble.

A person in whom the principle of reason has become inactive is intellectually dead, although his body may be full of animal life; lunatics are dead people, in whom reason has ceased to live. If the soul leaves the body, the form dies, although the soul lives if endowed with spirit; but if its connection with spirit ceases, either before or after the death of the body, it dissolves into the elements of the astral plane.

The astral soul, like the body, is a compound organism, composed of various elements. Some of these elements may be fit to assimilate with the spirit, others are not fit to do so. If a person, during his earthly life, has not purified his soul sufficiently, so as to enter the spiritual state immediately after the death of the physical body, a gradual separation of the pure and impure elements from the still impure remains takes place in the state after death. When the final separation is accomplished, the spiritual elements enter the spiritual state (which, in fact, they have never left); and the lower elements remain in the lower plane, where they gradually disintegrate.

If the organisation of the physical body becomes impaired to such an extent, that the principle of life cannot employ it any longer to serve as an instrument for its manifestation, it ceases to act. Death may begin at the head, the heart, or the lungs, but life lingers longest in the head, and is still active there to a certain extent after the body, to all exterior appearances, has become unconscious and ceased to live.

The power of thought continues for a time to work in its habitual manner, although sensation has ceased to exist in the nerves. This activity may even grow in intensity as the principles become disunited; and if the thought of the dying is intensely directed upon an absent friend it can impress itself upon the consciousness of that friend, and perhaps cause him to see the apparition of the dying. At last vitality leaves the brain, and the higher principles depart, carrying with them their proper activity, life, and consciousness, leaving behind an empty form, a mask, and illusion.

There need not necessarily be any loss of consciousness in regard to the persons and things by which the dying person is surrounded; the only consciousness which necessarily ceases is that which refers to conditions concerning his personality, such as physical sensation, pain, weight, heat and cold, hunger and thirst, which affected the physical form.

As his life departs from the brain, another state of consciousness comes into existence, because he enters into relation to a different order of things.

"The principle, carrying memory, emerges from the brain, and every event of the life which is ebbing away, is reviewed by the mind. Picture after picture presents itself with living vividness before his consciousness, and he lives in a few minutes his whole life again. Persons in a state of drowning have experienced that state. That impression which has been the strongest, survives all the rest; the other impressions disappear to reappear again in the devachanic state.

"No man dies unconscious, whatever external appearances may seem to indicate to the contrary; even a madman will have a moment, at the time of his death, when his intellect will be restored. Those who are present at such solemn moments should take care not to disturb, by outbursts of grief or otherwise, that process by which the soul beholds the effects of the past and lays the plan for its future existence."*(Extracted from the letter of an Adept.)*

Perispirit [astral body]

The process of the parting of the astral form [in the 8th edition, the "perispirit"] from the physical remains is described by a clairvoyant as follows: "At first I saw a beautiful light of a pale blue colour, in which appeared a small egg-shaped substance about three feet above the head. It was not stationary, but wavered to and fro like a balloon in the air. Gradually it elongated to the length of the body, the whole enveloped in a mist or smoke. I perceived a face corresponding in features to that which was so soon to be soulless, only brighter, more smooth, more beautiful, yet unfinished, with the same want of expression that we observe in a new-born infant.

With every breath from the dying body the ethereal form was added to and became more perfect. Presently the feet became defined, not side by side, as the dying man had placed himself, but one hanging below the other, and one knee bent, as new-born infants would be in an accidental position. The body appeared to be enshrouded in a cloudlike mist. A countless host of other presences seemed to be near. When the whole was complete, all slowly passed out of sight." *(A. J. Davis describes a similar scene.)*

This ethereal body is the soul-body or perisprit of the person that died. It is not the spirit itself, but still connected with the spirit, as it was connected with it during life. It still contains the good and evil tendencies which it acquired during life, unless its attraction towards one pole or the other was already so great that a separation of the highest principle has taken place before physical death.

The real man is an impersonal power, and his existence does not depend on a physical form, he only acquires such a form to manifest his activity on the lower planes. If his spirit rises above the attractions of his lower self, his lower self will be unconscious and disintegrate; but if he clings to his animal nature with a great intensity of desire, a centre of consciousness may become established therein, and its sense of personality still continue to exist for a while even after the physical body is dead. His soul will in such cases be a semi-conscious inhabitant of the Kama loca state. *(Purgatory)*

The time during which an astral corpse may remain in this state before it is entirely dissolved depends on the density and strength of its elements. It may differ from a few hours or days to a great many years. Man is made up of a great many living elements or principles, of which each one exists in its own individual state while they all receive their life from the spirit. When the spirit withdraws they become separated, while each retains for a while its own particular life in the same sense as a wheel which is once set into motion will continue to run until after the force is exhausted, even if the original motive power is withdrawn.

The remnant of a man in the Kama loca state is therefore not the man, but an elementary part of him which may or may not be conscious that it exists.

This Kama loca state is the "land of the shadows," the Hades of the ancient Greeks, and the "purgatory" of the Roman Catholic Church. Its inhabitants may or may not possess consciousness and intelligence, but the astral souls of average men and women possess no intelligence of their own; they can, however, be made to act intelligently by the power of the Elementals, who infuse their own consciousness into them.

Paracelsus says: "Men and women die every day, whose souls during their lives have been subject to the influence and guidance of Elementals. How much easier will it be for such Elementals to influence the sidereal bodies of such persons and to make them act as they please, after their souls have lost the protection which their physical bodies afforded! They may use their soul-bodies to move physical objects from place to place, to carry such objects from distant countries, and to perform other feats of a similar kind that may appear miraculous to the uninitiated."

The state of consciousness of the fourth principle (the animal soul) after the lower triad has become unconscious and lifeless, therefore, differs widely in different persons, according to the conditions that have been established during its connection with the body. The soul of an average person in Kama loca with only moderate selfish desires is not conscious and intelligent enough to know that its physical body has died, and that it is itself undergoing the process of disintegration; but the soul of a person whose whole consciousness was centred in self, chained to earth by fear, remorse, greed, or desire for revenge, *(Chinamen* kill themselves for the purpose of fastening their soul upon an enemy and taking revenge. Let those who "know" that this is a superstition try the experiment.) may be conscious and intelligent enough to make desperate efforts to enter again into physical life. Feeling its impending fate, seeking to prolong its existence, it clings for protection to the organism of some living being, and causes obsession. Not only weak-minded human beings but also animals may be subject to such an obsession.

Consciousness After Death

To a body without sensation or consciousness it can make no difference under what conditions it may continue to exist or perish, because it cannot realise its existence; but to a soul in which the divine spark of intelligence coming from the sixth principle has kindled consciousness and sensation, its surrounding conditions will be of importance, because it realises them more or less fully according to the degree of its consciousness.

Such surroundings, in the state after death, each man creates for himself during life by his thoughts, his words, and his acts. Man is creating all his life the world wherein he will live in the hereafter.

Thought is substantial and objective to those who live on the plane of thought. Even on the physical plane, every form that exists is materialised thought, grown or made into a form; the world of the souls is a world in which thought itself appears material and solid to those who exist in that world.

Man is a centre from which continually thought is evolved, and crystallises into forms in that world. His thoughts are things that have life and form and tenacity; real entities, solid and more enduring than the forms of the physical plane. Good thoughts are light and rise above us, but evil thoughts are heavy and sink. The world below us to which they sink is the sphere of the grossest, most diseased, and sensual thoughts evolved by evil-disposed and ignorant men. It is a world still more material and solid to its inhabitants than ours is to us; it is the habitation of man-created personal deities, devils, and monstrosities invented by the morbid imagination of man.

They are only the products of thoughts, but nevertheless they are relatively real and substantial to those who live among them and realise their existence. The myths of hell and purgatory are based on ill-understood facts. "Hells" exist, but man is himself their creator. Brutal man creates monsters by the working of his diseased imagination during life; disembodied man will be attracted to its creations.

There are few persons who are not subject to evil thoughts; such thoughts are the reflex of the lurid light from the region of folly, but they cannot take form unless we give them form by dwelling on them and feeding them with the substance of our own will. Love is the life of the good, malice the substance of evil.

An evil thought, evolved without consent of the heart, is without life; an evil thought, brought into existence with malice, becomes malicious and living. If it is embodied in an act, a new devil will be born into the world. The horrors of hell exist only for those who have been conscious, voluntary, and malicious colaborers of the imagination, peopling the mind with the products of fancy; the beauties of heaven are only realised by him who has created a heaven within himself during his life.

Pain is only caused if a being exists under abnormal conditions. Allegorically speaking, devils do not suffer in hell, because they are there in their own natural element; they would suffer if they had to enter into heaven. A man suffers if his head is kept under water: a fish suffers if he is taken out of the water.

Conscious Relationship

We can only be conscious of the existence of things, if a relation exists between ourselves and these things. A person who has created nothing during life that could have established a conscious relationship with his immortal self will have nothing immortal with which to remain in relation with after death.

If his whole attention is taken up by his physical wants, the sphere of his consciousness during life will be confined to those material wants. When he leaves his material habitation material wants will no longer exist for him, and his consciousness of them ceases. Having created nothing in his soul that can enter into relation with his own spirit, his soul will neither lose that which it never possessed nor gain that which it never desired, but remain a blank.

Death will clear away that which hinders our spiritual perception of truth; but it cannot enable us to develop that power. If we hire a priest or a professor to do our thinking for us, and to be guardian of our knowledge and spiritual aspirations, we create no spiritual aspirations or living thoughts for ourselves. If we are contented to live in the opinions of others, we have no truth of our own. The artificial consciousness, which has thus been created by the illusive reflection of the thought of others on the mirror of the individual mind, has no roots in the spiritual soul, and mere opinions have no immortal existence. Those minds which have been fed on illusions will have no substance after the illusions have passed away. The only knowledge which can remain with the soul is that which it loves and knows and is itself.

*"Whatever thou lovest, man,
that too, become you must.
God, if thou lovest God;
dust, if thou lovest dust."*
- Angelus Silesius

Every cause is followed by an effect. Illusions that have been created in the mind are forces that must become exhausted before they can die. They will continue to act in the subjective state and produce other illusions by the law of harmony that governs the association of ideas, and all illusions will end in the sphere to which they belong.

Selfish desires will end in the sphere of self, unselfish aspirations and thoughts will bring their own rewards if they were good, and their own punishment if they were evil. But after all the good and evil thoughts have been exhausted in Kama loca and Devachan, there can be left nothing of the individual but the self-consciousness of his spirit, that existed during his life in the innermost sanctuary of his heart.

If no such consciousness existed, if there were nothing in him to cause him to feel his own divine nature, the presence of truth, there will be nothing left but a blank, an empty mind, to become reincarnated for the purpose of trying again to attain the knowledge of self.

Death is a transformation or change of conditions under which we exist. Our desires for things change as the conditions under which we exist assume a different character. Before we are born our state of life depends on the state of the mother's womb; but having been born into the world, we care nothing more for that which furnished us with nutriment and life during our foetal existence. Being infants, our interests are centred upon the breasts of the mother, but these breasts are forgotten after we need them no more. Things which absorbed the whole of our consciousness during our youth are discarded as we grow older. If we throw off the physical body, the desire for that which was attractive to it and important for its existence is thrown off with it, or perishes soon afterwards. But if the soul again approaches the material plane, and again enters into relationship with it, the old consciousness and the old desires, that were gone to sleep, reawaken, and its physical sensations return, but vanish again after the influence of the medium is withdrawn. The "Elementary" then relapses in his unconscious state. *(The non-remembering of previous appearances is an essential feature in returning ghosts.)*

The Mystic Death

There are innumerable varieties of conditions and possibilities in the world of spirit and on the astral plane, as there are upon the physical plane. If the mind begins to investigate these things separately, and without understanding the fundamental laws of nature upon which such phenomena are based, it may as well despair of ever being able to form a correct conception of them.

If a botanist were to examine separately each one of the thousands of leaves of a large tree which he has never seen, for the purpose of finding out the true nature of that tree, he would never arrive at an end; but if he once knows the tree as a whole, the colour and shape of the individual leaves will be of secondary importance. If we once arrive at a correct conception of the spiritual nature of man, it will be easy to follow the various ramifications of the one universal law. There is no death for that which is perfect, but the imperfect must perish sooner or later. So-called death is simply a process of elimination of that which is useless. In this sense we all are continually dying every day, and even wishing to die, because every reasonable person desires to get rid of his imperfections and their consequences and the sufferings which they cause.

No one is afraid to lose that which he does not want, and if he clings to that which is useless, it is because he is unconscious and ignorant of that which is useful. In such a case he is already partly dead to that which is good, and must come to life and learn to realise that which is useful, by dying to that which is useless. This is the so-called mystic death, by which the enlightened come to life, which involves the unconsciousness of worthless and earthly desires and passions, and establishes a consciousness of that which is immortal and true.

The reason why men and women are sometimes afraid to die is because they mistake the low for the high, and prefer material illusions to spiritual truths. We ought not to live in the fear of death; but in the hope of coming to life. There is no death for the perfect, and the dead in life must throw away their imperfectness, so that that which is perfect in him may become conscious and live. This mystic death is recommended by the wise as being the supreme remedy against real death. This mystic death is a spiritual regeneration. *(John 3:3 [Jesus replied, "Very truly I tell you, no one can see the kingdom of God unless they are born again."])*

Hermes Trismegistus says: "Happy is he whose vices die before him"; and the great teacher Thomas de Kempis writes: "Learn to die now to the world" (to the attractions of matter), "so that you may begin to live with Christ"; and Angelus Silesius writes: "Christ rose not from the dead, he is still in the grave for those who do not know him." The true and only saviour of every man or woman is the self-knowledge of divine truth.

A person whose vices have died during his earthly life does not need to die again. His sidereal body will dissolve like a silver cloud, being unconscious of any desires for that which is low, and his spirit will be fully conscious of that which is beautiful, harmonious, and true; but he, whose conscience is centred in the passions that have raged in his soul during life, can realise nothing higher than that which was the highest to him during his life, and cannot gain any other consciousness by the process of death.

Physical death is no gain; it cannot give us that which we do not already possess. Unconsciousness cannot confer consciousness, ignorance cannot give knowledge. By the mystic death we arrive at life and consciousness, knowledge and happiness, because the awaking of the higher elements to life implies the death of that which is useless and low. "Neither circumcision nor uncircumcision availeth, but a new creature." *(Galat. vi. 15.)*

Premature Death

There are Esprits soufrantes, our suffering souls. They are the "revenants" or "restants" the astral bodies of victims of premature death, whose physical forms have perished before their time. They remain within the attraction of the Earth until the time arrives that should have been the termination of their physical lives according to the law of their Karma.

They are under normal conditions, not fully conscious of the conditions in which they exist; but they may be temporarily stimulated into life by the influence of mediumship. Then will their half-forgotten desires and memories return and cause them to suffer. To rouse such existences from their stupor into a realisation of pain for the purpose of gratifying idle curiosity is cruel, and very injurious to such irrational souls, as it reawakens their thirst for life and for the gratification of earthly desires.

The soul of the same suicide, however, or that of a malicious person, may be fully conscious and realise the situation in which it is placed. Such shadows wander about earth, clinging to material life, and vainly trying to escape the dissolution by which they are threatened. Partly bereft of reason, and following their animal instincts, they may become Incubi and Succubi, Vampires stealing life from the living to prolong their own existence, regardless of the fate of their victims.

The soul-bodies of the dead may be either unconsciously or consciously attracted to mediums for the purpose of communicating with the living. By using the astral emanations of the medium they sometimes become materialised, visibly and tangibly, and appear like the deceased person himself. But if a deceased person was in possession of high aspirations and virtues, his soul-corpse will not be the actual entity which it represents, although it may act in some respect as the person whose mask it wears.

If one blows into a trumpet it will give the sound of a trumpet and no other. The soul-corpse of a good person, if infused artificially with life, will produce the thoughts it used to produce during life; but there needs to be no more of the identity of that person in the corpse than there is the identity of a friend in a phonograph.

The revelations made by such "spirits" are the echoes of their former thoughts, or of thoughts impressed upon them by the living, as a mirror reflects the faces of those that stand before it. They do not give us a true description of the spirit's condition in the world of souls, because they are themselves ignorant of that condition.

At the time when Plato was living, such souls returned, giving descriptions of Hades and of the deities that were believed to exist in that place. At the present day the souls of Roman Catholics will return and ask for masses to be relieved from purgatory, while the Protestants refuse to be benefited by the ceremonies of the Catholic Church. The souls of dead Hindus ask sometimes for the performance of sacrifices to their gods, and every such "spirit" is domineered by those ideas in which he believed during his life. The discrepancy in their reports prove that their tales are only the products of the imagination of the irrational soul.

We do not deny the occurrence of so-called spiritual phenomena; and we are not opposed to "spiritualism"; but we are opposed to the misunderstanding of it. We believe in Spiritualism as belonging to the department of natural science and as having been very useful in overthrowing the blind materialism of the past. We also make a distinction between Spiritualism, which implies Spirituality and ennobling elevation of soul, and Spiritism, which consists in dealing with the inhabitants of the Astral plane, an intercourse whose dangers are unfortunately not sufficiently known.

Immortal Spirit

If man has a "spirit" that spirit must be immortal, but a man is not immortal if he does not realise the presence of the immortal spirit in him. Having become conscious in man, it cannot become unconscious again, because it is self-existent and independent of all conditions but those which it creates itself.

In him who IS, the consciousness of the I Am is indestructible, because it exists in the absolute eternal One. If that consciousness were to perish, the world would perish with it; because in the consciousness of the I Am the world came into existence, and by its power does it continue to exist. Its consciousness upholds the world, its unconsciousness would be annihilation, but that which not truly IS cannot have the true consciousness of being; it may at best fancy to be. It exists; but as an illusion and not in truth.

The object of man's life is to become conscious that He is -- not an illusive personal form -- but an impersonal, immortal reality, to render the unconscious spirit conscious and enable the immortal soul to realise its own immortality; the object of death is to release that which is conscious from that which is unconscious, and to free the immortal from the bonds of matter.

The tree of life grows and produces a seed, and this seed has to be planted again, to grow into a tree and produce another seed, and this process will have to be repeated over and over again, until at last the soul slumbering in the seed awakens to the realisation of its immortal life.

Unconscious of any relation to personalities, unconscious of its own self, it [the seed of life] will be attracted to such conditions as may be best suited for its further development, as its Karma decides. It will be attracted to overshadow a man whose moral and intellectual tendencies and qualities correspond to its own, careless whether it enters the world as a new-born babe through the door of the hut of a beggar or through the palace of a king.

It does not care for its future conditions, because it is unconscious of their existence. The unconscious spiritual monad, descending into the lower plane, gathering again the elements which belonged to the previous man of earth, building again the thought-body which it had created in former lives and which constituted its terrestrial character, and entering again into connection with a human physical organism, is born once more into the world of sorrow, builds up the house of flesh, and takes up once more the battle with life, the strife with its lower nature, to make a step forward and come nearer to God.

Thus a man that reigned as a king in a former incarnation may be reborn as a beggar, if his character was that of a beggar; and a liberal beggar may create as his future successor a king or a being of noble birth. Both act without freedom of choice at the time of their visit to the Earth, following unconsciously their Karma. But the Adept, who knows his own real self and has learned to realise his immortal existence, will be his own master. He has grown above the sense of personality, and thereby gained immortal consciousness during his earthly life. He has thrown away his lower self, and death cannot rob him of that which he no longer possesses and to which he attaches no value. Being conscious of his existence and of the conditions under which he exists, he may follow his own choice in the selection of a body, if he chooses to reincarnate, either for the benefit of humanity or for his own progression. Having entirely overcome the attractions of Earth, he is truly free. He is dead and unconscious to all earthly temptations, but conscious of the highest happiness attainable by man. The delusion of the senses can fashion for him no other tabernacle to imprison his soul, and before him lies open the road to eternal rest in Nirvana.

But now, them builder of the tabernacle, thou!
I know thee! Never shalt thou build again
These walls of pain,
Nor raise the roof-tree of deceits, nor lay
Fresh rafters on the clay.
Broken thy house is, and the ridge-pole split!
Delusion fashioned it.
Save pass I thence. Deliverance to obtain.

-- Sir Edwin Arnold: *"The Light of Asia."*

If a person has once attained spiritual self-knowledge he will not need to follow the blind law of attraction, but he will be able to choose the body and the conditions most suitable to him. He may then reincarnate himself in the body of a child, or in the body of a grown person, whose soul has been separated by disease or accident from the body, and that person will thus be brought to life again, if no vital organ is too seriously injured, to carry on the functions of life again.

Cases are known in which a certain person apparently died, and finally came to life again, when from that time he appeared to be an entirely different man; he may have died as a ruffian and after his recovery become suddenly like a saint, so that such a sudden change appeared inexplicable on any other theory than that an entirely different character had taken possession of his body. Such people may, after their recovery takes place, speak a language they never learned, talk familiarly of things they never saw; call people by their names, of which they never heard, know all about places, where their physical bodies never have been, &c., &c. If phenomena could prove anything, such occurrences might go to prove the theory of the reincarnation of living adepts.

"Shall we know our loved ones after death?" is a question which is often asked, and which answers itself if the true nature of the "Ego" is known. In all planes rules the law of harmony, and like is attracted to like; but an illusion can only know illusions. We do not know each other in this life, if we have not the knowledge of our own self.

He who, having become self-conscious of his own spiritual nature, knows his own real self, may rise up in his soul to the planes of the blessed, and by entering their individual spheres join their own happiness and partake of their joys; but the souls dreaming in heaven, being immersed in bliss, do not descend and join in the circus of life, before the time of their reincarnation arrives. Such a descent would be degradation. Heaven does not descend to earth; but if earth ascends to heaven it becomes heaven itself.

Degradation

To die is to become unconscious in relation to certain things. If we become unconscious of a lower state, and thereby become conscious of a higher existence, such a change cannot properly be called death. If we become unconscious of a higher condition, and thereby enter a lower one, such a change is followed by degradation, and therefore degradation is the only death to be feared.

Degradation takes place if a human faculty is employed for a lower purpose than that for which it was by nature intended. Degradation of the most vulgar, the lowest material type takes place, if the organs of the physical body are used for villainous purposes, and disease, atrophy, and death are the common result.

A higher and still more detrimental and lasting degradation takes place if the intellectual faculties are habitually used for selfish and degrading purposes. In such cases the intellect, that ought to serve as a basis for spiritual aspirations, becomes merged with matter, its consciousness is bound down to the plane of materiality and selfishness, and becomes inactive in the region of spirituality.

The lowest and most enduring degradation takes place if man, having reached a state in which his personality has, to a certain extent, merged with his impersonal I, degrades his spiritual self by employing the powers which such an amalgamation confers for villainous purposes of a low character. Such are the practices of black magic. A person who, for want of any better understanding, employs his intellectual faculties for his own selfish purposes, regardless of the principle of justice, is not necessarily a villain, but simply a fool.

The murderer may commit a murder to save himself from being discovered of some crime, and not for the purpose of robbing another person of life. A thief may steal a purse for the purpose of enriching himself, and not for the purpose of rendering another man poor. Such acts are the result of ignorance; persons usually act evil for selfish purposes and not for the pure love of evil. Such acts are the result of personal feelings, and personal feelings cease to exist when the personality to which they belong ceases to exist. Such a personal existence ceases when his life on the lower plane ceases to act. The higher spiritual I of the man is neither a gainer nor loser on such an occasion, it remains the same as it was before the compound of forces representing the late personality was born.

Black Magic

The real villain, however, is he who performs evil for the love of evil without personal considerations. A person who is no more influenced by his sense of personality, and has attained spiritual knowledge, is a magician. Those who employ such a power for the purposes of evil have been called black magicians or

Brothers of the Shadow, in the same sense as those who employ their spiritual powers for good purposes have been called Brothers of Light.

The white magician is a spiritual power for good; the real black magician is a living power of evil attached to a personality that performs evil instinctively and for the love of evil itself. This power of evil may kill the man or the animal that never offended it, and by whose death it has nothing to gain, destroys for the love of destruction, causes suffering without expecting any benefit for itself, robs to throw away the spoils, revels in torture and death.

Such an individuality attracts and calls to its aid other impersonal evil powers, which become a part of it, and which continue to exist after the personality ceases to live on the physical plane. Many incarnations may be needed before such a power will come into existence, but when it once lives it will perish as slow as it grew. "Angels," as well as "devils," are born into the world, and children with villainous propensities and malicious characters are not very rare. They are the products of such forces as in former incarnations have developed a spiritual consciousness in the direction of evil.

A power which may be employed for a good purpose, can also be used for an evil purpose. If we can by magnetism decrease the rapidity of the pulse of a fever-patient, we may also decrease it to such an extent, that the subject ceases to live. If we can force a person by our will to perform a good act, we may also force him to commit a crime. Everything is either good or evil according to the purpose for which it is used.

It is unnecessary to enter into details in regard to the practices of Black Magic and Sorcery. It is more noble and useful to study how we can benefit mankind than to satisfy our curiosity in regard to the powers for evil. To show to what aberrations of mind a craving for the power of working black magic may lead, it may be mentioned that the would-be black magician and great vivisector, Gilles de Rays, marechal of France, and better known as "Blue Beard," who was executed for his crimes at Nantes, killed and tortured to death during a few years not less than one hundred and sixty women and children in the interest of his science, and for the purpose of gratifying his curiosity in regard to Black Magic.

Truth is Everywhere

The white magician delights in doing good, the servant of the black art revels in cruelty. The former co-operates with the Divine Spirit of Wisdom, the latter co-operates with certain spiritual forces of nature; the former will be exalted in God and united with him; the latter will ultimately be absorbed by the beings with which he has associated and which he called to his aid.

To ennoble our character and to raise our consciousness into the spiritual plane is to live; to let it sink to a lower level is to die. The natural order of the universe is that the high should elevate the low; but if the high is made to serve the low, degradation is the result.

Everywhere in the workshop of nature the high acts upon the low by the power of the highest. The highest itself cannot be degraded. Truth itself cannot be turned into falsehood, it can only be rejected or misapplied. Reason itself cannot be rendered foolish, it can only be misused by reasoning foolishly. The universal and impersonal cannot itself become limited, it can only come into contact with such personalities as are able to approach it. The Law does not suffer by breaking its connection with the form, the form alone suffers and dies.

The truth is everywhere, seeking to manifest itself in the consciousness of man. Man's consciousness rotates between the two poles of good and evil, of spirit and matter. The omnipresent influence of the great spiritual Sun renders him strong to overcome the attraction of matter, and assists him to come victorious out of the struggle with evil.

Man is not entirely free as long as he is not in possession of perfect knowledge, which means, realisation of truth; but he is free to allow himself to be attracted by a love for the truth or to close his door against it. He may become united with the principle of wisdom, or he may sever his connection with it and sell his inherited rights to immortality for a comparatively worthless mess of pottage. The Centaur in his nature, whose lower principles are animal, while the upper parts are possessed of Intellect, may carry away his spiritual aspirations and lull them into unconsciousness by the music of its illusions.

Bodies may be comparatively long-lived, and some forms, compared with others, may be very enduring; but there is nothing permanent but the self-consciousness of love and the self-consciousness of hate. Love is light, and hate is darkness, and in the end love will conquer hate, because darkness cannot destroy light, and wherever light penetrates into darkness, there will love conquer, and evil and darkness will disappear.

Chapter IX - Transformations

"Be ye transformed by the renewing of your mind." -- **Rom. xii, 2**

Universal Mind

The Universe is a manifestation of Divine Wisdom and thought is an action of Mind. The Mind in which Wisdom can bring a universe into existence must be a Universal Mind, embracing in its totality all the individual minds that ever existed, and containing the germs of everything that will ever come into existence.

Ideas are states of mind, and the thoughts of the Universal Mind stored up in the Astral Light, after their representative forms have dissolved, grow again into visible forms, by being clothed with matter.

Man remembers his thoughts; that is to say, he enters again into one of his previous mental states. To remember a thing is to read it in the mind. The Astral Light is the book of memory, in which every thought is engraved and every event recorded, and the more intense the thought the deeper will it be engraved, and the longer will the picture remain.

Thought is a force, and its products remain in the Astral Light long after the person who gave them form has ceased to live. As the images of things which exist in the Astral Light remain there for ages, they may be seen by the clairvoyant. Such images are formed of thought, and as thought is something substantial, it is even possible for the Occultist to reproduce books, writings, &c., which have existed thousands of years ago.

Men do not create thought; the ideas existing in the Astral Light flow into their minds, and there they transform themselves into other shapes, combining with other ideas, consciously or unconsciously, according to the laws that control the correlations, interrelations, and associations of thought. A great mind can grasp a great idea, a narrow mind is only capable of holding narrow ideas. Thoughts are existing things and are sometimes grasped contemporaneously by several receptive minds. Some great discoveries have been made almost simultaneously by several minds. *(There are three claimants for the discovery of chloroform, two for the discovery of Uranus, two for the Bell telephone, &c.)*

Ideas contained in the imagination of nature throw their reflections upon the minds of men, and, according to the capacities of the latter to receive ideas, they come to their consciousness, clear or distorted, plain or shadowy, like images of pictures reflected in living mirrors, that are either clear or rendered dim by the accumulation of dust. In those living mirrors they are remodelled and transformed into new pictures, to people the currents of the Astral Light with new images, and to give rise to new forms of thought. Therefore a spiritually strong person who lives in solitude and silence may do a great work, by evolving ideas, which will remain impressed upon the Astral Light and come to the cognisance of those who are capable to grasp them.

The thoughts of men impress themselves upon the Astral Light, and every event that takes place on the physical plane is recorded in the memory of nature. Every stone, every plant, every animal as well as every man, has a sphere in which is recorded every event of its existence. They all have a little world of their own, made of thought, and whenever they move, they think; for their motions are motions of thought.

In the Astral Light of each is stored up every event of its past history and of the history of its surroundings; so that everything, no matter how insignificant it may be, can give an account of its daily life, from the beginning of its existence as to form up to the present, to him who is able to read. A piece of lava from Pompeii will give to the Psychometer a true description of the volcanic eruption that devastated that town and buried it under its ashes, where it remained hidden for nearly two thousand years; a floating timber carried by the Gulf Stream to the far North can give to the inhabitants of the North a true picture of tropical life; and a piece of bone of a Mastodon teach the vegetable and animal life of antediluvian periods. *(Prof. Wm. Denton: "Soul of Things.")*

The pictures impressed in the Astral Light react upon the mental spheres of individual minds and can create in them emotional disturbances, even if these pictures do not come to the full consciousness of their minds. Deeds committed with a great concentration of thought call living powers in the Astral Light into existence, tempting others to commit similar acts.

A case is known, for instance, in which a prisoner hung himself in his cell, and several other persons that were successively shut up in the same cell hung themselves also without any apparent cause. At another place a sentinel killed himself at his post, and several soldiers mounting guard after him did likewise, so that the post had to be deserted. Many similar examples may be cited. Crimes of a certain character often become epidemic in places where a criminal has been executed; murder becomes epidemic like measles or scarlatina.

Capital Punishment

Man does not know the influences which cause him to think and to act, as long as he does not know his own nature. He is therefore not a responsible being, except to the extent of his wisdom and power to control his own nature. Wisdom and strength can only be attained in life by experience and by the exercise of the power of overcoming temptation.

If the true nature of the constitution of man were properly understood, capital punishment would soon be abandoned as perfectly useless, unjust, and contrary to the law of nature. That which commits a murder or any other crime is a conscious and invisible power, which cannot be killed and which does not improve in character by being separated from its external form. The body is innocent, it is merely an instrument in the hands of the invisible culprit, the astral man. The face of even a criminal bears an expression of peace when the soul has departed.

By severing the bonds between this vicious power and the physical form, we do not change its tendency to act evil; but while during the life of the body the action of that power was restricted to only one form, having been liberated, it now incites numerous other weak-minded people to perform the same crimes for which the body was executed. Thus by capital punishment evil is not abolished, but its sphere of action increased.

As far as the theory of influencing other would-be criminals with fear, by making an example of one, and thus to prevent others from committing crimes, is concerned; it is well known that criminals do not look upon any punishment as being something which they have deserved for their deeds, but as being a consequence of having been so careless as to allow themselves to be caught, and they usually make up their minds, that if they were permitted to escape, they would be more careful -- not to be caught again.

Life is a school through which every one must pass for the purpose of acquiring experience, strength of character, and self-knowledge. To rob a person of this opportunity is a great crime if it is done knowingly. The fool who kills another man has little responsibility, because he has no actual knowledge of the nature of his deed; but the lawgiver who institutes legal murder is the true criminal.

Occult Properties

A lock of hair, a piece of clothing, the handwriting of a person or any article he may have touched, handled, or worn, can indicate to an intuitive mind that person's state of health, his physical, emotional, intellectual, and moral attributes and qualifications. The picture of a murderer may be impressed on the retina of his victim, and reproduced by means of photography; it is impressed on all the surroundings of the place where the deed occurred, and can there be detected by the psychometer who, thus coming en rapport with the criminal, can follow him and hunt him down just as the bloodhound traces the steps of a fugitive slave. *(Emma Hardinge Britten: "Ghost Land." The case cited in this book, in which a clairvoyant followed the tracks of a murderer through several towns and caught him at last, is quoted in several German publications of the last century.)*

This tendency of the Astral Light to inhere in material bodies gives amulets their power and invests keepsakes and relics with certain occult properties. A ring, a lock of hair, or a letter from a friend, can not only conjure up that friend's picture in a person's memory, but bring him en rapport with the peculiar mental state of which that person was or is a representation. If you wish to forget a person, or free yourself from his magnetic attraction, part from everything that reminds you of him, or select only such articles as call up disagreeable memories and are therefore repulsive. Articles belonging to a person bring us in sympathy with that person, and this circumstance is sometimes used for purposes of black magic.

Paracelsus in his writings about the Mumia and the transplantation of diseases gives many illustrations of this theory. The existence of a power, by which a disease may be transferred upon a healthy person, even in "non-contagious" cases, by means of some article belonging to the sick person, is generally believed in by the people in various countries. It must, however, be remembered that in making such experiments the success depends on the amount of "faith" which the magician can employ. Without that faith, which is soul-knowledge, nothing can be accomplished in any department of life.

As every form is the representation of a certain mental state, every object has such attributes as always belong to that state, and therefore every substance has its sympathies and its antipathies; the loadstone attracts iron, and iron the oxygen of the air; hygroscopic bodies attract water, affinities exist between certain bodies, some substances change their colours under certain coloured rays, while others remain unaffected, &c. These phenomena are all nothing else but the various manifestations of the One Life, in which the principle of Love is active and seeks to unite whatever is harmonious.

Every material object is condensed and solidified force. Looked at in this light, it does not seem impossible that the ancients should have attributed certain virtues to certain precious stones, and believed that the Garnet was conducive to joy, the Chalcedony to courage, the Topaz promoting chastity, the Amethyst assisting reason, and the Sapphire intuition.

A spiritual force, to be effective, requires a sensitive object to act upon. In an age which tends to extreme materialism, spiritual influence ceases to be perceived, but if a person cannot feel the occult influences of nature, it does not necessarily follow that they do not exist, and that there are not others able to perceive them because their impres-sional capacities are greater.

Chemistry

Only the fool believes that he knows everything. What is really known is only like a grain of sand on the shore of the ocean in comparison to what is still unknown. Physiologists know that certain plants and chemicals have certain powers, and they explain their effects. They know that Digitalis decreases the quickness of the pulse by paralysing the heart; that Belladonna dilates the pupil by paralysing the muscular fibres of the Iris; that Opium in small doses produces sleep by causing anaemia of the brain, while large doses produce coma by causing congestion, &c.; but why these substances have such effects, or why some chemical compound of Nitrogen, Oxygen, Carbon, and Hydrogen is poisonous in one chemical combination, while the same substances, if combined in a different stoechiometrical proportion, may be used as food, neither chemistry nor physiology can tell us at present.

If we, however, look upon all forms as symbols of mental states, it will not be more difficult to imagine why strychnine is poisonous, than why hate can kill, or fear paralyse the heart.

A simple idea which is once firmly rooted in the mind cannot be changed. If an idea is complicated it is less difficult to modify it in its details, so that gradually an entirely different compound will be the result. In physical chemistry the law is analogous. Compound bodies may be easily changed into other combinations, but single bodies cannot be changed. There are, however, indications that even these so-called single bodies are the results of combinations of still more primitive elements.

It has been observed that when lightning has struck gilded ornaments they have become blackened, and it has been found, on analysing the blackened matter, that the presence of sulphur was distinctly indicated. Unless sulphur exists in the lightning it must have existed in the gold, and have been evolved by the action of lightning. We may then fairly assume that gold contains the elements of sulphur, and this is no anomaly in the case of gold, as other metals have also been proved to contain the elements of sulphur, *(David Low, F.R.S.E: "Simple Bodies in Chemistry.")* and the dreams of physical Alchemy may have some foundation, after all.

But sulphur is supposed to be related to nitrogen, and the elements of nitrogen are believed to be hydrogen and carbon, and if we go still further, we find that even on the physical plane all bodies are only modifications of one primordial element, which is not of a sufficiently material nature to be detected by physical means, and that in this primordial element the germs of all other secondary principles must be contained.

Will and Imagination

The power to receive, preserve, and transform ideas, is the power of Will and Imagination. If an idea enters into the mind, the imagination clothes it into a form, with or without a conscious exercise of the will. We step upon a piece of rope in the dark and immediately imagine that we have stepped upon a snake. This is called passive imagination; while, if we determine to give a certain form to an idea, it is called active imagination; but in both cases the will is active; only in the former instance it is exercised instinctively, and in the latter this is done with intent and deliberation.

The will is, therefore, the active power, and it forms the basis of all artistic and magical operations. Art and magic are closely related together; both give objective form to subjective ideas. The artist exercises this power when he mentally projects the picture formed in his mind upon the canvas and chains it there by the use of his pencil or brush; the sculptor shapes the picture of a form on his mind and embodies it in the marble. He then employs mechanical force to free the ideal from all that is foreign to it, and raises it from the tomb, a materialisation of thought.

In the regeneration of man the will is entirely inactive as far as the creation of an ideal is concerned; but it is highly active in keeping away all the influences which will prevent the realisation of the ideal. God does not need the co-operation of man, his will alone is sufficient; he only requires that the will of man shall not prevent him in the performance of his work. The magician forms an image on his mind and makes it perceptible to others by projecting it into their mental spheres. Uniting his own mental sphere with theirs, they are made to participate of his imagination, and they see that as a reality what he chooses to fancy and think.

By this law many of the feats performed by Indian fakirs can be explained. They cause tigers and elephants to appear before a multitude, by forming the images of such things in the sphere of their mind. What the spectators see on such occasions is nothing else but the thoughts of the conjuror, rendered objective and visible by the latter. *(The fact, that what the spectators on such occasions believe to see does not actually take place, has been proved by means of photography.)*

In the case of an artist, mechanical labour executes the work; in the case of a magician, the will. But the greatest amount of labour will not enable a person who is not an artist to produce a real work of art, and the greatest concentration of thought will not enable a person who has no spiritual power to perform a true magical feat.

Alchemy

The "will" to which we refer is a spiritual self-conscious power, unknown to modern psychology. A person may be an excellent anatomist and know nothing whatever about living spiritual principles; he may be a splendid chemist and know-nothing whatever about Alchemy; he may have perfect control over the mechanical forces of nature acting on the physical plane and know nothing whatever about the chemistry of the soul.

For this reason the mysteries of Alchemy will for ever remain mysteries to a scientist who has no spiritual power at his command. This spiritual power is the spiritual will. Without this power he can only separate the substances of compound bodies and recombine them again as is done in Chemistry, but not employ the principle of life.

The processes of nature are alchemical processes; because, without the principle of life acting upon the chemical substances of the earth, no growth would result. If the force of attraction and repulsion were entirely equal, everything would be at a standstill. If growth and decay would go hand in hand, nothing could grow, because a cell would begin to decay as soon as it would begin to form.

The chemist may take earth, and water, and air, and separate them into their constituent elements, and recombine them again, and at the end of his work he will be where he began. But the Alchemy of nature takes water, and earth, and air, and infuses into them the fire of life, forming them into trees and producing flowers and fruits.

Nature could not give her life-imparting influence to her children if she did not possess it; the chemist, having no life-principle at his command, or not knowing how to employ it, cannot perform the wonders of Alchemy. The reason why we have at present very few alchemists, is because we have very few persons endowed with the life of the spirit.

There are three aspects of Alchemy. It deals with the physical substances of things, more especially with their souls, and in its highest aspect with their spiritual centres. In its physical processes it requires physical means, and from the study of these modern chemistry has taken its rise. By the developed powers of his soul the Alchemist may act upon the souls of material substances, and if he can change their qualities, the character of the physical form may be changed. If the spiritual "fire" is awakened within him, he attains the spiritual powers required to act upon the inferior elements. An insufficient degree of heat will not accomplish anything great: he must gradually attain within himself the fire of divine love until he becomes himself the Salamander, able to live in a light in which nothing impure can exist.

H. P. Blavatsky says: Everything in this world of effects is made up of three principles and four aspects, each object has an objective exterior, a vital soul, and a divine spark of spiritual fire. By these principles nature acts, and in order to imitate nature, Kriyasakti [or Kriya-Shakti] (the creative will) must be developed in man. This spiritual power is also called the "Word," of which it is written, that there is no need to seek it in distant places; "for it is close to you; it is in your mouth and in your heart."

Johannes Tritheim says: "The Spiritus Mundi resembles a breath, appearing at first like a fog and afterwards condensing like water. This 'water' (Aakaasa) was in the beginning pervaded by the principle of life, and light was awakened in it by the fiat of the eternal spirit. This spirit of light, called the soul of the world (the Astral Light), is a spiritual substance, which can be made visible and tangible by art; it is a substance, but being invisible, we call it spirit. This 'soul' or corpus is hidden in the centre of everything, and can be extracted by means of the spiritual fire in man, which is identical with the universal spiritual fire, constituting the essence of nature and containing the images and figures of the Universal Mind."

"This Light resides in the Water and is hidden as a Seed in all things. Everything that originated from the spirit of light is sustained by it, and therefore this spirit is omnipresent; the whole of nature would perish and disappear if it were removed from it; it is the principium of all things."(J. Tritheim: "Miraculosa," Chap. xiv.)

There were true Alchemists during the Middle Ages who knew how to extract that Seed from the soul-essence of the world, and there are some who have the power to perform that process to-day; but those who do not possess that power will not be inclined to admit the possibility of such facts. "It is an eternal truth, that without our secret magical fire nothing can be accomplished in our art. The ignorant will not believe in it because they do not possess that fire, and without this all their labour is useless. Without that fire spirits cannot be bound, much less can they be acted upon by material fire."

"I am the Light and the Truth"; but he who spoke those words and speaks them still, cannot be made the servant of those who are not themselves that Light; nor can any "Christian Scientist" turn himself into a Christ by believing himself to be Christ. Real knowledge is attained by nothing less than experience. No one becomes a Christ unless the Christ becomes revealed in him.

Some of the more enlightened modern chemists do not deny the possibility that a metal may be transformed into another; but the most serious objections made against the ancient Alchemists is that their object was to make artificial material gold. Such objections are based upon an entire misconception of alchemistical terms. The sole circumstance that certain planetary constellations in the microcosm were of the utmost importance for the success of alchemical processes is sufficient to show that the Alchemists experimented with the souls of things, of which their material forms are only the external representatives on the physical plane. Gold, the purest and most incorruptible metal, represented Spirit, Magnesia wisdom, and Calcinated Magnesia wisdom attained through suffering. Sulphur, Mercury, and Salt represent the trinity of all things, the fiery, watery, and material elements, and have nothing to do with material substances. They are essentially one, but threefold in their manifestation.

Here we are about to divulge one of the secrets of Alchemy, the truth of which will, however, be self-evident. On a preceding page we have explained that in every atom of the body of man are contained all the principles which go to make up the whole organism of man, with all its organs and functions; and likewise, in every atom of matter is contained a principle, which may grow into a whole universe of matter with its great variety of substances. A principle cannot be changed or transformed into another. Principles are eternal. Only the mode of their manifestation may be changed, and the basis of all material things, manifesting itself outwardly as iron or lead, may, under certain conditions, by changing the divine purpose of its existence, be made to manifest itself as silver or gold. The Alchemist does not create any new substance, he merely guides nature, and induces her to grow "the seeds of minerals," in the same sense as a gardener assists nature to grow the seeds of plants, and to develop them into flowers. The Alchemists, therefore, say: `We cannot make gold out of anything which is not gold. To make material gold, we must have spiritual gold; we can merely cause the spiritual gold which exists already to grow into a visible and material form. This process is taught by the science of Alchemy, but this science is necessarily incomprehensible to him who has not arrived at that stage of spiritual knowledge, in which he can exercise a spiritual will, and a "spiritual will" does not exist in a man whose will is not free of material or personal desires. As the gardener puts the seed into the ground, and supplies it with water and with the necessary temperature, likewise the Alchemist "waters" the seeds of the metals with spiritual influences proceeding from his own divine soul. If a true appreciation of these truths is arrived at, it will at once remove Alchemy from the realm of superstition, and bring it within the limits of an exact spiritual science.'

To answer the question whether or not any one ever succeeded in making gold grow in this manner, we will say that there is a German book in existence entitled, "Collection of historical accounts regarding some remarkable occurrences in the life of some still living Adepts." It was printed in 1780; and among many most interesting anecdotes about successful attempts of making gold grow, there are copies of the legal documents and decisions of the court at Leipzig in regard to a case where, during the absence of the Count of Erbach in the year 1715, an Adept visited the countess in the castle of Tankerstein, and out of gratitude for an important service which had been rendered to him by the countess, he transformed all the silver she had into gold. When the count returned, who, as it seems, kept his own property separate from that of his wife, he claimed that gold for himself, appealing to a certain statute of the law, according to which, treasures discovered upon or below the surface of a certain piece of land belong to the proprietor of that territory; but the court decided that as the material (the silver) out of which the gold had been made belonged legally to the countess, consequently this gold could not be classified as a hidden treasure, and did not come within the reach of that statute. The count thereupon lost his case, and his wife was permitted to keep the gold.

We have reasons to believe in the genuineness of these documents; and if looked at from the standpoint of Occultism, it does not at all seem improbable that gold can be made in that manner. Moreover, we have some personal experience to support our belief; for there lived about ten years ago a person whose name was Prestel, within a short distance of the town where we are now writing, who was a reputed Rosicrucian and Alchemist. We personally knew this man, and are well acquainted with two of his still living disciples. This man was generally known as an eccentric and mysterious person. He possessed great powers of projecting the images formed in his own mind upon the minds of others, so that they believed to see things which, however, had no objective existence. For instance he was once waylaid by an enemy, and as the latter bounced upon him, he caused him to see a terrible sight of a scaffold and an executioner, so that the person was terrified and ran away; and it was not Prestel who told this story, but the man himself who attacked him: the former kept silent about it.

Now, this man was not a full-fledged Alchemist, and could not make gold and the Elixir of Life, because, as he said, he could not find a woman sufficiently pure, and at the same time willing, to assist him in his labours; for, as it is known to all Alchemists, it requires the co-operation of the male and the female element to accomplish the highest process. This person could therefore not make pure gold; but he could change the nature of metals so that they would obtain certain chemical qualities, differing from substances of the same kind. He could, so to say, ennoble metals, so that, for instance, Iron or Brass would not rust if exposed to air and water; and we are now in possession of a Rosicrucian Cross made of brass, which, although it is over twenty years old, and has been exposed to salt-water air, and to climates where every other inferior metal rusts, is still as bright as it has been when first received, and it never needed any cleaning or polishing. This person also had the power to cause combustible substances to become incombustible, and he could perform many of the alchemical processes described in the books of T. Tritheim, abbot of Spandau. He insisted that he could have made himself to live a thousand years, if he had found a suitable person to assist him in his alchemical work.

The most important alchemical work is the generation of man; it requires not only the chemical combination of physical substances, but involves the chemistry of the soul and an influence of the spirit, and all must harmoniously act together, if a human being and not a human monster and mental homunculus is to be the result. If the rules of Alchemy were better understood and adhered to, scrofula, cancers, syphilis, tuberculosis, and other inherited diseases would disappear, and a strong and healthy generation of men and women would be the result.

The great alembic [distillation apparatus] in which the passions of men are purified and transformed is the mind. The true magic fire, without which nothing useful can be accomplished, is his self-conscious love, in other words, spiritual recognition of self. Man does not create or originate a thought. Ideas are already in existence. He does not invent ideas, the ideas are already present; he can only collect, elaborate, and modify their expressions.

Thoughts and Ideas

We cannot imagine anything that does not exist, we can only make new combinations of that which is already in existence. We may imagine a snake with the head of a man, because snakes and men do exist; but we cannot imagine the form of an inhabitant of the Sun, because we have no conception of the forms that may be existing under conditions of which we have no experience, and which therefore do not exist for us.

If -- as some modern physiologists believe -- thoughts were a secretion of the brain, as the bile is a secretion of the liver, a thought would be lost as soon as it was expressed, and we would have to wait for the brain to recuperate its power, and to form and secrete another one like it again, before we could have twice the same thought. We would have to be careful not to express our thought or impart our knowledge to others, as by doing so it would be lost to ourselves. Verily, if we seek for absurdities, we need not look for them in ancient books on Alchemy, but find them sufficiently represented in the works of modern scientific authorities. Thoughts and ideas are entities, and exist independently of the perception of man; they do not need man for their existence, but man needs them to enable him to think. Thoughts and ideas, set in motion by the Will, move through space; a thought set in motion in the Astral Ether resembles the expanding ripples upon the surface of a lake; a thought projected to a certain destination by the power of an Adept may be compared to an electric current passing with lightning-velocity through space.

Thoughts directed towards an object are like a mountain stream rushing towards that object, and if the wills of several persons combine to direct it, it grows in extension and force, provided their wills are single-minded and without any secondary designs. *(This law is said to be well known to certain "Jesuits" and employed for the purpose of influencing minds at a distance.)* If a mountain stream strikes a rock, whose resistance it cannot conquer and which it cannot pass, the waters will swell into a lake, devastating the shore and surging back towards its source.

If a thought-current cannot enter the sphere of mind of the individual towards whom it is directed, it rebounds upon the mind of the individual from whom the impulse came. A person who concentrates the full power of a malicious thought upon another may, if he fails to succeed, be killed by the energy which he has called into action.

An illustration of this law may be seen when a person dies of grief on account of disappointment. The ray of force continually projected by long and intense desire, unable to accomplish its purpose, returns to the heart, producing a sudden revulsion of feeling; it changes love into grief, attraction into repulsion, desire into contempt, it may cause sickness and death.

Light travels through the air with a velocity of over 180,000 miles per second; thoughts pass with a similar velocity through space. A ray of light is seen to flash through the air and is intercepted by some nonconducting material. An idea flashes through space and is intercepted by a receptive mind. A sound is heard by an indefinite number of persons, and an idea may affect the world. As a pebble thrown into water produces concentric waves, which grow wider and wider, but less distinct as distance increases, so a thought affects some person, and spreading from that centre creates a ripple in the family, the town, the country, or all over the world.

A biogenesis of thought-infections and mental epidemics might be written. To such an investigation would belong the histories of all great reformations originating from some central idea; also the history of the crusades, the flagellants, the inquisition, mediaeval witchcraft, and modern materialism, and the absurdities of fashion.

Thought Transfer

To give presupposes the ability to receive. The possibility to impress a thought upon another mind presupposes the ability of that mind to receive that impression. A person who is sufficiently sensitive and in a passive condition, will without difficulty be brought under the control of the will of another, and be made to act unconsciously in obedience to that will. A sleeping person may be impressed with such dreams as another may call up in his imagination, by projecting a picture formed in his mind into the mind of the sleeper; a person in a mesmeric trance may have his imagination identified with that of the person who mesmerised him, and be made to comply implicitly with the will of the master.

We see in everyday life that one person subjects another one to his will and causes him to obey his commands without putting him to sleep, and even without expressly stating a wish. A general does not need to hypnotise his soldiers to make them obey his orders. The difference between such an obedient person and one in the hypnotic sleep is merely that the former will not and the latter cannot resist.

An impulse created by the will continues until the energy is exhausted. If the first impulse is followed by a series of others acting in the same direction, the effect will be correspondingly greater, and one person may affect the thoughts of another at a distance of thousands of miles by continually directing his thoughts upon him.

It would be impossible to move inanimate bodies at a distance by the mere power of will, if there were no substantial contact between such objects and the person who attempts to move them. Nevertheless such movements take place, and prove that there must be a contact of some kind, even if it is an invisible one. The Aakaasa furnishes that contact, and the developed willpower of a person may act through the substance of his soul upon the soul of the object, and set that object in motion. In this way tables may be made to talk and bells be made to ring. This, however, cannot be accomplished by everybody; to accomplish this an astral organism is required, and it can therefore be done only by such persons as have their astral body developed and are capable to use its organs at will.

H. P. Blavatsky writes in a private letter to the author: "I proved that all that mediums can do through 'spirits,' others could do at will without any 'spirits'; that the ringing of bells, thought-reading, raps, and physical phenomena could be achieved by anyone who had the faculty of acting in his physical body through the organs of the astral body, and I had that faculty ever since I was four years old. I could make furniture move and objects fly apparently, and by my astral arms that supported them, which remained invisible; all this before I even knew of the Masters."

The thoughts and consciousness of a person or of a number of persons may be projected and concentrated upon any object or to any place that exists within the sphere of their minds. It may be made to inhere in material objects by entering their astral elements and producing corresponding vibrations. Plants or precious stones may be brought in this manner into sympathetic relation with persons, so that if the person is sick or dies, the plants wither and the stones lose their brilliancy. No object in nature is entirely inanimate, and the life-principle is the same in all, whether it be a man or a stone; only the state of their activities differ. If we can induce corresponding vibrations in the souls of a lower order of life, their life will be united with us, because all individual forms are only centres in which the Universal Mind has crystallised into forms, and all forms are related together and bound together by the universal cement of Love. A bird may drop down dead when its mate is killed, a mother may feel the pain of an accident happening to her child, twin-brothers have been known to have become affected simultaneously with the same disease and to die at the same time, although their bodies were far apart from each other. No being stands entirely isolated in nature, all are united by divine love, and the more they become conscious of the love that unites them the more do they realise that they are one.

Unity

Separation and differentiation exists only in regard to the form, the fundamental power is one, and those who have united their minds with that principle know that they are one, and distance forms no impediment to the actions of their minds. Spirit is substance, inseparable, impenetrable, indivisible, and eternal; form is an aggregate, separate, penetrable, divisible and subject to continual change.

The "communion of the saints "is a reality, for they are all one in the spirit. Light is only one. A number of lights in a room are as one light composed of that number. There is only one "Sound" but many expressions. If an orchestra is played in a room, each instrument produces sound, the sound of each fills the whole room and is heard according to its intensity. One instrument may sound louder than another; one light may shine brighter than the rest; but they do not annihilate or extinguish each other. Sound is one, and Light is one, and Spirit is one, only their manifestations differ in quality and in strength.

Love is one, but it manifests itself in various ways. Love unites all. Love is a state of the Will. Thought is directed by will, but the will to be powerful must be pure. If we desire two things at the same time, the will acts in two different directions: but division causes weakness, only in unity is strength. Will is one. The will is an universal principle and not confined within a form. If we concentrate our will and thought united upon a cloud in the sky, we can cause that cloud to dissolve, and the rapidity with which it dissolves will be proportionate to the strength of our concentration of mind.

There will be very few of our readers who have never noticed, that if they pass a certain person in the street, and then turn around to look after him or her, it very often happens that the latter turns at the same time to look after them. This happens so frequent, to be a mere matter of coincidence, and is caused by the fact that the impulse of will of one person can communicate itself to another person. But if one desires to make a person turn around by the effort of his will, and for the purpose of seeing whether he can do so, he will probably fail; because the desire to gratify hi3 curiosity weakens the force of his will; he desires two things at once, and he fails.

Magic Power

As all forms are only external expressions of thought, if we could hold on to a thought and project it, we could create a form. But men do not control thought, they are the victims of it; they do not think what they choose, but what they are forced to think, by the thoughts flying into their minds.

To obtain magic power the first requirement is to learn how to control thought; to command our own moods of mind, and to allow only such ideas to enter the mind as we voluntarily choose to admit. Whoever has for the first time attempted to command a thought, and to hold on to it for five minutes, will have experienced the difficulty, and yet without this first requirement no progress in magic will ever be made.

Before one can become a magician he must learn to control his own mind; for mind is the substance with which the magician acts, and the power to control it is the beginning of magic. No one can control the mind of another as long as he cannot control his own. The will acts outwardly from within the centre of the heart, and no one can make it act beyond the periphery of his body as long as he has not become strong enough to guide it within the body. The neophyte must learn first to control his own emotions before he can control the emotions of others, he must know how to master his thoughts before he can make them objective.

But the mind cannot control its own self, it cannot rise above its own nature. To control the action of the mind a Master is required; this Master is the spirit of man. But spirit without substance is without power; without an organism through which to act, it is merely a spirit. That which controls the mind is the spiritually awakened inner man, the divine nature in man, which is superior to his terrestrial mind.

To change a form we change the state of mind, of which the form is an expression. Certain states of mind find their expressions in certain attitudes, and these attitudes induce corresponding mental states. A proud man will walk erect, a coward will creep, a continually practised creeping walk will develop a cowardly nature, and a habitually erect posture will make a man proud or conscious of his dignity. An actor who can identify himself fully with the personality whose part he plays, need not study attitudes to appear natural; an angry person who forces himself to smile lessens his anger; a person with a continual scowl on the face will find it difficult to be gay. It is on account of the desire to facilitate the entering into certain mental states that certain attitudes have been prescribed in religious ceremonies and acts of devotion.

If the Mind were its own Master, if the actions of the Universal Mind were not subject to the eternal divine law of cause and effect, but guided by the arbitrary whims and notions of some invisible power constituted of Mind without wisdom, the most extraordinary results were liable to follow and the age of actual miracles would begin. The earth would perhaps stand still for a day or a year and begin to revolve again the next; sometimes it might turn fast and at other times slow, and there is no end to the absurdities which might take place; especially if this imaginary power could be induced to follow the advices of its worshippers.

Nature

To the superficial observer the processes of nature seem to be the results of chance. The sun shines and the rain falls upon the land of the pious as well as upon that of the wicked; storms and fires rage, careless whether they destroy the life and property of the learned or that of the ignorant, because they are the necessary results of the law of cause and effect. The interest of individuals cannot control the welfare of the whole. While the welfare of the human body seems to be, to a certain extent, under the control of the will of the individual, the processes of nature, as a whole, appear to be unguided by the reason of the Universal Mind.

The intellect, being unreasonable, is disposed to gauge the absolute reason of the Universal Mind by the relative understanding of comparatively microscopic man. By the same right might the insect crawling in the dust doubt the intelligence of the wanderer, by whose foot it is maimed or killed without consideration and without remorse; such an insect, if capable of reasoning, would discover no intellect in that foot, and yet the man, whose foot is the destroyer, may be highly intellectual.

The cause, why we cannot comprehend the eternal principle of reason in nature, is because it acts according to law, being one with the law; while our intellect, being filled with considerations of self-interests, is not free of desire, and therefore always inclined to act contrary to the law.

Invisible causes produce visible effects, and the same cause, acting under similar conditions, will always produce similar results. Whenever a certain amount of energy has been accumulated, the time will arrive when it will be expended. The accumulated tension between the particles of explosives finds its equilibrium at the approach of a spark; the electric tension established in the upper regions of the air finds its relief in lightning; accumulated emotions will be equilibrised by an outburst of passion; accumulated energies in the soul of the earth produce earthquakes in the body of the earth, in the same manner as an outburst of grief causes the human form to tremble and to shake.

Man's reason may prevent an outburst of his emotions; but where is the personal god to control the emotions of the soul of the world? God does not prevent the growth of warts, or cancers, or tumours; God being the law cannot act in contradiction with himself. His blessings are accompanied by curses. Man's foot crushes the insect, because man's perception and intelligence does not pervade his feet; God does not prevent the growth of a stone in the bladder, because the high cannot manifest itself in the low, wisdom cannot be active in an unconscious form; the means must be adapted to the end.

When universal Man will have so far perfected himself as to be a self-conscious sphere of wisdom without any material parts, then will nature itself be a god. The music that can be made with a harp cannot be made with a stick. The absolute intelligence of the Universal Mind can only manifest itself relatively through instruments adapted to intellectual manifestation. Consciousness can manifest itself as relative consciousness only in conscious forms.

Wisdom

Wisdom is not a product of the organisation of man. It is eternal and universal. It finds its expression in the fundamental laws upon which the universe with all its forms is constructed. It is expressed in the shape of a leaf, in the body of an animal, in the organism of man. Its action can be found everywhere in nature, as long as the beings in nature live according to natural law.

There are no diseases in nature, which have not been originally created by powers which acted contrary to the laws of nature and became therefore unnatural. Outward appearances seem to contradict this assertion; because we find animals affected with diseases, and epidemic diseases are even of frequent occurrence in the vegetable kingdom.

But a deeper investigation into the occult laws of nature will go to show that all the forms of nature, minerals, vegetables, and animals, are merely states or expressions of the Universal Mind of Universal Man. They are the products of the imagination of Nature, and as the imagination of Nature is acted on, influenced and modified by the imagination of man, a morbid imagination of man is followed by a morbid state of Nature, and morbid results follow again on the physical plane. This law explains why periods of great moral depravity, sensuality, superstition, and materialism are always followed by plagues, epidemics, famine, wars, &c., and it would be worth the while to collect statistics to show that such has invariably been the case.

The elementary forces of nature are blind and obey the law that controls them. A motion originated by an impulse continues until the original energy is expended. Stones have no intelligence, because they have no organisation through which intelligence can become manifest, but if an intelligent power sets them into motion, they obey the law of its nature. As the organisms rise in the scale of evolution and development of form, their consciousness becomes more manifest. Consciousness becomes manifest as instinct in the animal creation. It teaches the bird to fly, the fish to swim, the ants to build their houses, the swallows to make their nests. Acting through the nerve centres and the spinal cord it induces the actions of the heart and lungs and other organic and involuntary actions of the body.

As the spinal cord, in the course of evolution, develops into a brain, the principle of consciousness obtains a more perfect instrument for its manifestation. Intellectual power takes the place of instinct, and the Universal Mind begins to think through the individual brain of man, in the same sense as universal nature uses his body for manifesting her powers.

With the highest development of the human brain, the most perfect instrument for the external manifestation of mind is attained. But the essential man is a spirit, and with the development of the most perfect physical form the climax of his spiritual evolution is not reached. The essential man is a spirit and requires a spiritual organisation for the display of his powers. He has within himself the latent power to realise his own divine and universal existence, and to awaken this power hidden within his psychical constitution another light than the light of nature is required.

This Light is the light of Divine Wisdom, one and infinite, and beyond the conception of the brain. It is itself the one eternal Life into which man must enter, if he desires to realise his own immortal existence. To realise that divine universal existence, an organised soul as wide as the universe is required. This soul belongs to the divine man, the Divinity in Humanity, whose material body is the world and whose self-consciousness is Divine Wisdom, the self-recognition of Truth, the Redeemer of All.

Chapter X - Creation

"And God said: Let us make Man." – Bible

What is Man?

The term Creation is frequently misunderstood. Neither the Bible nor any other reasonable book says that anything had ever been created out of nothing. Such a superstition belongs entirely to modern materialistic Science, which believes that life and consciousness could grow out of dead and unconscious things. The word "Creation" means the production of forms out of already existing formless materials; form in the absolute is not a thing, it is nothing but an illusion, and therefore if a form is produced nothing but an illusion has been created.

The most important question that was ever asked, and is still asked with anxiety and often with fear, is the same that was propounded thousands of years ago by the Egyptian Sphinx, who killed him that attempted to solve the riddle and did not succeed: What is Man? Ages have passed away since the question was first asked, nations have slain each other in cruel religious warfare, making vain efforts to impose upon each other such solution of the great problem as they believed they had found, but from the tombs of the past only re-echoes the same question -- What is Man?

And yet the answer seems simple. Reason, if divested of religious or scientific prejudices, tells us that man, like every other form in the universe, is a collective centre of energy, a solitary ray of the universally present Divine Light "which is the common source of everything that exists"; he is a true child of the great Spiritual Sun. As the rays of our sun only become visibly active in contact with dust, so the divine ray is absorbed and reflected by matter.

The sun-ray plays with the waves of the ocean: the heat created by the contact of water with light from above extracts from below the refined material, and the vapours rise to the sky, where, like the ghosts of the seas, they wander in clouds of manifold shapes, travelling freely through the air, playing with the winds, until the time arrives when the energies which keep them suspended become exhausted and they once more descend to the earth.

In a similar manner a divine ray of the spiritual sun mingles with matter while dwelling on Earth, absorbing and assimilating whatever corresponds to its own nature. As the butterfly flits from flower to flower, tasting the sweets of each, so the human monad passes from life to life, from planet to planet, gathering experience, knowledge, and strength; but when the day of life is over, night follows, and with it follows sleep, bringing dreams of vivid reality.

The grossest elements remain to mingle again with earth, the more refined elements -- the astral elements -- which are still within the attraction of the planet, float about, driven hither and thither by their inherent tendencies, until the energy which holds them together is exhausted, and they dissolve again in the plane to which they belong.

But the highest spiritual energies of man, held together by love, freed from the attraction of Earth, ascend to their source like a white-robed spirit, bringing with them the products of experiences beyond the limits of matter.

Man's love and aspiration do not belong to Earth. They create energies which are active beyond the confines of the grave and the funeral-pyre; their activity lasts for ages, until it becomes exhausted, and the purified ray, still endowed with the tendencies impressed upon it by its last visit to the planet, again seeks association with matter, builds again its prison-house of animated clay, and appears an old actor in a new part upon the ever-changing stage of life.

Some of the greatest philosophers have arrived at a recognition of this truth by speculation and logical reasoning, while others, whose minds were illumined by wisdom, have perceived it as a self-evident fact by the power of intuition.

Experience

To build the new house the impressions gathered by its previous visits furnish the material. The slothful rich man of the past may become the beggar of the future, and the industrious worker in the present life develop tendencies which will lay the foundation of greatness in the next. Suffering in one life may produce patience and fortitude that will be useful in another; hardships will produce endurance, self-denial will strengthen the will; tastes engendered in one life will be our guides in another; and latent energies will become active whenever circumstances require it during an existence on the material plane either in one life or another according to the eternal law of cause and effect.

A child burns its fingers by touching the flame, and the adult does not remember all the circumstances under which the accident occurred; still the fact that fire will burn and must not be touched will remain impressed upon the mind. In the same manner the experiences gained in one life are not remembered in their details in the next, but the impressions which they produce will remain. Again and again man passes through the wheel of transformation, changing his lower energies into higher ones, until matter attracts him no longer, and he becomes what he is destined to be, a god.

There is a certain stage in the spiritual evolution of man, when he will remember the events of his previous lives; but to remember them in his present state of imperfection would be merely a hindrance in his progress. It has been said, that by not remembering the errors of our past lives, and their evil consequences, man is liable to commit his previous errors again; but we ought not to do good merely as a matter of speculation and to avoid evil consequences resulting therefrom, but from an inherent sense of duty, regardless of what the resulting consequences may be.

Man, like the majority of organised beings, is an atom in the immensity of the universe; he cannot be divided and still remain a man; but unlike other and lower organised beings, whose realisation of existence is confined to the physical or astral plane, that which constitutes him a Man and distinguishes him from an animal is an integral and conscious part of the highest spiritual energy of the universe, which is everywhere present, and his spiritual consciousness is, therefore, not limited to a certain locality in the physical world.

Evolution

Who made Man? -- Man makes himself during every day of his life. He is his own creator. The clay -- the material body -- that clings to the ray of the manifested Life, is taken from Earth, the energies, called the astral soul, are the products of the astral plane, the highest energies belong to the spirit. Animal man, like the lower orders of nature, is a product of the blind law of necessity, and may even be produced artificially. *(See Paracelsus. "Homunculi.")*

The physical attributes of the child and its mental qualifications are the result of inheritance of previously existing conditions. Like the tree that can send its roots into the neighbouring soil and gather the nutriment by which it is surrounded, but cannot roam about in search of food at distant places, so physical man has only a limited choice in the selection of such means of development as he may require; he grows, because he cannot resist the law of necessity and the impulses given by nature.

But as reason begins to enlighten him, the work of creation begins. The intelligence within says to the will: "Let us make man." She urges the will, and the will sullenly leaves its favourite occupation of serving the passions and begins to mould man in accordance with the divine image held up before him by wisdom. Let us make Man, means: Let us make a divine man out of an animal man; let us surround the divine ray within us with the purest of essences; let us throw off everything which is sensual and grossly material, and which hinders our progress; let us transform the emotions into virtues in which the spiritual ray may clothe itself when it reascends to its throne.

Let us make man! It depends entirely on our efforts what kind of a man we shall make. To make an average man or even a superior one in the common acceptation of the term is not a very difficult matter. Follow the rules of health and the laws of diet, provide above all for yourself and never give anything away, unless by doing so you are sure to get more in return. You will then make a respectable animal, a "self-made" man, prominent, independent, and rich -- one who lives and dies on the plane of selfishness, an object of envy for many; respected perhaps by many, but not by his conscience.

There is another class of self-made men; those on the intellectual plane. They stand before the world as the world's benefactors, as philosophers, teachers, statesmen, inventors, or artists. They have what is called genius, and instead of being mere imitators, they possess originality. They benefit themselves by benefiting the world.

Intellectual researches that benefit no one are unproductive; they resemble physical exercise with dumbbells, by which muscular strength may be gained, but no labour accomplished. An intellectual pursuit may be followed for merely selfish purposes; but unless there is a love for the object of that study, little progress will be made, and instead of a sage, a bookworm will be the result. True genius is a magician who creates a world for himself and for others, and his power expands as he grows in perfection.

Mind and Spirit

The lower intellectual labour alone cannot be the true object of life; the truth cannot be grasped by the unaided efforts of the brain, and he who attempts to arrive at the truth merely by the intellectual labour of the brain, without consulting the heart, will fail. The heart resembles the Sun as the seat of Wisdom, the brain corresponds to the Moon; it is the seat of the reasoning intellect, and receives its light and life from the Sun. If the Sun stands guard over the Moon, thoughts which are distasteful to the heart will not enter the brain. The heart and the head should work together in harmony, to kill the dragon of ignorance, dwelling upon the threshold of the temple, and to arrive at the truth.
In the allegorical books of the Alchemists the Sun represents Intelligence; he is the "heart" of our solar system; the Moon represents dreams and desires or the "brain"; Earth represents the physical Body. If the male Sun cohabits with the female Moon in the water of Truth, they will produce a son whose name is Wisdom. The intellect is the material man whose bride is spiritual understanding, the divine woman; no man or woman is perfect as long as the celestial marriage has not taken place through the power of Divine Love. *(Compare "The Perfect Way, or the Finding of Christ.")*
The materials of which Man is constructed are the principles that flow into him from the store-house of universal nature, the builder is the will, reason the superintendent, and wisdom the supreme architect. The building goes on without noise, and no sound of the hammer is heard, because the materials are already prepared by nature; they only require to be put into their proper places.

The highest is the Spirit or "Consciousness," and Spirit alone is immortal. Such of the lower elements as harmonise with it amalgamate with the spirit, and are rendered conscious and immortal. Spirit can only find its corresponding vibrations in the highest spiritual elements of the soul such as are furnished by the higher principles, and consist of the purest thoughts, aspirations, and memories produced by the fifth, in which resides the intellectual power of man. Pure intelligence is Spirituality, but intellectual activity confined within the lower planes of thought can bring to light no spiritual treasures. Intellectual activity is not a power; but the result of the power of spirit acting within the mind. A very intellectual and learned person may be very unhappy and unharmonious, if his tendencies are towards selfishness, and his mind incapable to be illuminated by the light of truth. Wisdom is the self-recognition of the truth; it resides in the spiritual soul of man, and sends its light down into his fifth principle, shining through the clouds of matter like the sunlight penetrating a fog.

The fifth principle receives its stimulus from the fourth, the irrational nature of man. We cannot build a house without solid material, and we may just as well attempt to run a steam-engine without fuel or water as to make a genius out of a being without any emotions. The stronger the emotions are, the more enduring will be the spiritual temple, if they can be made to fit into the walls and pillars. A person originally without any emotions is without virtues, he is without energy, a shadow, neither cold nor warm, and necessarily useless. The passionate man is nearer to the spirit, if he can guide his passions in the right direction, than the man who has nothing to guide and nothing to conquer.

Emotion

To produce a perfect building, or a perfect man, the proportions must be harmonious. Wisdom guides the work and love furnishes the cement. An emotion is either a virtue or a vice according to the manner in which it is applied. Misapplied virtues become vices, and well-directed vices are virtues. A man who acts according to the dictates of prudence alone is a coward; one who indiscriminately exercises his generosity is a spendthrift; courage without caution is rashness; veneration without knowledge produces superstition; charity without judgment makes a beggar, and even one-sided justice, untempered by mercy, produces a miserly, cruel, and despicable tyrant.
The irrational soul, impelled only by its desires and unguided by wisdom, resembles a drunken man who has lost his physical balance; it totters from side to side, falls from one extreme into another, and cannot guide its steps. Only an equilibrium of forces can produce harmony, beauty, and perfection. The irrational soul, swayed by uncontrollable emotions, forms an unfit habitation for the divine ray, that loves peace and tranquillity.
The control of the emotions is the difficult struggle that is allegorically represented by the twelve labours of Hercules, which the oracle of Zeus commanded him to perform. Every man who desires to progress is his own Hercules and works for the benefit of the king (his Atma), whose orders he receives through the divine oracle of his own conscience. He is constantly engaged in battle, because the lower principles fight for their lives and will not be conquered. They are the products of matter and they cling to their source.

Whence do the emotions come?

The cosmologies of the ancients express under various allegories the same fundamental truth; that "in the beginning" the Great First Cause evolved out of itself, by the power of its own will, certain powers, whose action and reaction brought the elementary forces that constituted the world into existence. These elementary forces are the Devas of the East, the Elohims of the Bible, the Afrites of the Persians, the Titans of the Romans, the Eggregores of the book of Enoch. They are the active agents of the cosmos, beneficial or detrimental according to the conditions under which they act, intelligent or unintelligent according to the nature of the instrument through which they work. They are not necessarily self-conscious rational entities, but may manifest themselves through conscious organisms endowed with reason; they are not persons, but become personified by finding expression in individual forms.

Love and hate, envy and benevolence, lust and greed are not persons, but become personified in human or animal forms. An extremely malicious person is the embodiment of malice, and if he sees the demon in an objective form, he beholds the reflection of his own soul in the mirror of his mind. Spirit exists everywhere, but we cannot perceive a spirit unless it first enters the sphere of our soul.

The spirit that enters our soul obtains its life from ourselves, and if we do not expel it from our soul it grows strong by vampirising our life. Like a parasite growing on a tree and feeding on its substance, it fastens its feelers around the tree of our life and grows strong while our own life grows weak. A thought, once taking root in the mind, will grow until it becomes expressed in an act, when, obtaining a life of its own by that act, it leaves its place to a successor.

Those elementary forces of nature are everywhere, and always ready to enter the soul if its doors are not defended. To call up a wicked spirit we need not go in search of him, we need only allow him to come. To call up a devil means to give way to an evil thought, to vanquish him means to resist successfully a temptation to evil.

Elementary Powers

The elementary powers of nature are innumerable, and their classification gave rise to the pantheons of the Greeks and to the mythologies of the East. The greatest power is Zeus, the father of the gods, or the source from which all other powers take their origin. Minerva, the goddess of wisdom, springs from his head, her origin is the noblest of all, but Venus, the daughter of the Sun, arising from the ocean of the universal Soul, conquers all by her beauty. She holds together the worlds in space by the power of her attraction, binds souls to souls, chains the like to like, and binds the evil to evil.

She is the mother of the minor gods that combat each other, because love of self, love of possession, love of fame, love of power, &c., are all only children of the universal power of love. They fight among themselves like children, because action gives rise to reaction, love is opposed by hate, hope by fear, faith by doubt, &c. To control them the god of Power (Mars) must be united with the goddess of Love -- in other words, the passions must be held in obedience by the Will.

Each power exists and is held in its elementary matrix or vehicle, the Aakaasa, the Universal Proteus, the generator of form, which finds its outward expression in Matter, and these powers constitute the eternal circle, or the snake, "whose head shall be crushed by the heel of the woman," meaning Wisdom, the eternal virgin, whose "daughters" are faith, hope, and charity.

The snake cannot enter the soul, if the soul is defended by wisdom. If an evil thought enters the soul and we do not reject it, we harbour a devil in our heart, whose claims we take into consideration; we give him a promise and induce him to remain, and, like an unwelcome creditor, he will continually urge his claims until they are fulfilled.

The lower triads of principles in the constitution of man receive their nutriment from the inferior kingdoms of nature. If the body is overfed or stimulated by drink, the emotional element will become excessively active and the intellect will become weak. Too stimulating food or drink is injurious for higher development, because life will in such cases withdraw its activity from the higher principles and be made to work in the lower principles of man. Large quantities of otherwise healthy food will be injurious for the same reason.

Vegetable Diet

The principle of life which transforms the lower energies into higher ones is the same principle which causes the digestion of food. If it is squandered in the lower organs, the higher organs will starve. Some men are habituated to meat-eating, and they require it; others are used to alcohol, and if they would suddenly discontinue its use they will suffer; but meat and alcohol are, under normal conditions, unnecessary for the human system, and often they act positively injurious.

The principle argument of the lovers of animal food is that it "gives bodily strength, and is necessary for those who have to perform manual labour." This argument is based upon an erroneous opinion, because animal food does not give as much strength as a vegetable diet *(According to the calculations made by Prov. J. v. Liebig, the same amount of albuminous [protein] substances for which, if in the form of animal food, is paid 100d., can be bought in the shape of peas for 9d., and in that of wheat for 4d.);* it only stimulates the organism, and induces it to use up the strength which it already possesses in a short period of time instead of saving it up for the future. The consequences of an exclusive animal diet, gluttony, extreme sensuality, combativeness, cruelty, and stupidity, indolence, physical and psychical apathy, are the necessary consequences of over-stimulation. Darwin says that "the hardest-working people he ever met are the persons that work in the mines of Chili, and that they are living on an exclusively vegetable diet." The country people in Ireland live almost without meat-eating, and yet they are strong and enduring. The common Russian eats very little meat and enjoys good health.

The strongest people that can perhaps be found anywhere are the country people in the South of Bavaria, and they eat meat only on exceptional occasions and holy-days. Horses, bulls, elephants, are the strongest animals, and live on vegetable food, while the prominent traits of character of the flesh-eating animals are cowardice, irritability, and cunning. A bear kept at the Anatomical Museum at Giessen showed a quiet, gentle nature as long as he was fed on bread, but a few days' feeding on meat made him, not stronger, but vicious and dangerous.

Let those who desire to know the truth in regard to meat-eating seek the answers to their questions, not with the intellect of the head, but through the voice of wisdom speaking in the interior of their heart, and they will not be mistaken. *(See Dr A. Kingsford: "The Perfect Way in Diet.")*

Another question arises in regard to the eating of flesh; it is the question whether or not man has a right to kill animals for his food. To the professed Christians who claim to believe in the Bible there seems to be no cause for any doubt, because the command is plain: "Thou shall not kill." And yet this command is disregarded daily by millions of professed "Christians," who base their illusory right to kill animals upon a misunderstood verse of their Bible. It is said that God permitted man to "have dominion over the fish of the sea, and over the fowls of the air, and over the cattle, and over every living thing that moveth upon the earth,"*(Genesis i. 26.)* if he kills his inferiors, his dominion over them is at an end. Man's prerogative is to appease suffering, not to cause it; not to interrupt the work of evolution, but to assist it. Christianity and murder are incompatible terms.

Meat is stimulating, and stimulating food creates a desire for stimulating drink. The best cure for the desire for alcoholic drink is to avoid the eating of meat. It is doubtful whether there is any passion in the world more devilish and more detrimental to the true interests of humanity and of individual happiness than the love of Alcohol. As meat-eating endows man with illusory strength, that soon fades away, leaving its possessor weaker than he was before; likewise stimulating drinks lull him into an illusory happiness, which soon disappears, and is followed by lasting and real misery, causing suffering to himself and to others.

It causes a long list of diseases of the internal organs, and leads to premature death; it is the cause of by far the great majority of all crimes committed in civilised countries. To those who look upon man as a rational being, it seems incomprehensible why civilised nations will suffer an evil in their midst that fills their jails, hospitals, lunatic asylums, and graveyards; and why men will "put an enemy in their mouths" that destroys their health, their reason, and their life. But those who look deeper see that in our present age the dawn of reason has only begun, and that the spiritual faculties of the majority of men still sleep in the icy embrace of ignorance. Reforms are necessary, but they cannot be inaugurated by merely external means; the only redeemer is knowledge. *(See Dr A. Kingsford: "The Alcoholic Controversy.")*

The body politic resembles the individual body. It is of no use to destroy the means to gratify a desire as long as the desire itself is suffered to exist. The evils that affect mankind are the outcome of their desires for such evils. Means to gratify evil desires will exist as long as they are patronised, and if they are abolished other means will be found. Weeds are not destroyed by cutting their leaves, if the roots are allowed to remain. These roots grow in the dark soil of ignorance, they can only be destroyed by the light of the truth.

To eat and drink and sleep for the purpose of living, and not to live for the purpose of eating, drinking, and sleeping, is a maxim which is often heard, but which is not frequently carried out. A great deal of nutriment daily taken by men serves no other purpose than to comply with habit, and to gratify an artificially created desire. The more a man is gross and material, the greater is the quantity of food he desires, and the more food he takes the more gross and material will he become. Noble and refined natures require little nutriment, ethereal beings and "spiritual" entities require no material food.

The means should always be adapted to the end in view. If the end is low and vulgar, low and vulgar means will be needed; if it is noble and high, equally high and noble means are required. A prize-fighter, whose main object is to develop muscle, will require a different training from that of one who desires to develop the faculty to perceive spiritual truths. Conditions that may be suitable for the development of one person may be impracticable for another.

One man will develop faster through poverty, another through wealth; one man may need as his initial psychic stimulus the gentle and exalting influences of married life, while another one's aspirations rise higher, if independent of earthly ties. Each man who exercises his will for the purpose of his higher development is, to the extent he exercises it, a practical occultist. Every one grows necessarily in one direction or in another; none remain stationary. Those who desire to outstrip others in growth must act.

Perfection

One of the Tibetan Adepts says in a letter --

"Man is made up of ideas, and ideas guide his life. The world of subjectivity is the only reality to him even on this physical plane. To the occultist it grows more real as it goes further and further from illusory earthly objectivity, and its ultimate reality is Parabrahm. Hence an aspirant for occult knowledge should begin to concentrate all his desires on the highest ideal, that of absolute self-sacrifice, philanthropy, divine kindness, as of all the highest virtues obtainable on this Earth [the paramitas], and work up to it incessantly.

"The more strenuous his efforts to rise up to that ideal, the oftener is his willpower exercised, and the stronger it becomes. When it is thus strengthened, it sets up a tendency, in the gross shell of Stula-sharira, [gross or physical body] to do such acts as are compatible with the highest ideal he has to work up to, and his acts intensify his will-power doubly, owing to the operation of the well-known law of action and reaction. Hence in Occultism great stress is laid on practical results.

"Now the question is: What are these practical results, and how are they to be produced? It is a well-known fact, derived from observation and experience, that progress is the law of nature. The acceptance of this truth suggests the idea, that humanity is in its lower state of development, and is progressing towards the stages of perfection. It will approach the final goal when it develops new sensibilities and a clear relation with nature. From this it is obvious that a final state of perfection will be arrived at when the energy that animates man co-operates with the One Life operating in the Cosmos in achieving this mighty object; and knowledge is the most powerful means to that end.

"Thus it will be clear that the ultimate object of nature is to make man perfect through the union of the human spirit with the One Life. Having this final goal before our mind, an intellectual brotherhood should be formed by uniting all together, and this is the only stepping-stone towards the final goal. To produce this practical result, union, we must hold up the highest ideal, which forms the real man, and make others see that truth and act up to it. To lead our neighbours and fellow-creatures to this right path, the best means should be pursued with self-sacrificing habits. When our energy as a collective whole is thus expended, in working up to the highest ideal, it becomes potent, and the grandest results are produced on the spiritual plane.

"As this is the most important work in which every occultist should be engaged, an aspirant for higher knowledge should spare no efforts to bring about this end. With the progressive tide of evolution of the body as a whole, the mental and the spiritual faculties of humanity expand. To help this tide on, a knowledge of philosophical truths should be spread. This is what is expected from an aspirant for occult knowledge, and what he should do."

Faith and Will

The will is developed through action and strengthened by faith. The movements of the body, such as walking, are only successfully performed by a person because he has a full and unwavering faith in his power to perform them. Fear and doubt paralyse the will and produce impotency; but hope and faith produce marvellous results. The lawyer or physician who has no faith in his own ability will make blunders, and if his clients or patients share his doubts, his usefulness will be seriously impaired; whereas even the ignorant fanatic or quack may succeed, if he has faith in himself.

Lord Lytton says: "The victims of the ghostly one are those that would aspire and can only fear." Fear and Doubt are the hell-born daughters of ignorance that drag man down to perdition; while Faith is the white-robed angel that lends him her wings and endows him with power. "Samsayatma Vinasyati" (the doubter perishes), said Krishna to Arjuna, his favourite disciple.

Faith is soul-knowledge; therefore, even without intellectual knowledge, it is more useful than intellectual knowledge without faith. Strong faith, even if resting upon an erroneous conception, acts powerfully in producing results; faith produces an exalted state of the imagination, which strengthens the will, banishes pain, cures disease, leads to heroism, and transforms hell into heaven. The only way to develop will-power is to act according to law. Each act creates a new impulse, which, added to the already-existing energy, increases its strength. Good acts increase the power for good; evil acts, the power for evil. A person who acts only from impulse manifests no will of his own. If he obeys his lower impulses he passively develops into a criminal or a maniac; he who acts by the impulse of divine wisdom is a god.

The most horrible crimes are often committed without any proportionate provocation, because the perpetrators had not the power to resist the impulses that prompted them to such acts. Such persons are not necessarily wicked; they are weak and irresponsible beings; they are the servants of the impulses that control them, and they can be made the helpless instruments and victims of those who know how to call forth their emotions. They are like the soldiers of two opposing armies, who are not necessarily personal enemies; but are made to hate and kill each other by appeals to their passions.

The oftener such persons give way to impulses, the more is their power of resistance diminished, and their own impotency is their ruin. It is of little use to be merely passively good, if abstinence from wrong-doing may be so called. A person who does neither good nor evil accomplishes nothing. A stone, an animal, an imbecile, may be considered good, because they do no active evil; a person may live a hundred years, and at the end of his life he may not have been more useful than a stone. *("He who is neither hot nor cold, but lukewarm, will be spued out by nature." -- Bible. [Revelation 3:16])*

Development of the Will

There is nothing in nature which has not a threefold aspect and a threefold activity. The Will-power forms no exception to this rule. In its lowest aspect the Will is that power which induces the voluntary and involuntary functions of the physical organism; its centre of activity is the spinal cord. In its higher aspect it is the power which induces psychic activity; it is diffused through the blood which comes from the heart and returns to it, and its actions are governed, or can be governed, by intellect acting in the brain by means of the impulses, influences, and auras radiating from there. In its highest aspects the Will is a living and self-conscious power having its centre in Wisdom.

The will, to become powerful, must be free of desire. If we desire an object, we do not attract that object, but the object attracts us. Eliphas Levi says: "The Will accomplishes everything which it does not desire"; and the truth of this paradox is seen in every-day life. Those who crave for fame or riches are never contented; the rich miser is poorer than the beggar in the street; happiness is a shadow that flies before him who seeks it in material pleasures. The surest way to become rich is by being contented with what we have; the safest way to obtain power is to sacrifice ourselves for others; and if we desire love, we must distribute the love we possess to others, and then the love of others will descend upon us like the rain descends upon the earth.

The development of the will is a process of growth, and the only true way to develop the Will is by being obedient to the universal Law. If we wish to use nature, we must act according to natural law; if we wish to use spiritual powers, we must act in obedience to the spiritual law. Then will we become masters of Nature and God, and our Will will become a serviceable instrument for the fulfilment of law; but as long as the Will is governed by personal desire, it is not we who control our will, but it is our desire. As long as we do the will of the lower animal I, we cannot be gods; only when we perform the will of the Divinity, we will become free of the bondage of the animal elements, and our true Self will be the Master.

Man in his youth longs for the material pleasures of earth, for the gratification of his physical body. As he advances, he throws away the playthings of his childhood and reaches out for something higher. He enters into intellectual pursuits, and after years of labour he may find that he has been wasting his time by running after a shadow. Perhaps love steps in and he thinks himself the most fortunate of mortals, only to find out, sooner or later, that ideals can only be found in the ideal world.

He becomes convinced of the emptiness of the shadows he has been pursuing, and, like the winged butterfly emerging from the chrysalis, he stretches out his feelers into the realm of infinite spirit, and is astonished to find a radiant sun where he only expected to find darkness and death. Some arrive at this light sooner; others arrive later, and many are lured away by some illusive light and perish, and like insects that mistake the flame of a candle for the light of the sun, scorch their wings in its fire.

Life is a continual battle between error and truth; between man's spiritual aspirations and the demands of his animal instincts. There are two gigantic obstacles in the way of progress: his misconception of the nature of God and of Man. As long as man believes in an extracosmic personal God distributing favours to some and punishing others at pleasure, a God that can be reasoned with, persuaded, and pacified by ignorant man, he will keep himself within the narrow confines of his ignorance, and his mind cannot expand. To think of some place of personal enjoyment or heaven, does not assist man's progression.

If such a person desists from doing a wicked act, or denies himself a material pleasure, he does not do so from any innate love of good; but either because he expects a reward from God for his "sacrifice," or because his fear of God makes him a coward. We must do good, not on account of any personal consideration, but because to do good is our duty. To be good is to be wise; the fool expects rewards; the wise expects nothing. The wise knows that by benefiting the world he benefits himself, and that by injuring others he becomes his own executioner.

Power of Life

What are the powers of Man, by which he may benefit the world? Man has no powers belonging to himself. Even the substance of which his organisation is made up, does not belong but is only lent to him by Nature, and he must return it. He cannot make any use of it, except through that universal power, which is active within his organisation, which is called the Will, and which itself is a function of an universal principle, the Spirit.

Man as a personal and limited being is merely a manifestation of this universal principle in an individual form, and all the spiritual powers he seems to possess belong to the Spirit. Like all other forms in nature he receives life, light, and energy from the universal fountain of Life, and enjoys their possession for a short span of time; he has no powers whatever which he may properly call his own.

Thus the sunshine and rain, the air and earth, does not belong to a plant. They are universal elements belonging to nature. They come and help to build up the plant, they assist in the growth of the rosebush as well as the thistle; their business is to develop the seed, and when their work is done, the organism in which they were active returns again to its mother, the Earth. There is then nothing which properly belongs to the plant; but the seed continues to exist without the parental organism after having attained maturity, and in it is contained the character of the species to which it belongs.

Life, sensation, and consciousness are not the property of personal man; neither does he produce them. They are functions of the Spirit and belong originally to God. The One Life furnishes the principles which go to build up the organism called Man, the forms of the good as well as those of the wicked. They help to develop the germ of Intelligence in man, and when their work is done they return again to the universal fountain.

The germ of Divinity is all there is of the real man, and all that is able to continue to exist as an individual, and it is not a man, but a Spirit, one and identical in its essence with the Universal God, and one of his children. How many persons exist in whom this divine germ reaches maturity during their earthly life? How many die before it begins to sprout? How many do not even know that such a germ exists?

To this Universal Principle belong the functions which we call Will and Life and Light; its foundation is Love. To it belong all the fundamental powers which produced the universe and man, and only when man has become one and identical with God or to speak more correctly, when he has come to realise his oneness with God, can he claim to have powers of his own.

But the Will of this Universal Power is identical with universal Law, and man who acts against the Law acts against the Will of God, and as God is man's only real eternal Self, he who acts against that Law destroys himself.

The first and most important object of man's existence is, therefore, that he should learn the law of God and of Nature, so that he may obey it and thereby become one with the law and live in God. A man who knows the Law knows himself, and a man who knows his divine Self knows God.

The only power which man may rightfully claim his own is his Self-knowledge; it belongs to him because he has required it by the employment of the powers lent to him by God. Not the "knowledge" of the illusions of life, for such knowledge is illusive, and will end with those illusions; not mere intellectual learning, for that treasure will be exhausted in time; but the spiritual self-knowledge of the heart, which means the power to grasp the truth which exists in ourselves.

What has been said about the Will is equally applicable to the Imagination. If man lets his own thoughts rest, and rises up to the sphere of the highest ideal, his mind becomes a mirror wherein the thoughts of God will be reflected, and in which he may see the past, the present, and future; but if he begins to speculate within the realm of illusions, he will see the truth distorted and behold his own hallucinations.

Rules of Life

The knowledge of God and the knowledge of man are ultimately identical, and he who knows himself knows God. If we understand the nature of the divine attributes within us, we will know the Law. It will then not be difficult to unite our Will with the supreme Will or the cosmos; and we shall be no longer subject to the influences of the astral plane, but be their masters. Then will the Titans be conquered by the gods; the serpent in us will have its head crushed by Divine Wisdom; the devils within our own hells will be conquered, and instead of being ruled by illusions, we shall be ruled by Wisdom.

It is sometimes said that it does not make any difference what a man believes so long as he acts rightly; but a person cannot be certain to act rightly unless he knows what is right. The belief of the majority is not always the correct belief, and the voice of reason is often drowned in the clamour of a superstition based upon erroneous theological doctrine. An erroneous belief is detrimental to progress in proportion as it is universal; such belief rests on illusion, knowledge is based on truth. The greatest of all religious teachers therefore recommended Right Belief as being the first step on the Noble Eightfold Path.

The eight stages on the noble eightfold Path to find the truth are, according to the doctrine of Gautama Buddha, the following:

1. Right Belief
2. Right Thought
3. Right Speech
4. Right Doctrine
5. Right Means of Livelihood
6. Right Endeavour
7. Right Memory
8. Right Meditation

The man who keeps these augas in mind and follows them will be free from sorrow, and may become safe from future rebirths with their consequent miseries.

Perhaps it will be useful to keep in mind the following rules:

Do not believe that there is anything higher in the universe than your own divine self, and know that you are exactly what you permit yourself to become. The true religion is the recognition of divine truth; idols are playthings for children.

Learn that man is essentially a component and integral part of universal humanity, and that what is done by one individual acts and reacts on all.

Realise that man's nature is an embodiment of ideas, and his physical body an instrument which enables him to come into contact with matter; and that this instrument should not be used for unworthy purposes. It should neither be worshipped nor neglected.

Let nothing that affects your physical body, its comfort, or the circumstances in which you are placed, disturb the equilibrium of your mind. Crave for nothing on the material plane, live about it without losing control over it. Matter forms the steps upon which we may ascend to the kingdom of heaven.

Never expect anything from anybody, but be always ready to assist others to the extent of your ability, and according to the requirements of justice. Never fear anything but to offend the moral law, and you will not suffer. Never hope for any reward and you will not be disappointed. Never ask for love, sympathy, or gratitude from anybody, but be always ready to bestow them on others. Such things come only when they are not desired.

Learn to distinguish and to discriminate between the true and the false, and act up to your highest ideal. Grieve not if you fall, but rise and proceed on your way. Learn to appreciate everything (yourself included) at its true value in all the various planes. A person who attempts to look down upon one who is his superior is a fool, and a person who looks up to one who is inferior is mentally blind. It is not sufficient to believe in the value of a thing, its value must be realised, otherwise it resembles a treasure hidden in the vaults of a miser.

Louis Claude de Saint Martin (the Unknown Philosopher) [First to translate the writings of Jakob Böhme from German into French: Wikipedia] says:

"This is what should pass in a man who is restored to his divine proportions through the process of regeneration:

"Not a desire, but in obedience to the law.

"Not an idea, which is not a sacred communication with God.

"Not a word, which is not a sovereign decree.

"Not an act, which is not a development and extension of the vivifying rule of the Word.

"Instead of this, our desires are false, because they come from ourselves.

"Our thoughts are vague and corrupt, because they form adulterous alliances.

"Our words are without efficacy, because we allow them to be blunted every day by the heterogeneous substances to which we continually apply them.

"Our acts are insignificant and barren, because they can but be the results of our words."

The best of all instructions for becoming spiritual and ultimately divine are to be found in the Bhagavad Gita. They also teach that man needs not to exert his self-will for the purpose of saving himself; for Krischna says: "Devote thy heart to Me, worship Me, sacrifice yourself to Me, bow down before Me, so shalt thou surely come to me";*(Bhagavad Gita, xviii. 65.)* and the prayer of the Christians says: "Let thy will be done on earth (in our mortal nature) as it is done in heaven (in our spiritual nature)."

Such and similar instructions are nothing new; they have been pronounced in various forms by the philosophers of all ages, and have been collected in books, and men have read them without getting any better for it, because they could not realise the necessity for following such advice.

These doctrines have been taught by the ancient Rishis and Munis, by Buddha and Christ, Confucius, Zoroaster and Mahomed, Plato, Luther and Shakespeare, and every reformer. They have been preached in sermons, and written in poems and prose, in works of philosophy, literature, fiction, and art. They have been heard by all, understood by some, and practised by a few. To learn them is easy, to realise them is difficult, to adopt them in practical life is divine.

The highest spiritual truths cannot be intellectually grasped, the reasoning powers of half-animal man cannot conceive of their importance; terrestrial man can only look up to those ideals which are perceptible to his spiritual vision in moments of aspiration, and only gradually can he grow up into that plane when, becoming less animal and more spiritual, he will be able to realise the fact that this growth is not necessary to please a god whose favour must be obtained, or to insure a happy animal life; but that he himself becomes a god by that growth, and learns to experience his own immortal existence.

The highest energies are latent in the lower ones; they are the attributes of the spiritual soul, which in the majority of men is still in a state of infancy, but which in future generations will be more universally developed, when humanity as a whole, having progressed higher, will look back upon our present era as the age of ignorance and misery, while they themselves will enjoy the fruits of the higher evolution of Man.

Chapter XI - Light

"Let there be Light." – **Bible**

Form and Light

Form, personality, and sensuality are the death of spirit: the dissolution of form, loss of personality and unconsciousness of sensuous perceptions, render spirit free and restore it to life. The elementary forces of nature, bound to forms, become the prisoners of the forms. Being entombed in matter they lose their liberty of action and move only in obedience to external impulses; the more they cling to form, the more dense, compact, heavy, and dull will they become, and the less will they be self-acting and free.

Sunlight and heat are comparatively free; their elements travel from planet to planet, until they are absorbed by earthly forms. Crystallised into matter they sleep in trees and forests and fields of coal, until they are liberated by the slow decomposition of form, or forcibly restored to freedom by the god of fire.

The waves of ocean and lake play joyfully with the shore. Full of mirth they throw their spray upon the lazy rocks. The laughing waters of the wandering brook glide restlessly through forest and field, dancing and whirling and playing with the flowers that grow by the side of their road. They rush without fear over precipices, falling in cascades over the mountain sides, uniting, dividing, and uniting again, mingling with rivers and resting at last for a while in the sea.

But when winter arrives and King Frost puts his icy hand upon their faces, they crystallise into individual forms, they are then robbed of their freedom, and like the damsels and knights of the enchanted castle, they are doomed to sleep until the warm breath of youthful Spring breaks the spell of the sorcerer, and kisses them back into life.

The fundamental laws of nature are the same in all her departments, and man forms no exception to the general rule. He is a centre around which some of the intelligent as well as some of the unintelligent forces have crystallised into a form. Bound by the laws of the Karma which that centre created, they are doomed to dwell in a form, and to partake of the accidents to which forms are exposed; imprisoned in a personality, they partake of the sufferings which the tendencies of that personality have called into existence.

They may be exposed to desires whose thirst increases in proportion as they are furnished with drink, to passions whose fire burns hotter in proportion as their demand for fuel is granted, they are tempted to run after shadows that ever fly, to grasp at hopes that ever beckon and vanish as soon as they are approached, to sorrows that enter the house although the doors may be closed against them, to fears whose forms have no substance, to illusions that disappear only with the life of the form. Like Prometheus bound to a rock, the impersonal spirit is chained to a personality, until the consciousness of his herculean power awakes in him, and bursting his chains he becomes again free.

The Spirit of Man

Not all the elements that go to make up a complete man are enclosed in his material form. The far greater part of them is beyond the limits of his physical body; the latter is merely a centre in which those invisible elements meet. The body of man does not enclose the sphere of his spirit; his soul is far greater than the circumference of his form. *(For this reason persons manifesting great genius have been called "great souls" or "Mahatmas," from "maha" great and "atma" the soul.)* The elements that exist beyond the limits of his visible organism stand in intimate relation with those that are within, although the elements within the form may not seem to be conscious of the existence of those beyond. Still they act and react upon each other.

The mind of man is far more important than his physical form. Thought can create a form, but no form can produce a thought; and yet the substance of thought is invisible as long as it has not clothed itself in a form. Air exists within and beyond the physical body; it is invisible and yet it is an important element of the body, a man who could not breathe would be very incomplete. The ocean of mind in which man exists is as necessary to his soul-life as the air is to his body, he cannot breathe if deprived of air; he cannot think if deprived of mind. The outer acts upon the inner, the inner upon the outer, the above upon the below, the great upon the little, and the little upon the great. A man who could live independent of his surroundings would be self-existent, he would be a god.

The spirit is not confined by the form, it only overshadows the form; the form does not contain the spirit, it is only its outward expression; it is the instrument upon which the spirit plays, and which reacts upon its touch, while the spirit responds to its vibrations. An ancient proverb says: "Everything that exists upon the Earth has its ethereal counterpart above the Earth, and there is nothing, however insignificant it may appear in the world, which is not depending on something higher; so that, if the lower part acts, its preceding higher part reacts upon it."*(Sohar Wajecae.)*

The greatest philosophers in ancient times taught that the νομς (Greek: noms) that alone recognised noumena, always remained outside the physical body of man; that it overshadowed his head, and that only the ignorant believed it existed within themselves. Modern philosophers have arrived at similar conclusions. Fichte writes: "The real spirit which comes to itself in human consciousness is to be regarded as an impersonal pneuma -- universal reason -- and the good of man's whole development therefore can be no other than to substitute the universal for the individual consciousness."

The Real Self

The Bhagavad Gita says: "The Supreme Brahma is within and without all beings; motionless and yet moving. Not distributed in beings, yet constantly distributed in them. He is the light of all luminous things and in everything its perfection." *(Bhagavad Gita, xiii.)* And the same truth, speaking through the mouth of Jesus of Nazareth, says: "I am the Light of the world. He that followeth me shall not walk in darkness but shall have the light of life." *(St John, viii. 12.*

The greatest of all teachers, Gautama Buddha, says:
"The permanent never mingles with the impermanent, although the two are one. Only when all outward appearances are gone, is that one principle of life left, which exists independently of all external phenomena. It is the fire that burns within the external light when the fuel is expended and the flame is extinguished, for that fire is neither in the flame nor in the fuel, nor yet inside either of the two, but above, beneath, and everywhere."

This principle, in which rests the self-recognition of eternal truth is the real Ego of every human being, and he who succeeds in attaining self-knowledge of it has found the Christ. It is the true and living Christ of the real Christians, not the dead "Jesus" but the living Saviour, the Divinity, who, being born in our Humanity, remains with his followers unto the end of the world. Everyone who unites his own soul with that Christ -- no matter what his creed or confession may be -- will become as true and veritable a Christ as ever lived upon the Earth. It is the λογος (Greek: logos) of the ancients, the Adam Kadom of the Hebrews, the Osiris of the Egyptians, the Iswar of the Hindus, the way, the light, and the truth, the divine Self of every man and the Redeemer for all.*("Though Christ a thousand times in `Bethlehem' is born; If he's not born in thee, thy soul is all forlorn."- Angelus Silesius)*

Hermes Trismegistus says of that being called Man: "Its father is the Sun (Divine Wisdom), his mother the stars (the Astral light) and his body the generations of men."

The whole of a man is not enclosed within the small circle that circumscribes his terrestrial life. He who has found the "Father" within himself knows the true insignificance of his own personal self. The life of the personality is made up of a comparatively small number of years passed among the illusions of the terrestrial plane; the experience of the inner man is made up of the essence of a great many of such lives; he has retained of them only that which is useful and grand, while the worthless materials have been rejected, but the life of the Divine man is eternal, universal, self-existent, and infinite.

He who has once realised the presence of his God laughs at the idea of having ever imagined himself to be something more than a bundle of semi-conscious elements from which the inner Self draws nutriment, if it finds anything therein compatible with its own nature.

What is all the power and glory of earthly kings compared with the divine Man, the King in the realm of the soul? What is all the science of this earth but nonsense, if compared with the self-knowledge of the regenerated? Well may he who has welcomed the Lord in his soul be willing to renounce money, power and fame, terrestrial loves and all the illusions of life, if it can be called "renunciation" to refuse to touch things upon which one looks with indifference.

How can he, who has never seen the image of the true Saviour, in his heart love him, and how can he who has once beheld his own real ideal Self cease to love and adore it with his whole mind and with all the faculties of the soul? But such things will not be understood by those who cannot yet rise above limitation; let those who know them rejoice and worship in silence.

Regeneration

He who has succeeded in merging the higher elements of his soul with that divine Self will know its power in his own heart. This principle baptises his soul with fire, and he who receives this baptism of fire is ordained a priest and a King. He who is full of its influence is the true "vicegerent of God," because the supreme power of the universe acts through his instrumentality.

The recognition of this principle fills his heart with a peace "which passeth understanding," it attracts the affections of men to him, and sheds blessings upon every one who approaches his presence. It forgives the sins of men, by transforming them into other beings who have not sinned and need therefore not to be pardoned; it does not require to hear confession to give advice, because it understands the innermost thoughts of every being, and its admonishing voice is heard in the heart that has learned to understand the language of conscience.

The development of the power to perceive its power confirms men's faith, by enabling them to recognise that to be true which they heretofore only believed to be true; and being taught by the truth itself, they can make no mistake.

It communicates with man by being absorbed by man, and by absorbing the soul of man into itself; it brings the dying to life, because, being immortal, he who is consciously united with it enjoys its own immortality. The marriages it celebrates can never be dissolved, because in its power all humanity is bound together to one indissoluble whole; to separate from it would be death to the part that separates itself from the whole.

The world in which this principle exists is the sphere of eternal life; it is the only true and infallible "church" and its power cannot be taken away. This church is truly universal, nothing can live without its jurisdiction, because nothing can continue to exist without the authority of life. Still it has no particular name, requires no other fee for initiation but self-sacrifice, no ceremonies or rites except the "crucifixion" and death of the irrational man. "Heathens" and "Infidels" may enter it without changing their faith; opinions cease to exist where the truth is revealed.

The True Christ

But this true Christ is not the Christ of popular Christianism. He has long ago been driven away from the modern Christian temples, and an idol has occupied his place. The money-changers and tradesmen have again taken possession of the temple of the soul, sacrificing the life-blood of the poor at the altars of wooden gods, closing their eyes to the truth and worshipping tinsel, squandering the wealth of nations for the glorification of the illusion of self.

The true "Son of Man" is still scoffed at by his nominal followers, traduced [slandered] by his pretended friends, tormented by the lusts of the flesh, crucified by men who do not recognise in him the only scource of their life, killed by men in their own hearts, ignorantly and foolishly, because they do not know what they are doing, and that their own life-substance departs at the time when he departs from their life.

Modern hypocrisy adores the religion of selfishness and rejects the gospel of love. Humanity debases her own dignity by crouching at the feet of idols, where she should stand up in her own dignity and purity as the queen of the whole creation.

The soul of humanity is still dreaming and has not yet awakened to life. She seeks for a god whom she does not know, and cannot realise the fact that in herself is that god, and that there can be no other god besides him. Men and women clamour for the coming of a god, and yet this god is there and everywhere, and ever ready to manifest his presence as soon as he is admitted into the heart.

This unknown god is attainable to all and may be recognised by everyone. It is a principle ever ready to be born as a power in every heart where the conditions for its birth are prepared. It always begins to come to life in a "manger" between the elemental and animal forces in man. It can only be born in a lowly place, because pride and superstition are its enemies, and in a heart filled with vanity it would soon perish.

The news of its birth sends a thrill of pleasure through the physical body, and the morning stars in the soul sing together for joy, heralding the dawn of the day for the resurrection of the celestial spirit. The three magicians from the East, Spirit, Soul, and Matter, representing Love, Wisdom, and Power, appear at the manger and offer their gifts to the new-born babe. If the king of pride and ambition does not succeed in driving it out of the country, it begins to grow, and as it grows its divinity becomes manifest.

It argues with the intellectual powers in the temple of the mind and silences their sophistry by its superior knowledge. It penetrates into mysteries, which intellectuality, born of sensual perceptions, cannot explain. Grey-headed material science, superstition hoary with age, old logic based upon misconceptions of fundamental truths, give way, and are forced to acknowledge the wisdom of the half-grown god.

Living in the wilderness of material desires, it is vainly tempted by the devil of selfishness. It cannot be misled by personal considerations, because being superior to them, it has no personal claims. The "devil" can give to it nothing that it does not already possess, because being the highest it rules over all that is low. This principle is the first emanation of The Absolute. It becomes the "only-begotten son" of its father, and is as old as the father, because the Absolute could only become a "father" at the time when the "son" was born. *(Bible: St John i. 1;*

Hebrews i. 3.) It is the living Word, and every man is that Word, in whom this "son of god" becomes manifest. It is the divine self of every man, his own divine ethereal counterpart without any infirmities, because the latter only belong to the terrestrial form.

It is not a personality, but it may become individualised in man and yet remain in its essence impersonal, a living being, ubiquitous, incorruptible, and immortal. This is the great mystery before which the intellect, reasoning from particulars to universals, stands hopelessly still, but which the soul, whose inner spiritual perceptions are alive, beholds with astonishment and wonder. Only that which is infinite and immortal in man can comprehend infinitude and immortality.

True Faith

As long as the wavering intellect doubts the existence of God, it cannot become conscious of His existence, because only the steady light of unclouded reason can penetrate into the depths where divine wisdom dwells. Mere "belief" is a confession of ignorance; true faith is based upon experience. We cannot be convinced of the existence of something we do not know, and of which we are unconscious, except by becoming conscious of its existence.

Consciousness, knowledge, and realisation of the existence of something can only begin at the moment when that something begins to become conscious within ourselves. We may search for the god within us, but we cannot artificially bring him to life. We can prepare the conditions under which he may manifest his consciousness within ourselves, by divesting the mind from all predilections and prejudices; the divine principle awakes within us by the power of its own grace. Such a grace is not a favour conferred by a partial, whimsical, and personal god, it is the effect of a free will which has the power to grant its own prayers. As well may an acorn enclosed in a stone pray to be developed into an oak, as a man whose heart is filled with desires for the low ask to become conscious of the high. To put implicit belief in the statement of bonze [monk] or priest is weakness; to keep the soul pure, so that it can be taught by wisdom itself, is strength, to arrive at conviction through the knowledge of the soul confers the only true faith. Tennyson speaks of the beginning of true faith when he says --

"We have but faith, we cannot know,
A beam in darkness, let it grow."
[From "In Memoriam"]

When the beam has grown, it constitutes spiritual knowledge, which is identical with the living power of faith.

When the divine being becomes conscious in the personal man, the body begins to feel new sensations, the pulse begins to throb with more vigour, the animal forces stirred up in their "hells" by the arrival of the new light, become more active, pains will be experienced in various parts of his body, and the candidate for immortality will physically experience a process resembling the martyrdom of the crucified Christ. *(The pains referred to are the result of the penetrating power of the spirit, infusing a new life into the physical form.)* The penetration of the mortal by the new life will necessarily cause suffering until the lower elements are entirely subjected and that which is impure eliminated.

There is no salvation except through suffering; pains accompany man's entrance into the world, pains accompany his regeneration. The low must die so that the high may live. Only he who has tasted the bitterness of evil can fully realise the sweetness of good, only he who has suffered the heat of the day can fully appreciate the cool of the evening breeze. He who has lived in darkness will know the true value of light when he enters its realm.

What is true in regard to individual man is equally true in regard to humanity as a whole, but that which may be accomplished in a few suitable individual organisms in a comparatively short time, will require ages to take place in the body of humanity as a whole.

*"Though other things grow fair against the sun,
Yet fruits that blossom first will first be ripe."*
- **Othello, ii. 3.**

Infinite love radiating from the centre of the All, eternally descends into the hearts of mankind. Divine wisdom has no separate will of its own, but is doing the will of the Father. Christ takes upon His shoulders the sins of the world, for he who has entered into the realisation of divine truth, has stepped out of the realm of ignorance and illusions and become free, is without sin, He can gain no personal benefit by His descent into matter; being perfection itself, He needs no further perfection. *(Bhagavad Gita, iii. 22.)*

As men and women become conscious of His divine presence, they become aware not merely of their own individual evils, but of the sufferings of humanity as a whole; they begin to suffer with and for each other, they recognise in the divinity in humanity the universal link that binds them all together into one harmonious whole.

Realising their high nature as sons of the eternal God, they die to all that is low, and the more they die to it the more will they become alive in the only true, real, and immortal life. The motto of the ancient Rosicrucian fraternity was: In Deo nascimur, in Jesu morimur, reviviscimus in Spiritu Sando; that is to say, they recognised that their souls were born from the universal fountain of all; they died to their lower natures by entering into the spiritual body of Christ, and gained eternal life by being penetrated, illuminated, nourished and glorified by the light of divine truth.

The temple where they worshipped was that of the "Holy Ghost," the spirit of divine wisdom, pervading the soul of the world. This they represented by the symbols of Mercury and the earth joined in one.

Eternal Truths

These ideas are not new, they have not come into existence with the advent of modern Christianity; they are eternal truths, as old as the world, and they have been represented in various fables and allegories among the nations of this globe.

In the "Old Testament" we find the doctrine of salvation represented in the story of Noah's ark. Noah represents the spiritual man, and the ark the plane of divine self-consciousness. Only those elements of the psychic organism of man which enter this spiritual realm can be saved, while those who remain in a lower state are doomed to destruction.

Upon the waters of thought floats the ship containing many compartments; the window of knowledge is open to enable the inner man to look out upon the watery waste. The intellectual raven is sent out to discover dry land, but it can find no place to rest, and returns to the ark; the dove of spiritual knowledge alone can find solid ground in the realm of the spirit; it returns carrying the emblem of peace, the doubts recede, and the ark is turned into a temple resting upon the top of the mountain of self knowledge.

Blessed is he whose ark during his terrestrial life is guided upon this Ar-ar-at of true Faith; it will enable him patiently and with indifference to bear the ills of terrestrial life until the soul is released from its bonds, and returns to its home in the eternal kingdom, having become separated from all the attractions of earth.

How grand and sublime are the mysteries of true religion! How superior is knowledge of the soul to speculative science! How infinitely great the living spirit of Truth!

Those who cling to external forms, cling to illusion. To convert an ignorant person by substituting one form of illusion for another is useless, and the money and labour expended for such "conversions" is wasted. Ignorance exchanged for ignorance remains ignorance still; a change of opinion cannot establish self-knowledge and an imaginary knowledge does not make a man wise.

If a man has religion, it matters little by what name he may call it, or under what form he may attempt to express that which cannot be expressed in a form. The Buddhist, who looks upon the image of Buddha as a figurative representation of a living principle, and who, in memory of a once living person in whom that principle found its fullest expression, and whose example he wishes to follow, offers flowers and fruits at his shrine, is as near the truth as the Christian who sees in the picture of Jesus of Nazareth the representation of his highest ideal. For it is not the person, however much he may be venerated, that ought to be worshipped, but Divine Wisdom itself, without whose light Gautama could not have become a Buddha, nor Jesus a Christ.

There has been a great deal of time and labour spent to prove or disprove that the founder of Christianity was a person living in Palestine at the beginning of the Christian era. To know whether or not such a person by the name of Jesus, or perhaps Jehoshua, ever existed, and whether he existed at the time indicated by theologians, may be a matter of great historical interest, but it cannot be of supreme importance for our salvation; because the personality of even a God incarnate is only a mask, and the knowledge of another man is not our own. The "Light of Asia" says:

"Within thyself salvation must be found"

and Angelus Silesius (John Scheffler) expresses the same truth, when he says:

*"The cross of Golgotha can never save thy soul,
The cross in thine own heart alone can make thee whole."*

The doctrines of the Jesus of the Gospel grow in sublimity in proportion as their secret meaning is understood; the tales of the Bible in regard to His deeds and the miracles which He performed, and which to the superficial observer appear incredible and absurd, represent eternal truths and psychological processes which are not merely things of the past, but which occur even now within the realm of the soul of man, and in proportion as man comes nearer to the true living Christ, veil after veil drops from his eyes.

The theory of the redemption of man does not date from the time when the historical Christ is supposed to have been born. The history of Christ finds its prototype in the history of Krishna. The Greeks taught the redemption of the soul under the allegory of Amor and Psyche.

Psyche (the human soul) enjoys the embraces of her divine lover every night (in each incarnation). She feels his divine presence and hears the voice of intuition in her heart, but she is not permitted to see the source from which that voice proceeds. At a time when the god is sleeping her curiosity awakes and she wishes to see him objectively. She lights the lamp of the intellect and proceeds to examine critically the source of her happiness; but at that moment the god disappears. Despairingly she wanders through the lower regions of her intellect and through the sphere of sensual perceptions. She cannot find her god by the power of reasoning from the material plane. Ready to die (giving up her self-will), she is saved by the power of love. Losing her "self" in love, she becomes united with him, knowing his attributes, which are now her own.

Modern Christianity has not destroyed the Olympian gods, it only destroyed the forms in which they were represented. They were allegorical representations of truths, and truths cannot be killed. The laws of nature are the same to-day as they were at the time of Tiberius; Christianity has only changed the symbols and called old things by new names. Dead heathen idols have been resurrected in the form of Roman Catholic saints.

Faust

Modern writers have represented the same old truths in other forms, in prose and in verse. Goethe represents it beautifully in his "Faust." Dr Faust, the man of great intellect and celebrated for his learning, in spite of all his scientific accomplishments, is unable to find the truth.

*"The unknown is the useful thing to know;
That which we know is useless for our purpose."*

Despairing at the impotency and insufficiency of speculative research, he enters into a pact with the principle of evil. By its assistance he attains wealth, love, and power, he enjoys all that the senses are capable to enjoy, still feeling intuitively that selfish enjoyment cannot confer true happiness. Neither the splendour of the imperial court, nor the beauty of Helen of Troy, who returns from the land of shadows at his request, nor the orgies of the Blocksberg, where all human passions are let loose without restraint, can satisfy his craving.
Lord of the Earth, he sees only a single hut which is not yet his own, and he takes even that, regardless of the fate of its inhabitants. Still he is not satisfied until, after having recovered a part of land from the ocean by his labours, he contemplates the happiness which others may enjoy by reaping the benefit of his work. This is the first unselfish thought that takes root in his mind. It fills him with extreme happiness, and in the contemplation of the happiness of others his sense of self dies and his impersonal soul is saved.
The soul knows that it is, but it cannot intellectually and critically examine itself unless it steps out of itself, and, stepping out of itself, it ceases to be one. The eye cannot see itself without the aid of a mirror; good becomes only known to us after we have experienced evil, to become wise we must first become foolish and gain experience by eating of the forbidden fruit. A spiritual power not having been embodied in a form, would not know the nature of freedom. To learn the conditions of existence man becomes embodied in form and acquires knowledge; having gained that knowledge, form is no longer required.

Liberation

The selfish desire for existence imprisons the inner man into a mortal form; he who during his life on Earth conquers all selfish desire for existence becomes free.
The divine Buddha, resting under the Boddhi-tree of wisdom, and having his mind fixed on the chain of causation, said: "Ignorance is the source of all evil. From ignorance spring the Sankharas (tendencies) of threefold nature- productions of body, of speech, and thought (during the previous life); from the Sankharas originates (relative) consciousness, from consciousness spring name and form, from this the six regions (the six senses); from this springs desire, from desire attachment, from attachment existence, birth, old age, death, grief, lamentation, suffering, dejection, and despair.
"By the destruction of ignorance the Sankharas are destroyed, and their consciousness, name, and form, the six regions, contact, sensation, desire, attachment, existence, and its consequent evils. From ignorance spring all evils, from self-knowledge comes cessation of this mass of misery. The truly

enlightened one stands, dispelling the hosts of illusions like the sun that illuminates the sky."

The power which destroys selfishness and the sense of personality is the same which caused the existence of man; it is the power of universal love, and the more the love of a person expands over all others the more will the consciousness of personality be diffused.

We esteem a person according to the degree in which he prefers common interests to the interests of his own personality. We admire generosity, and unselfishness, and benevolence, and yet such qualities are absurd and useless, if we believe that the highest object of man's existence is his own personal happiness on the physical plane; because the highest happiness in that plane consists in the greatest amount of possessions pertaining to that plane.

To give is to experience a personal loss. But if man strives for spiritual power, to sacrifice personal possessions will be his gain, because the less he is attracted by personal possessions the more will his soul become free. To give with the view of expecting some benefit in return is useless for such a purpose, because a person having such an object in view simply gives up one personal possession for another. He is a tradesman that clings to his goods, and is only willing to part with something good provided he can get something better in exchange.

According to the unselfishness and the spiritual power of a person his individual influence may extend over a family, a village, a town, a country, or over the whole Earth.

Every one desires influence, and seeks to obtain power by obtaining wealth and position. But the influence gained by such possessions is not spiritual power. A fool may be a pope, a king, or a millionary, and people bow in obedience before him on account of his position and wealth. They may despise his person and adore his possessions, which he himself adores, and to which his person is as subject as the lowest one of his slaves.

Such a person is not a commander; it is his wealth that commands him and the others. His wealth and not he is, in such a case, the object of the world's admiration. When his wealth is squandered, those who used to crouch at his feet spurn him away from their table.

The spiritual power of a person is independent of such external conditions, a virtuous person is esteemed in proportion as his qualities become known, and the spiritually strong exerts a powerful invisible influence over all his surroundings.

Man may be compared with a planet revolving around its own centre and circling around an invisible sun. Above the orbit in which he turns is light, and below is the darkness. The light above and the darkness below attract him. The farther he travels from the invisible sun, from which the light proceeds, the more will he approach the shadow; and having reached a certain point at which either one or the other attraction ceases, he will either rise up to the source of light or sink into the darkness.

A change from darkness to light, from evil to good, is only possible as long as man, in his revolutions around the centre of his own self, has transcended the orbit where the attractions of light and shadows are equal. Having transcended that orbit, no return is possible.

Only he who has attained the knowledge of self will be able to choose free, because he will know the nature of that which he chooses; the blind have no freedom of choice. The unpardonable sin is to knowingly and wilfully reject spiritual truth when it becomes manifest in the heart. In a certain sense all sins are "unpardonable," because they all cause effects, which have to become exhausted before they can cease; but if a person knowingly and wilfully rejects the truth revealed to him by his own inner self-consciousness, it proves that he loves evil better than good, and that his nature is evil.

He who is ignorant is not responsible for his acts. But he who knows the truth by its interior self-revelation his own consciousness and rejects it, condemns himself. Truth alone will survive in the end while evil will perish in evil. It is therefore dangerous for men to seek for occult spiritual knowledge for the gratification of scientific curiosity, before they have become sufficiently wise to select only that which is true.

Chapter XII - Theosophy

"He to whom time is like eternity, and eternity like time, is free." - **Jackob Boehme**

Inexpressable Truth

To picture the eternal and intellectually incomprehensible in forms, and to describe the unimaginable in words, is a task whose difficulty has been experienced by all who ever attempted it. The formless cannot be described in forms, it can only be represented by allegories which can only be understood by those whose minds are open to the spiritual illumination of truth.

The misunderstanding of allegorical expressions in the sacred books has led to religious wars, to the torturing, burning, and killing of thousands of innocent victims, it has caused the living wives of dead Hindus to be burned with the corpses of their husbands, it has caused ignorant men and women to throw themselves before the wheels of the car of the Juggernath, it causes the endless quarrels between some 200 Christian sects, and while the truth unites all humanity into one harmonious whole, the misunderstanding of it produces innumerable discords and diseases.

Far, in the unfathomable abyss of space, far beyond the reach of the imagination of man, unapproachable even by the highest and purest angel or thought, and nevertheless omnipresent in his own essence and power, self-existent, eternal, resplendent in his own glory is the Shining One, whose Centre is rest, peace and happiness, whose heart is invisible Fire, whose rays are Light and Life, pervading the Universe to its utmost limits, penetrating every form and causing it to live and to grow.

Their harmonious vibrations are undulating through space, nourishing all animate and inanimate beings with the substance of Love. Meeting with the sleeping forms of thought in space, the products of a previous day of creation, the divine rays of wisdom endow them with life, causing them to become living systems of worlds, chained together by the power of mutual recognition, manifesting itself as attraction and guiding them on in their restless revolutions. Penetrating into the hearts of animals and men, they create sensation and relative consciousness, cause the form to feel, to perceive and to know its surroundings, call into life the emotions, instincts, and the power of reasoning. Penetrating deep into the hearts of men, they kindle there the divine fire in whose light man may see the image of the Shining One, and know it to be his own immortal ideal, to be realised within himself.

But it is beyond the power of man to describe in language that which cannot be described, to combine words, so that the reader may form an intellectual conception of something, for which no intellectual conception exists, because it is beyond the experience of the limited mind. In the presence of the highest, the unthinkable ideal, intellectual labour ceases, and spiritual recognition begins. "The secret things belong to the Lord"; only divine wisdom itself can know that which is divine; it being the self-knowledge of God in man; the self-realisation of truth. Intellectual labour is a function which man shares with certain animals; but the prerogative of spiritual man is to realise within his own self-consciousness the presence of Truth, to become himself one with the God of the universe and join His self-knowledge, and this self-realisation of truth is called Divine Wisdom or Theosophia.

Universal Source

In this eternal universal source of all that exists is all magic power contained, even to the extent of creating new worlds. The realisation of its existence is the Philosopher's Stone and the Elixir of life or Universal Panacea, which can be had everywhere and at any time without expense by every one. It is attainable only by man, because the lower animals are not yet far enough advanced to be used as vehicles for the manifestation of divine wisdom; but he whom it has awakened to life shares its attributes and is a living temple of God.

The man whom this principle has not awakened from its sleep is merely an intellectual animal, and can possess no spiritual or magical powers. Some modern "philosophers," who say that man has no magical powers, are right from their own point of view; for the "man" known to modern science has no spiritual life and therefore no spiritual power; the real man only begins to exist when he awakens to the realisation of his divine nature.

True philosophers have recognised this fact. Schopenhauer says: "In consequence of the action of 'grace,' the entire being of man becomes remodelled, so that he desires no longer anything of that for which he was craving heretofore, and becomes so to say a new man." *("God is as much in a stick of wood as in a human being; but the difference is that a stick of wood knows nothing of God; while man may attain the realisation of his presence in him." -- Eckhart.)*

The Path

Everything in nature has a threefold nature, and likewise the allegories of the sacred books of the East as well as those of the West have a threefold meaning: an exoteric, an esoteric, and a spiritual signification. The vulgar -- the learned as well as the unlearned -- can see only the external side, which is often so absurd, that its very absurdity should serve as a warning to people endowed with reason not to accept such fables in their literal meaning.

Those who are willing to learn can be instructed, but they that believe that they already know, refuse to be taught. For this reason the man-appointed guardians of the truth, the learned teachers of science and religion are often the last ones to recognise that which is true.

How can we enter the path? -- Only in practical experience is life. Petrified speculative science, mouldy speculative philosophy, and dried-up speculative theology stand in our way. Humanity awakes from its slumber and asks for bread, but receives only a stone. It turns to science, but science is silent, wraps itself up in its vanity and turns away; it turns to philosophy, and old philosophy answers, but its talk is an incomprehensible jargon, and confuses matters still more. It turns to theology, but theology threatens the obnoxious questioner with curses, and bids him to be satisfied with a blind faith.

But the people, as a whole, are no longer satisfied with such answers; they are no longer contented with the assertion that the truth is to be known to a few privileged classes, and that they themselves must remain ignorant. Wisdom is not to be monopolised by any sectarian body or any Society.

If we wish to enter the path to infinite life, the first requirement is:

1. TO KNOW

Knowledge is the perception and understanding of truth. We can only know that which we perceive. There are two principal modes of perception, namely, seeing and feeling. Each of these modes, if unaccompanied by the other, is unreliable; only if we simultaneously see and feel a thing do we experience that it exists. Thousands of years have passed away since mankind first saw the sun and the stars, and modern telescopes have brought them nearer to us. Nevertheless our knowledge of these cosmic bodies and the conditions of life existing upon them, consists merely of speculations and opinions, which may be overthrown at any time, when our means for observation are supplanted by better ones. We give names to the substances discovered by the spectroscope, but we will not know the true nature of the stars as long as we are not able to partake of their consciousness and experience the qualities of life and characters embodied in their forms.

For thousands of years mankind has intuitively felt the presence of the Unknown. Those who experienced the presence of the universal Spirit, know that it exists. Generations after generations have disappeared from earth after spending their lives in vain efforts to know objectively that God whose power they felt in their hearts; but whom they could not see with their eyes.

If we are able to see and to feel the external qualities of a thing, we may understand what these qualities are, but we will still be ignorant of its interior character. To know its spirit it will be necessary to enter into its spirit, and this can only be done by the spirit of man, not by his external senses. The spiritual principle in man, if once awakened to self-consciousness, has attributes and functions far superior to those of the external man; it has the power to perceive, to see and to feel the internal qualities of things which are imperceptible to the external senses; it can identify itself with the object of its observation and partake of its consciousness, it becomes for the time being united with that object and shares its feelings, it partakes of its subjective sensations.

Thus does a lover partake of the joys and sorrows of the object he loves, and feel as if he were one with it in spirit; for love is the power by which such a divine state is attained, it penetrates all things, and coming from the heart it goes to the heart.

What is it that prevents us to love and to know all things but our own dislikes and misconceptions? We do not see things as they are but as we imagine them to be. He who desires to know all things should not look upon them with his own eyes, but with the eyes of the truth; he should not think the thoughts suggested by external appearances, but he should let Divine Wisdom do his thinking within his mind.

To obtain true knowledge we must be able to receive the light of the truth; we must free our minds from the learned rubbish that has accumulated there through the perverted methods of education of modern civilization. The more false doctrines we have learned the more difficult will be the labour to make room for the truth, and it may take years to unlearn that which we have learned at the expense of a great deal of labour, money, and time.

The Bible says that "we must become like little children before we can enter the kingdom of truth." The principal thing to know is to know our own true Self; if we know ourselves, we will know that we are to be the kings of the universe. The essential Man is a Son of God, he is something incomparably greater, far more sublime and far more powerful than the insignificant, changeable and impermanent and unconscious being described as "man" in our scientific works on anthropology.

Well may Man who knows his true nature be proud of his nobility and power; well may the man of earth be ashamed of his weakness. The real Man is a divine being whose power extends as far as his thoughts can reach. The illusive man is a compound of semi-animal forces, subject to their caprices and whims, with a spark of divine fire in him to enable him to control them, but which spark is only too frequently left to smoulder and vanish. The former is immortal, the latter exists a few years among the illusions of life. The real man realises his own immortality; the deluded illusion, having the appearance of a human being, deludes itself with the hope of obtaining permission, by the favour of some personal god, to carry its falsehoods into a sphere in which only the truth exists. *(Revelations xxi. 27. ["Nothing impure will ever enter it, nor will anyone who does what is shameful or deceitful, but only those whose names are written in the Lamb's book of life."])*

There are three kinds of knowledge, the useful, the useless, and the harmful. The useless knowledge is the knowledge of, or rather the adherence to, illusions and falsehoods; it is no real knowledge, although it embraces a great deal of what is considered of great importance in civilized countries that men should know. It is true that modern science has on many occasions drawn away a part of the veil which hides the wonders of Wisdom in Nature; but as our science has not reached the foundation of truth; it is mixed up with illusions. Our scientific systems are continually subject to change, and what is considered to be final truth by one generation, is often rejected as false by the next. Our "scientific attainments" confer no real knowledge of fundamental law of nature, because they are based upon ignorance, in regard to the fountain of All, and, however logical the deductions made from false premises may be, falsehoods can produce only falsehood.

What can be more erroneous than the assertion of rationalistic speculators, that the intellect is a product of the material organization of the physical body; that life is a product of the mechanical action of a dead force; that effects can be produced without any adequate causes; that something can come out of something having elements therein capable to produce it; that man's mind exists within the narrow limits of his skull; that man can know nothing except what he perceives with his external senses; that consciousness is the result of the chemical action of unconscious substances; that man can will, think, imagine, love, and hate without having a soul; that wisdom, knowledge, spiritual perception, prophecy, etc., were results of pathological conditions of the body and other endless absurdities and scientific hallucinations.

As long as the true nature of man is not known, his lower interests are mistaken for his higher ones. Scientific attainments are often only used for the purpose of obtaining the power to speculate on the ignorance of those that have no such intellectual acquirements, and by taking advantage of their beliefs to obtain money and material comfort. Such scientific attainments may be good for such purposes, but they retard the progress of man in a spiritual direction, because they make men more selfish, and cause them to worship matter; they are therefore useless for the only true and permanent interest of man.

If science wishes to find the foundation of truth, it must begin to realise the unity of the universe and know that the world of appearances manifested in nature is a revelation of truth originating in divine wisdom. This realisation cannot be attained by arguments and inferences, it is only realised by the power of universal love, which is the recognition of truth.

"To bring thee to thy God,
love takes the shortest route;
The way which science leads
is but a round about."
- Angelus Silesius.

The harmful knowledge consists in scientific attainments without any corresponding perception of the moral aspect of truth. It is only partial knowledge, because it recognises only a part of the truth. A high intellectual development without any corresponding growth of spirituality is a curse to mankind. Knowledge to be good must be illuminated by Wisdom; knowledge without wisdom is dangerous to possess. Misunderstanding and misapplication of truths are the sources of evil.

"A little knowledge is a dangerous thing." **- Pope**

Such an attainment of knowledge without wisdom may become detrimental. The invention of the fulminates of mercury, of gunpowder and nitro-glycerine, has caused much suffering to a large part of humanity. Not that the substances applied, or the forces which are liberated, are intrinsically evil, but their misapplication in the hands of those without wisdom leads to evil results. If all men were intelligent enough to understand the laws which govern the world, and wise enough to employ their knowledge for good purposes only, no evil results would follow.

One of the most harmful acquisitions is the so-called "religious knowledge"; that is to say the holding on to theological doctrines which are wrong or misunderstood, because it is unaccompanied by any unfoldment of true spirituality. Such a "religion" results in bigotry, hypocrisy and intolerance; it is based upon fear and not upon faith. A religion without universal love is an absurdity; because that Love is the link which relates man to God. A faith without love is only a superstition. Nevertheless it is that foolish "faith" which clamours the most for its rights.

*"Faith without love will make
the greatest roar and din;
The cask sounds loudest
when there is nought within."*
- **Angelus Silesius.**

If we proceed a step further and imagine intellectual but wicked and selfish people possessed not only of the power to employ explosives, and poisonous drugs, to injure others, but able to send their own degrading poisonous thoughts to a distance, to leave at will the prison-house of the physical body to kill or injure others, the most disastrous results would follow. Such forbidden knowledge has been and is sometimes possessed by people with criminal tendencies, a fact which is universally known in the East, and upon the possibility and actuality of such facts have been established on many occasions, and among others by many of the witch trials of the Middle Ages.

Modern scientists may now laugh at these facts, but the doctors of law, of medicine, and of theology of their times, were as sure of their knowledge as modern representatives of science are of their own opinions to-day, and the former had as many intellectual capacities as the latter. The only difference is that the former knew these facts, but gave a wrong explanation; the latter find it easier to ignore than to explain.

Man is continually surrounded by unseen influences, and the astral plane is swarming with entities and forces, which are acting upon him for good or for evil, according to his good or evil inclinations. At the present state of evolution man has a physical body, which is admirably adapted to modify the influence from the astral plane, and to shelter him against the "monsters of the deep."

If the physical body is in good health, it acts as an armour, and, moreover, man has the power, by a judicious exercise of his will, to so concentrate the odic aura by which he is surrounded, as to render his armour impenetrable to the influences of the astral world and its inhabitants; but if by bad health, by a careless expenditure of vitality, or by the practice of mediumship, he disperses his protective power, his physical armour will become weakened and unable to guard him; he becomes the victim of elementaries and elemental forces, his mental faculties lose their balance, and sooner or later he will, like the symbolical Adam and Eve, know that he is naked, and exposed to influences which he cannot repel.

Such is the result for which those ignorantly crave who wish to obtain knowledge without corresponding morality. To supply the ignorant or weak with powers of destruction would be like providing children with gunpowder and matches for play.

Only an intelligent and well-balanced mind can discriminate properly and dive into the hidden mysteries of Nature. "Only the pure in heart can see God." He who has reached that stage need not search the world for a person to instruct him; the higher intelligences will be attracted to him, and become his instructor, in the same manner as he himself is attracted by the beauty of an animal or of a flower.

A harp does not invent sound but obeys the hand of a master, and the more perfect the instrument, the sweeter will be the music. A diamond does not originate light, but reflects it, and the purer the diamond the purer will be its lustre. Man does not invent or create thought, will, and intelligence. He is a mirror in which the thoughts of the world are reflected, an instrument through which the will of nature expresses itself; a pearl filled with a drop of water from the universal ocean of intelligence.

The only true knowledge is the knowledge of one's own true self, which knows neither "good" nor "evil," but is the realisation of truth. He who ate from the tree of the knowledge of illusion has died; because by experiencing the illusion of self, he has died to his spiritual nature and become an illusion himself. *(Gen. ii. 17.)* If you eat of the tree of divine knowledge, which is the tree of life, your illusion will die and you will live. Your personality will be swallowed up by a realisation of the fact that "you" are nothing, and that God in you is the only true self and the All. Realising this, you will not be "as one of the gods;" but a self-conscious power in God, unlimited and immortal.

How can self-knowledge be attained? The answer is: "By the realisation of truth." The truth is everywhere, always ready to manifest itself in you and around you, if you only permit it to become manifest. Wisdom requires no other teacher but wisdom itself. Rise up to it in your soul and it will descend upon you and fill your heart. He who ascends to the top of a high mountain need not enquire for somebody to bring him pure air. Pure air surrounds him there on all sides. The realm of wisdom is not limited, and he whose mind is receptive will not suffer from want of divine grace to feed his holy aspiration.

The school in which the occulist graduates has many classes, each class representing a life. The days of vacation may arrive before the lesson is learned, and what has been learned may be forgotten during the time of vacation; but still the impression remains, and a thing once learned is easily learned again. This accounts for the different talents with which men are endowed, and for their propensities for good or for evil.

No effort is lost, every cause creates a corresponding effect, no favours are granted, no injustice takes place. Blind to bribes and deaf to appeals is the law of justice, dealing its treasures out to every one according to his capacities to receive, but he who has no selfish desire for reward, and no cowardly fear of punishment, but who dares to act rightly because he will not do wrong, identifies himself with the law, and in the equilibrium of the law will he find his Power. The second requirement is

2. TO WILL

If we are not willing to receive the truth we will not obtain it.

Men believe that they love the truth, but there are few who loving for its own sake desire it. They desire welcome truths; those that are unwelcome are rejected. Opinions which flatter the vanity and are in harmony with accustomed modes of thought are accepted; strange truths are regarded with astonishment and driven away from the door. Men are often afraid of that which they do not know, and, not knowing the truth, they are afraid to receive it. They ask new truths for their passports, and if they do not bear the stamp of some fashionable authority they are looked upon as illegitimate children, and are not permitted to grow.

How shall we learn to love the truth? By learning to know it. How can we know the truth? By learning to love it. The deluded asks for external proofs, but the wise requires no other certificate for the truth but its own revelation. There can be no difference between speculative and practical knowledge; because knowledge is one, an opinion based upon mere speculation is no knowledge. Knowledge can only be attained by speculation, if the speculation is accompanied by experience. Those who want to know the truth must practise it; those who cannot practise it will not know it; speculation without practice is only a deceitful dream.

Man can have no actual desire for a thing which he has never experienced, and which he therefore not knows. How can we love a thing of which we know not that it exists? How can we know its existence, except by realising its presence? How can we realise its presence if we do not enjoy it? How can we enjoy it if we do not love it? Neither inductive nor deductive reasoning can give us a realisation of truth. Divine Reason itself alone can cause it to become manifest in ourselves.

To know that a thing is good, is to desire it; for it is a law acting within the constitution of man, no less than among the planets, that we should be attracted to that which we know to be good and be repulsed by that which we know to be evil. A strong desire to be good, causes man to perform good actions; a desire to be evil, causes him to commit evil deeds. Man is the product of his own thoughts and acts; if he thinks and acts good, he becomes good; if he thinks and acts evil, he becomes evil. In an occult sense "willing" is identical with "feeling"; for the substance of the Will, if infused with the consciousness of the Spirit, feels and grasps its object. Willing, knowing, and acting are ultimately identical; because we can only will what we know, and we can only know that of which we have an experience.

The only way to obtain true practical knowledge of spiritual truths is by the practice of the truth -- in other words, the awakening of the inner consciousness to the recognition of truth existing within oneself. Only a mind which has been purified from all selfish desires, and is filled with a strong determination to learn the truth, is thereby "duly and truly prepared" to enter the temple of wisdom. Every time that a person, either for selfish purposes or to gratify the whim of another, or for any other personal consideration, gives his consent to something, of which his reason or conscience tells him that it ought not to be; however insignificant such an act may be; it will nevertheless involve for him a loss of a certain amount of will.

Man is chained to the kingdom of his illusions with a thousand chains. The inhabitants of his earthly soul appear before him in their most seductive forms. If they are driven away they change their masks and appear in some other form. But the chains by which man is bound are forged by his own desire. His vices do not cling to him against his will. He clings to them, and they will desert him as soon as he rises up in the strength and dignity of his manhood and shakes them off. There is a method, by which we may, without any active effort, obtain that which we desire, and this is that we should desire nothing except what the divine spirit wills within our own heart.

The third requirement is...

3. TO DARE

We must dare to act and throw off low desires, instead of waiting inactively until they desert us. We must dare to tear ourselves loose from accustomed habits, irrational thoughts, and selfish considerations, and from everything that is an impediment to our recognition of truth. We must dare to conquer ourselves and the world by becoming like a disinterested spectator, taking no part in the performance, *(Bhagavad Gita.)* -- not on account of any stupid indifference or mournful acquiescence to the decrees of fate, nor on account of being a "pessimist" or a misanthrope; but on account of having outgrown the follies of the lower world and realising the beauties of the high.

We must learn to overcome our own ignorance, dare to face the ridicule of the ignorant, the vilifications of bigots, the haughtiness of the vain, the contempt of the learned, and the envy of the small; dare to proclaim the truth if it is useful to do so, and dare to be silent if taunted by the fool. *(Prov, xxvi. 4.)* We must dare to face poverty, suffering, and isolation, be superior to all ills that may affect us, and act under all circumstances according to our highest conception of truth.

All this might be easily accomplished, if the will of man were free, if man were his own master and not bound with the chains of the soul; but man is only free to a certain extent. Man may perform certain acts and leave others undone if he chooses; but his wisdom determines his choice. A man knowing and wise has the power to will that which he does not desire personally, and not to will that to which his desires attract him. To make the will free, action is required, and each action strengthens the will, and each unselfish deed increases its power.

There is only one divine Law and one divine Will; the Will of divine Wisdom. He who follows the law executes the will of God; he who opposes it may become individually strong in his self-will; but will finally be crushed by the opposing force, which is immeasurably stronger than he. Dare to obey the Law, and you will become your own Master, and the Lord over all.

There are three ways to develop the power of will:

The first is to act against our own desires by forcing ourselves to perform acts which are disagreeable and painful. This method used to be prevalent in the West during the Middle Ages, and is to-day practised in the East by Fakirs and the lower class of ascetics. It is a method by which people disposed to witchcraft may obtain sufficient strength of will to control some of the lower Elementals, and acquire power to affect men and animals at a distance by the influence of their will. It consists in the endurance of pain with indifference, and the accounts given by travellers in the East show to what height of absurdity such practices of Hatha yoga have been carried out. But while such practices may strengthen the will, they do not eradicate selfishness; but they rather increase it. Seen in the proper light, people given to such practices do not act against their desires; because their desire is the attainment of personal power. Penances and tortures are therefore worse than useless for the higher development of the soul.

The second way is not to follow our unlawful desires on account of being afraid of the consequences which we might have to experience if we were to be disobedient to the law. This is the kind of morality which is usually to be found in the world; but which is based upon cowardice and not upon recognition of truth. Its foundation is the idea to forego a small pleasure for the purpose of enjoying a greater pleasure of an equally selfish kind.

Philosophical courage is a quality for which men are admired everywhere; its foundation is personal vanity. The Red Indian prides himself at his indifference to physical pain, the Fakir undergoes tortures to strengthen his will-power, the civilised soldier is eager to prove his contempt for danger, and to measure his strength with the strength of the enemy.

But there are deeds to perform [i.e., the third way] that require a courage of a superior kind. It requires only momentary outbursts of ambition to perform a daring deed on the physical plane, but a continual and unremitted strain is needed to keep the emotions subjected, and this strain is rendered still more fatiguing by the circumstance that it depends entirely on our own will whether or not we will endure it, and that if we relax the bridle and allow our emotions to run free, sensual gratification will be the result.

The performance of such deed of valour requires not merely a philosophical, but a theosophical courage; namely the courage to do one's duty because it is one's duty to do it, and for no other reason. Therefore, the best way is, not to make any selfish attempts at all to overcome our desires; but to let the recognition of truth overcome these desires; to sacrifice not merely our desires, but our own self with all its desires to the fountain of Divine Wisdom, which is to be found in the temple of our own heart, and to remain there even while we attend to the duties of life.

If we enter that place, all desires will remain outside; they cannot enter the sacred precinct. It requires a courage of the highest order to act under all circumstances in obedience to divine law. Long may the battle last, but each victory strengthens the will; each act of submission renders it more powerful, until at last the combat is ended, and over the battlefield where the remnants of the slain desires are exposed to the decomposing action of the elements hovers the spiritual eagle, rising towards the sun and enjoying the serene tranquillity of the ethereal realm.

Metals are purified by fire and the spirit is purified by suffering. Only when the molten mass has cooled can we judge of the progress of the purification; only when a victory over the emotions is gained, and peace follows after the struggle, can the spirit rest to contemplate and realise the beauty of eternal truth. In vain will men attempt to listen to the voice of truth during the clash of contending desires and opinions, only in the silence that follows the storm can the voice of truth be heard. *("Light on the Path," by Mabel Collins.)*

The fourth requirement to the recognition of the truth is therefore

4. TO BE SILENT

This means that we must not allow any desire to speak in our heart, but only the voice of the truth; because the truth is a jealous goddess and suffers no rivals. He who selects wisdom for the bride of his soul must woo her with his whole heart and dismiss the concubines from the bridal chamber of his soul. He must clothe her in the purity of his affection and ornament her with the gold of his love, for wisdom is modest, she does not adorn herself but waits until she is adorned by her lover. She cannot be bought with money nor with promises, her love is only gained by acts of devotion. Science is only the handmaid of wisdom, and he who makes love to the servant will be rejected by the mistress; but he who sacrifices his whole being to wisdom will be united with it.

The Bhagwat Gita says: "He who thinketh constantly of me, his mind undiverted by any other object, will find me. I will at all times be easily found by a constant devotion to me."

The Christian Mystic, Jackob Boehme, an illuminated seer, expresses the same truth, in the form of a dialogue between the master and his disciple, as follows:

The disciple said to the master: "How can I succeed in arriving at that supersensual life, in which I may see and hear the Supreme?"

The master answered: "If you can only for a moment enter in thought into the

formless, where no creature resides, you will hear the voice of the Supreme."
The disciple said: "Is this far or near?"
The master answered: "It is in yourself, and if you can command only for one hour the silence of your desires, you will hear the inexpressible words of the Supreme. If your own will and self are silent in you, the perception of the eternal will be manifest through you; God will hear, and see, and talk through you; your own hearing, desiring, and seeing prevents you to see and hear the Supreme."
(Jackob Boehme: "Theosophical Writings," book vi.)
These directions are identical with those prescribed by the practice of Raja Yoga, by which the holy men of the East unite their minds with the formless and infinite. All religious ceremonies are calculated to elevate the mind into the region of the formless, and, in fact, all religious systems can have no other ultimate object than to teach methods how to attain such states.
All churches are not worthy the name of "church," which means a spiritual union, unless they serve as schools in which the science of uniting oneself with the eternal fountain of life is practically taught. But it is easier to allow one's mind to revel among the multifarious forms and attractions of the material plane, or to go through forms of external "worship"; than to enter into nothingness, where at first no sound is heard but the echo of our voice.
It is easier to let our minds be controlled by thoughts that visit the mind than to close the doors of the soul to all thoughts that have not the seal of truth impressed upon their forms; and this is the reason why the majority of men and women prefer the illusions of finite life to the eternal realities of the infinite; why they prefer ignorance to a knowledge of truth.
To be silent means to let no other language be heard within the heart but the language of God, to listen to the voice of Divine Wisdom speaking within the heart. *(H. P. Blavatsky. "The Voice of the Silence")*
He who has learned to know, to will, to dare, and to be silent, is upon the true path that leads to immortal life, but by those who move merely in the sensual plane, or whose minds are absorbed in external things of the intellectual plane, even the meaning of these words will not be understood.
Various instructions are given in the books of the East in regard to the practice of this silence and interior meditation, but they all teach the same thing, namely, a concentration of man's higher consciousness to a single point within his own centre.
In the Oupnekhata the following directions are given: --
"Breathe deep and slow, and concentrate your unwavering attention into the midst of your body, into the region of the heart. The lamp in your body will then be protected against wind and motion, and your whole body will become illuminated. You must withdraw all your senses within yourself like a turtle, which withdraws its members within the shell. Enter your own heart and guard it, and Brahma will enter it like a fire or a stroke of lightning. In the midst of the big fire in your heart will be a small flame, and in the centre of it will be Atma."
Herocarcas, an abbot of a convent upon the mount Athos, gives to his monks the following directions to acquire the power of true clairvoyance:

"Sit alone in your room, after having the door locked against intrusion, concentrate your mind upon the region of the navel and try to see with that. Try to find the seat of your heart (sink your consciousness into your heart), where the centre of power resides. At first you will find nothing but darkness; but if you continue for days and nights without fatigue, you will see light, and experience inexpressible things. When the spirit once recognises its own centre in the heart, it will know what it never knew before, and there will be nothing hidden before its sight, whether in heaven or upon the earth."

Let us compare with these statements one received from an unknown uneducated person, who is an illuminate of our times. He has never heard of the Oupnekata nor of Herocarcas; but he possesses the power to see interior truths. He says:

"Sink your thoughts downward into the centre of your being, and you will find there a germ which, if continually nourished by pure and holy thoughts, will grow into a power that will extend and ramify through all parts of your body. Your hands and feet and your body will become alive; a sun will appear within your heart and illuminate your whole being. In this light you will see the present, the past, and the future, and by its aid you will attain the true knowledge of self."

Wisdom

Man is himself a creation of thought, pervading the ocean of Mind. If his soul is in perfect accord with the truth, the truth will be one with his soul. A talented musician will not need a scientific calculation of the vibrations of sound to know whether a melody which he hears is melodious or not; a person who is one with the truth will recognise himself in the mirrors of every external manifestation of truth.

The highest magical power in nature is Wisdom; it is the oneness of Intelligence, Will and Law. It is the highest ideal that man can possess. The highest power of the soul is to express wisdom in language, the highest power of physical man is to embody that language in acts.

Every form in Nature is a symbol of an idea and represents a sign, or a letter, or a word; and a succession of such symbols forms a language. Nature is therefore the divine language, in which the Universal Mind expresses its ideas.

The individual mind which is developed to such a state of perfection as to form the best instrument through which the highest intelligence can manifest itself, will be the most apt to realise the meaning of that language. The highest secrets of Nature are, therefore, accessible to him whose mental constitution is so perfected as to enable him to understand the language of Nature.

Such a language means a radiation of the essence of things into the centre of the human mind, and a radiation from that centre into the universal ocean of mind. Man in a state of purity, being an image and an external expression of the highest spiritual power, is able to reflect and reproduce the highest truth in its original purity, and man's expressions ought therefore to be a perfect reproduction or echo of the impressions which he receives from the sphere of eternal truth.

But average man being immersed in matter, as a result of a combination of principles on a lower scale of evolution, receives the pure original rays only in a state of refraction, and can therefore reproduce them only in an imperfect condition. He has wandered away from the sun of truth, and beholding it from a distance it appears to him only as a small star, about to vanish from sight. Everything in Nature has its natural name, and he who has the power to call a thing by that name can call its form into existence. This proper name of a thing is its character, the expression of the totality of its powers and attributes, to cause the truth in a thing to become manifest by the spiritual power of the living word, is to call it into existence. This cannot be done by any merely external language; but by the living power of the spirit, of which the external expression is merely an outward symbol and form. *("There are three states of Vach or 'word,' each more interior than the other, and each has three elements; the meaning, the thought and its expression in sound." Subba Rao, "Lectures on the Bhagavad Gita.")* There is only one genuine and interior language for man, the symbols of which are natural and must be intelligible to all, and this language is an interior direct communication of thought. This interior language is the parent of the exterior one, and being caused by the radiation of the first cause which is unity and with whom all men are one, it follows that if the original radiation of the supreme ray were existing in all men in its original purity, all men would understand the same language.

There exists such an external language, which is a perfect expression of that interior one; but this language is known to only few and it cannot be artificially acquired. He who knows the internal language will also know the external one. The interior language breathes spirit; while the exterior one is only a succession of sounds. The key to that interior language is in the divine Word, the key to the exterior one is the mental organisation of collective bodies of men. Man in his present condition hears the voice which speaks that interior language, but does not understand it; he sees the sacred symbols, but does not comprehend them; his ear is accustomed to connect certain meanings with certain sounds, but the true vibrations are lost; he understands human writings in books, but he cannot divine the hieroglyphics that express the true nature of things.

Each character has its own true symbol and form, which expresses its nature; each symbol is a thing representing the essential character of a certain power, and this character can therefore be recognised by him who knows the language of nature in the same way as an artist recognises the character of another artist, by simply beholding his work.

Men have ever been desiring an universal language. Such an universal language cannot be arbitrarily constructed, or if so constructed, would be more difficult to learn than any other. True language must express the harmony of the soul with the nature of things, and as long as there is a differentiation of national character and disharmony there can be no universal harmonious language.

There is a threefold expression of divine essence; a physical, an intellectual, and a divine word. The first is the language of nature, the second the language of reason, the third one is the language of God, which is thought, speech and action in one, and which is therefore a creative power. Each true symbol or form is an external image of an internal state. Each body is the symbol of an invisible and corresponding power, and Man, in whom the highest powers are contained, is the most noble symbol in nature, the first and most beautiful letter in the alphabet of earth.

If he were true to his own divine nature, his body would be a body of light, a perfect expression of beauty. For every thought there is an outward expression, and if we have a thought which we cannot express by symbols, it does not follow that such symbols do not exist, but that we are unacquainted with them.

Man's Actions

A word or a language is the expression of thought, and to be perfect it must give perfect expression to the thought it is intended to convey. By giving a false expression to thought the true power of language is lost. In our present state of civilisation words are used more for the purpose of concealing than revealing thought. Lying involves a loss of spiritual power.

To give pure and perfect expression to thought is White Magic; to act upon the imagination so as to create false impressions is witchcraft, deception, and falsehood. Such witchcraft is practised every day and almost in every station of life, from the priest in the pulpit who wheedles his audience into a belief that he possesses the keys of heaven, down to the merchant who cheats with his goods, and the old maid securing a husband by means of artificial teeth and false hair. Such practices are publicly denounced but silently followed; they lead to a universal disappearance of faith and trust, they will necessarily lead to active evil and bring destruction upon the nation that allows them to grow; because, as the power of good increases by practice, in the same manner increases the power of evil.

Man's mission is to do the highest good to himself; that means to do that which is most useful for his highest development, and being in his true nature universal and unlimited, his highest good can only be obtained by working for the benefit of the whole world and not for his own limited personality.

In this way his nature will become more refined, and its interior illuminated by the light of divine wisdom. By living attached to "self" he attracts to himself the unintelligent and material principles of Nature, his constitution becomes more material, degraded and heavy until, unable to rise to the true light, he becomes metaphysically petrified, lost in the astral plane.

Man's actions are his writings. By putting his thoughts into action, he expresses them and records them in the book of life. Every evil act is followed by a degradation of character, a metaphysical incrustation of the soul. Good actions dissolve existing incrustations produced by evil deeds, and re-establish the soul in its former condition. Repentance, unless followed by a change of nature, is useless. It is like the inflammation caused by a thorn in the flesh; it causes pain, and unless the cause is removed putrefaction will be the result. Man's acts are his creations, they give expression to his thoughts. The motive endows them with character, the will furnishes them with life.

An intention is practically useless as long as it is not put into practice. A sign, a letter, or a word is useless unless it conveys a meaning; a symbol represents an idea, but no symbol can be efficacious unless one masters that which it represents. The most potent magical signs are useless to him who cannot spiritually in his soul realise what they mean, while in him who has soul-knowledge, the use of a single point, a line, or any geometrical figure, may put spiritual powers into action.

Magical Symbols

Let us in conclusion attempt to explain exoterically and esoterically a few of the most important magical signs. We may succeed to a certain extent in giving these explanations in words; but their spiritual meaning cannot be expressed in language nor even in music. Language can merely attempt to guide the reader into a region of thought in which he may be able to perceive the secret meaning with the eye of the spirit; if he has the power of perceiving the truth spiritually by the light of the truth.

The Pentagram or the Five-pointed Star.

In its external appearance it is merely a geometrical figure, found everywhere as a trade-mark or ornament. Superstitious and credulous people once believed, that if it were drawn upon the doors of their houses it would protect them against the intrusions of the sorcerer and the witch.

In its esoteric signification it symbolises Man. The four lower triangles represent the four elementary forces of nature, and as the lines of each triangle are intimately connected or identical with those forming the other lines, the sum of these lines forming only one broken line without any interruption, likewise the four lower elements are intimately connected and identical with the fifth element, the quintessence of all things, situated at the top of the figure; representing the head, the seat of intelligence.

The spiritual knowledge of the Five-pointed Star is identical with its practical application. Let us beware that the figure is always well drawn, leaving no open space, through which the enemy can enter and disturb the harmony existing in the Pentagon. Let us keep the figure always upright, with the topmost triangle pointing to heaven, for it is the seat of Wisdom, and if the figure is reversed perversion and evil will be the result.

Let the lines be straight, so that all the triangles will be harmonious and of equal size, so that the symbol will grow without any abnormal development of one principle at the cost of another. Then the lower triangles will send their quintessence to the top, the seat of intelligence, and the top will supply the lower triangles with power and induce them to grow. Then, when the time of probation and development is over, the triangles will be absorbed by the Pentagon in the centre, and form into a square within the invisible circle connecting the apices of the triangles, and our destiny will be fulfilled.

There is no higher duty for man to perform, than to keep the Five-pointed Spiritual Star intact; it will be his protection during life and his salvation in the hereafter.

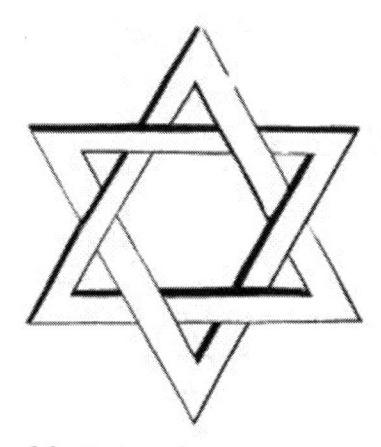

The Double Triangle or Six-pointed Star.

This is one of the most important magical signs, and practically applied it invests man with magic power. Its exoteric meaning is merely two triangles joined together, so that they partially cover each other, while the apex of one points upwards and the apex of the other downward. It is sometimes surrounded by a circle or by a snake biting its tail, and sometimes with a tau in the middle.

Its esoteric meaning is very extensive. It represents among other things the descent of spirit into matter, and the ascension of matter to spirit, which is continually taking place within the circle of eternity, represented by the snake, the symbol of wisdom. Six points are seen in the star, but the seventh cannot be seen; nevertheless the seventh point must exist unmanifested, it not having become manifest; because without a centre there could be no six-pointed star, nor any other figure existing.

But who can describe in words the secret spiritual and universal signification of the six-pointed star and its invisible centre? Who can intellectually grasp and describe the beauties and truths which it represents? Only he who experiences in his own divine nature the power of this sign can practically apply it, and he who can apply it practically is an Adept.

Knowing that sign practically means to realise the nature of "God," to be God and know, and the laws of eternal nature, it means to know by experience the process of evolution and involution of matter and spirit; to realise how the life-impulse travels from planet to planet, beginning with the evolution of the elemental kingdom, rising up through the mineral, vegetable, and animal kingdom, and at last evolving a god-like being out of animal man.

To him who cannot realise within his heart the divine mysteries of nature, the blinding light shining from the centre of the figure has no existence; but the Adept knows that invisible centre, the great Spiritual Sun, the heart of the Cosmos, from which Love and Light and Life are radiating for ever.

He sees the seven primordial rays of that light shining into invisible matter and forming visible worlds upon which men and animals live and die, and are happy or discontented according to their conditions. He sees how by the breath of that invisible centre suns and stars, planets and satellites are evolved, and how if the day of creation of forms is over, it reabsorbs them into its bosom. Verily the six-pointed star is a most potent magical sign, and it requires the wisdom of God to understand it, and the omnipotent power of Life to apply it to its fullest extent.

In its external signification the Christian Cross is a symbol of torture and death. The sight of a cross calls up in the mind of the pious the memory of a historical event said to have taken place in Palestine some two thousand years ago, when a noble, good, and just man, an incarnation of God, is said to have been executed as a criminal upon a cross.

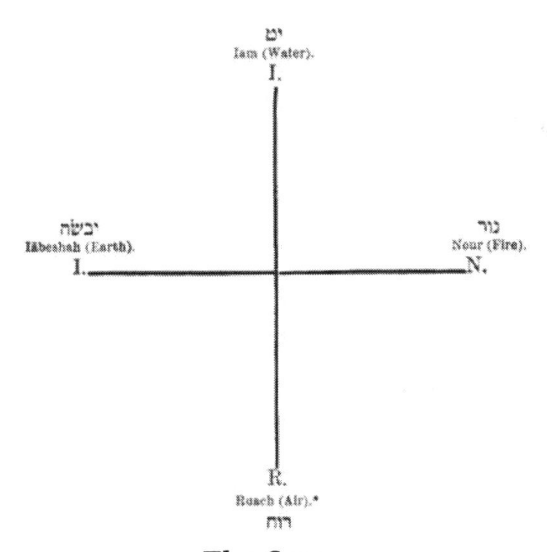

ים
Iam (Water).
I.

יבשה
Iâbeshah (Earth).
I.

נור
Nour (Fire).
N.

R.
Ruach (Air).*
רוח

The Cross.

Compare J. R. Skinner, "Key to the Hebrew-Egyptian Mystery."

The esoteric meaning of the Cross is very ancient, and the Cross has existed as a secret symbol probably thousands of years ago, before the Christian era. It is found in the ancient cave-temples of India and Egypt, where it was hewn in stone long before Christianity was known. The philosophical Cross represents, among other things, the principle of matter and that of spirit intersecting each other, forming the quaternary which, when it is inscribed in the square, forms the basis of knowledge for the Occultist.

The horizontal line represents the animal principle, for the heads of animals are bowed to the earth. Man is the only being upon the globe who stands erect; the divine principle within him keeps him morally erect, and therefore the perpendicular line is the symbol of his divinity. The cross represents Man, who has acted against the law and thereby transformed himself into an instrument for his own torture.

From the beginning of his existence as a ray of the divine spiritual Sun he represented a perpendicular line, cutting in the direction of the source from which he emanated in the beginning. As the distance from that source increased, and as the ray entered into matter, it deviated from the originally straight line and became broken; creating thereby a division in its own essence and making two parts out of the original Unity; thus establishing a will and imagination of its own, acting not in accordance with the Law, but even in opposition to it. If man follows again the dictates of the Law, he will then be taken from the Cross and resume his former position. "To take up one's Cross," means to submit one's own desires to the rule of divine Law.

Who can know the practical spiritual signification of the Cross except spiritual man, who by his incarnation in a terrestrial human form has become nailed to the cross of suffering the ills of the flesh and its temptations, nor can he regain his freedom unless the terrestrial man dies the mystic death for him, by nailing his self-will to the cross of the law and dying the mystic death, so that the true man may live.

On the head of the Christian cross there are inscribed the letters I.N.R.I., which in its exoteric meaning is said to read "Jesus Nazarenus, Rex Iudeorum." This means that the light of Divine Wisdom is the king of all knowledge, and must rule over all intellectual speculations, to which not only the Jews, but also our modern philosophers are devoted. But the Rosicrucian meaning of these letters was: In Nobis Begnat Jesus, and this truth will also be realised only by those who are in possession of immortal life; and because in them the true Jesus, the spiritual soul, illumined by the light of Divine Wisdom, has awakened to life and is actually the Lord and ruler of their interior kingdom.

In its practical application the Cross represents the self-recognition of Divine Truth. He whose spiritual perception is open sees the living Cross in its glory. Sublimely stands that Cross upon the mountain of self-knowledge, magnificent is its aspect.

Far into heaven shines the light radiating from its centre and illuminating the darkness with its beneficent rays. Rise, oh man, up to your true dignity, so that you may see the meaning of the true Cross. Not the dead wooden Cross, the emblem of ignorance and suffering, nor the glittering cross made of brass, the emblem of vanity, sectarianism and superstition; but the true Cross, made of the pure gold of the light of Wisdom which each true Brother of the Golden and Rosy Cross carries deeply buried within his own heart.

This cross is the full-grown Tree of Life and of Knowledge, bearing the fruits of salvation and immortality, the dispenser of Life, the protector against evil. He who knows practically the true mystery of the Cross is acquainted with the highest wisdom; he who is adorned with the true Cross is safe from all danger. Infinite power of the Cross! In thee the Truth is revealed. Buried deep in the darkness of Earth is thy foot, teaching us Patience; high into the light of heaven reaches thy crown, teaching us Faith. Lifted by Hope and extended by Charity are thy arms, light and sunshine surround thee. Link upon link the chain of creation encircles the Cross; worlds within worlds, forms within forms, illusions upon illusions. But in the Centre is the Reality in which is hidden the jewel of priceless value, the Truth.

Let the dew of heaven which comes from the true Cross descend into your hearts and penetrate into your soul and body, so that it may crystallize into form. Then will the darkness within your mind disappear, the veil of matter will be rent, and before your spiritual vision will stand revealed the angel of truth. Truly! no one can be a real Christian unless he practically realises in his soul the meaning of the symbol of the Cross; the self-revelation of Truth.

The present material age is ever ready to reject without examination the symbols of the past whose meaning it cannot realise because it does not possess the treasures which they represent. Engaged in the pursuit of material pleasures, it loses sight of divine wisdom and exchanges spiritual wealth for worthless baubles. Losing sight of his divine destiny, man runs after shadows, closing his eye to the Light of the World.

Ruled by fear, man bows before the Moloch of superstition and ignorance, rushes madly into the arms of a dead and cold agnostic science to perish in its stony embrace; but the wise, whose far-seeing perception reaches beyond the narrow circle of his material surroundings and beyond the short span of time which includes one of his lives on this earth, knows that it is in his power to control his future destiny.

He raises the magic wand of his will and quiets the tempest of the soul. The forces which were rushing to his destruction obey him and execute his orders, and he walks safely upon the waters under whose calm surface is hidden the abyss of death, while above his head shines that bright constellation formed of Truth, Knowledge, and Power, whose centre is the Law and whose germs can be found in the spiritual self-consciousness of every human being.

Appendix

A New Guide on the Path: For Those Who Desire to Follow the Practical Way

Know that All is One.
Know that everything is Thyself.
Know that the One in a state of vibration produces the great multiplicity of forms and activities in the Universe.
Know that if you examine this multiplicity from the standpoint of your intellectual reasoning, you will arrive at the following deductions:
Everything that you call "Life," "Energy," "Substance," is a Duality.
Everything has a tendency to return to Unity.
All desire and therefore all suffering originates from duality.
Let thy aspiration be for enlightenment.
Know that the result of the joys experienced by the attainment of enlightenment is happiness.
Rise above the state of condensation.
Know that the result of the joys experienced in the state of condensation is suffering.
On the road from Unity in motion to tranquillity is the state of condensation. It is the cause of your illusions, because you imagine it to be tranquillity; and it is the cause of your doubts, because you regard it as the object of your desires.
Know that the striving after the unification of the duality is the only source of your will, your desires, and of those joys whose results you call "suffering."
Know that the door for the solution of that which is fixed is what is called "Matter."
Know that everything has to pass through that door.
Know that the door for the solution of the fixed is also called "Life."
Know that everything has to pass through that door.
And that the long sojourn in "Matter" and the interruption of the voyage by "Life" means retardation in the solution of the fixed and procrastination in the unification of the duality.
Enforce the practice of the power of that which is solved over that which is condensed.
Direct your attention to the consciousness of that which is dissolved over that which is condensed.
Carry this consciousness through all the planes of your being.
Elevate your whole body to the capacity to think, to hear, and to see.
Cause it thereby to become a fit instrument for the use of your self-consciousness of the One and of your self-power (resulting from unification).
Conquer the pains resulting therefrom.
When the divine Language is once heard within thy heart -- when the King within thy interior has once obtained dominion -- when thou hast passed through water and fire, and thy spirit has become the life of thy blood -- then you may say: I am, I go, and I remain.